HISTORICAL
PARALLELS IN THE
DEVELOPMENT OF
PHYSICS
AND
PSYCHOLOGY

Second Edition

Michael J. Scavio
California School of Professional Psychology, Los Angeles

Susan Regas
California School of Professional Psychology, Los Angeles

KENDALL/HUNT PUBLISHING COMPANY
4050 Westmark Drive   Dubuque, Iowa 52002

To Debbie . . .

Taken away from here so soon,
your joyous spirit endures forever!

Copyright © 1989, 1997 by Kendall/Hunt Publishing Company

Library of Congress Catalog Card Number: 97-72318

ISBN 0-7872-3771-X

Printed in the United States of America

10 9 8 7 6 5 4

Contents

Preface to the Second Edition

The first edition of this book was published by Kendall/Hunt in 1989. In the first edition, a status report was given how well humans have answered two questions that have endured throughout history. The first question pertains to an understanding of the Universe and the second question addresses an understanding of the human Self. These questions have been pursued within the respective domains of physics and psychology. Moreover, physics and psychology have joined, sometimes unwittingly, with mythology, biology, and philosophy in an attempt to provide answers to the two questions. As a result, a vast amount of information has been gained over the millennia that bears witness to the incessant human desire to know.

The second edition of this book expands upon the first but still provides only a glimpse of the vast amount of knowledge accumulated in physics and psychology. The two fields were once united by the pre-Socratic Greek philosophers. However, physics and psychology separated long ago. Thus, the exploration of the Universe and the Self became separate domains of inquiry. Yet, psychology's search for a unifying paradigm beckons a return to physics. Accordingly, the second edition represents a further report on the success of physics and psychology in finding answers to the two ultimate questions. In particular, suggestions based upon physics are offered for the nature of the paradigm that will allow psychology to become a true pathway for the understanding of the Self.

The completion of the second edition was immensely helped by the efforts of Kendall/Hunt Publishing. We are very grateful to them.

Michael J. Scavio
Susan Regas

Preface to the First Edition

Since the dawn of Western Civilization, humans have been captivated by two questions. The first question concerns the origins of the Universe and the second question addresses the origins of Self. The first issue falls within the province of physics and the second one is in the domain of psychology. It is the purpose of this book to review the parallel development of the two fields in order to ascertain their progress and also to understand their mutual influences upon each other's development. Our treatment will begin with the ancient Greeks and carry to the present times. The wealth of knowledge gained in 2600 years has been staggering and serves as a strong testimonial for the human penchant to know. Also, we hope that the material presented here will stimulate thinking about some of the fundamental issues that have confronted humans. Many of the issues to be discussed still beg for solutions, especially in the area of psychology.

Many thanks go to the people who have made this book possible. We wish to acknowledge the contributions of the following for their dedicated library work: Vicki Dowling, Todd Cartmell, Rosemary Cleveland, Heba Elkobaitry, Laura Kaff, William Helvogt, Toni-Rose Shegina, Lisa Wellington, Brenda Wheeler, and Melissa Kester. Special thanks is given to A. Louise Fix and Leslie Anne Mathis for their patient reading of the manuscript.

Michael J. Scavio
Pamela Scavio Clift

The Meaning of Reality: Ancient Views

1

In the very distant past, perhaps as long ago as 15 to 20 billion years, a cataclysmic explosion occurred and, at that moment, space, time, and reality began. The explosion, known as the "Big Bang" in cosmology, eventually led to the formation of our Milky Way galaxy with its 100 billion stars. In addition, at least another 100 billion galaxies have emerged after the Big Bang. This small planet Earth orbits a relatively minor star that travels in one of the spiral arms of the Milky Way. As insignificant as Earth may be in the grand Cosmos, it still is home to six billion human beings who, throughout the collective history of the species, have tried to understand their existence and how the Universe came to be. However, the answers to such questions have proven to be elusive, even in modern times. Our purpose in this book is to give a progress report regarding the success of physics in explaining the Universe and psychology in explaining human nature. The treatment of both disciplines begins at the same time with the ancient Greeks and carries to the contemporary age. Examining the parallel development of physics and psychology indicates how intertwined the two sciences are in the history of thought. Both disciplines are required to give humans the answers to the timeless questions regarding outer and inner existence.

Greek Cosmology

The Greek Myth of Creation

The Greeks, along with all other ancient peoples of the world, attempted to explain existence with the aid of mythical tales. The purpose of myth is to inspire understanding of very abstract issues by offering explanations and analogies drawn from the realms of human imagination and experience. The master myth-maker in the Greek world was Hesiod, who in the 8th century B.C., told the story of creation in his

1

two works, *Theogony and Works and Days*. Several sources, such as Barthell (1971), Hamilton (1940), Morford & Lenardon (1985), and Pinsent (1985), can be consulted for the full story of Hesiod's myth which is summarized below.

In the beginning, all that existed was Chaos, the personification of the endless void of the Universe. Eventually, Chaos was joined by three others, Gaea (Mother Earth), Eros (Love), and Tartarus (the Underworld). However, Chaos was supreme and, since no light shone on him, his appearance could not be described. Eventually, Chaos tired and was replaced by his son Erebus, who represents the darkness that surrounds the rim of the Earth. Hesiod unblushingly has Erebus marry his mother Nyx (Night) and they conceive two beautiful offspring, Aether (Light) and Hemera (Day). Also, from this wedlock was born the frightening Charon, a ghostly figure, whose function is to ferry the dead across the river Styx to the Underworld. Gaea, the Earth, now dazzling in light for the first time, fostered several offspring including Pontus (the Sun), Uranus (the Starry Heavens), and Typhon (the Sea Monster).

Afterwards, Uranus married his mother Gaea and both assumed absolute power. From this union came 12 gigantic children known as the Titans and three Cyclopes with the characteristic single eye in the middle of the forehead. Uranus, threatened by the immense size and power of his children, banished them all to the underworld. Gaea, seeking vengeance against Uranus, encourages their children to rebel. Eventually, one of the Titans, Cronus, who is personified as time, the devourer of all things, succeeds in overthrowing Uranus. The triumphant Cronus establishes tranquility and releases his sibling Titans from the Underworld. However, the fearsome Cyclopes still remain imprisoned.

Cronus, remembering how he came to power, worried that one of his children might be tempted to take command. To prohibit this possibility, Cronus decided to swallow whole each infant child born to his wife Rhea. Aghast at the treatment of her children, Rhea became determined to preserve her next child Zeus. Rhea, after safely hiding Zeus in a cave, presented to Cronus a stone wrapped in baby blankets. Thinking that this offering was another infant, Cronus immediately engulfed the bundle without first examining it.

Over the years, Zeus grew strong and defeated Cronus who was then forced to drink an emetic. The medicine dislodged the large stone in Cronus's belly and he then regurgitated Zeus's brothers and sisters. Zeus and his siblings, now rulers of the world, decided to live on Mount Olympus. Meanwhile, the stone from Cronus's stomach was placed outside the entrance to the Oracle of Delphi to commemorate Zeus's victory.

Several of the Titans, distressed at the demise of their brother Cronus, refused to give allegiance to Zeus. Consequently, a fierce war broke out between the Olympians and the Titans which was fought in Thessaly for 10 years. Zeus, searching for a means of victory against his powerful foes, finally released the Cyclopes from imprisonment in return for their help. The Cyclopes were the only ones who knew how to make thunder and lightning, and these terrors from the sky proved decisive in defeating the Titans.

Zeus and his brothers and sisters now ruled supreme. However, these deities felt lonely with no one to worship them. So Zeus asked Prometheus, a descendant of the Titan Iapetus who, nevertheless, had supported the Olympians against the Titans, to make human beings. From a mixture of clay and water, Prometheus made man to physically resemble the Olympian gods. Prometheus greatly admired his creations and was determined to attend to their welfare. Consequently, Prometheus gave humans the greatest gift in the ancient world. The gift was fire that served to inspire man to attain knowledge, art, and civilization.

Zeus became jealous of man and took fire away, only to have Prometheus restore the gift again. Now feeling vengeance, Zeus was determined to punish Prometheus for his insubordination. Accordingly, Prometheus was captured, chained to a mountain, and mutilated by a vulture that constantly gnawed at his liver. This agony endured for 30,000 years until Achilles killed the vulture and freed Prometheus.

Zeus's fury against humans continued and he devised a wicked plan to bring man everlasting punishment through the innocence of a beautiful woman. Thus, Zeus created Pandora, the first woman, to have remarkable loveliness. Zeus initially presented Pandora to Prometheus, before he was subjected to his chained punishment, but he rejected her. However, Epimetheus, Prometheus's brother, accepted her with plans for marriage. As a dowry gift, the wily Zeus gave Pandora a box with instructions never to open it. What happens next is related by Edith Hamilton (1940, pp. 70–72):

> For Pandora, like all women, was possessed of a lively curiosity. She *had* to know what was in the box. One day she lifted the lid—and out flew plagues innumerable, sorrow and mischief for mankind. In terror Pandora clapped the lid down, but too late. One good thing, however, was there—Hope. It was the only good the casket had held among its many evils, and it remains to this day mankind's sole comfort in misfortune. So mortals learned that it is not possible to get the better of Zeus or ever to deceive him.

Zeus's hatred for humans was still not satisfied. Angry at their impiety and growing independence, Zeus was moved to destroy the Earth by a great flood. As the rains fell and the sea waled against the land, the humans drowned. However, two of them, Deucalion, son of Prometheus, and Pyrrha, daughter of Pandora, were allowed to survive because of their goodness. Once the waters receded, Deucalion and Pyrrha replenished the Earth with new children. One of their sons, Hellen, became the forerunner of the Greeks. In turn, Hellen's descendants, Aeolus, Dorus, Ion, and

Achaeus, fathered the Aeolian, Dorian, Ionian, and Achaean branches of the Greek nation.

Milesian Philosophy

The Greeks, no doubt inspired by their mythological account of creation, made the understanding of the world the first question of their philosophy. Greek philosophy was initiated by the Ionians who were living in the prosperous trade-city of Miletus located on the Aegean coast of Asia Minor. The effort to use philosophy as a rational basis for the understanding the world started with Thales (624–546 B.C.). He was succeeded by Anaximander (611–545 B.C.) and Anaximenes (585–524 B.C.).

From his home in Miletus, Thales regularly took long trips to explore the world. He appears to have journeyed to Egypt to observe the flooding of the Nile, study geometry, and measure the heights of the Pyramids. He also ventured to Babalonia to learn astronomy. According to Heroditus, Thales was able to predict the occurrence of a solar eclipse which was so frightening that the event served to end a war between Lydia and Media. With such sagacity, Thales was chronicled to be one of the seven wisest men of all the Greeks and certainly earned the credentials to become their first philosopher.

As a philosopher, Thales speculated about the origins of all things and considered that everything must be composed of a single underlying unit. Thales decided that the fundamental unit of nature is water (Rogers, 1932). Later, Aristotle in his *Metaphysics,* quoted Thales as saying that the land itself rides on a cushion of water and, when the water moves, earthquakes result. Thales's reasons for making water the fundamental unit can only be conjectured. Moisture is found everywhere and is required to sustain life. Since it is indispensable and universal, Thales made it the primary unit.

The choice of water as the fundamental unit, however, was challenged by Thales's student Anaximander. The primary substance had to be more basic than water, and Anaximander called it the "unlimited" or the "boundless" (Martin, Clark, Clarke, & Ruddick, 1941). Anaximander's meaning of the "unlimited" is vague. Like Chaos in Greek mythology, the unlimited is the primordial form of existence that cannot be directly sensed. All things come from the unlimited and will eventually return to it. Creation from the unlimited is based upon the intermingling of opposite forces. The Earth is assumed to have once been a cold-moist mass enveloped within fire. The first living creatures came from sun-baked mud, and humans evolved from fish-like forms.

The last member of the Milesian school was Anaximenes. He rejected Anaximander's concept of the unlimited and searched for the fundamental unit in a determinant form. The conclusion now was that air is the fundamental unit (Martin et al.,

1941). In Anaximenes's cosmology, air can condense to form solid objects such as the Earth. The significance of air is even more important. Anaximenes believed that air is a spiritual force that maintains life. Thus, humans are kept alive by the soul whose presence is revealed by respiration. The atmosphere of the Earth also indicates that it too is pervaded by a spiritual force.

The Philosophy of Eternal Change

The great work started by the Milesian philosophers influenced thinkers in other Ionian regions. About 25 miles north of Miletus is the city of Ephesus, home of the enigmatic philosopher Heraclitus (circa 500 B.C.). According to the ancient biographer Diogenes Laertius, Heraclitus camped in the shade of the temple of Artemis, took vegetarian meals, played with children, and mocked adults visiting the city. Even to the Greeks, Heraclitus was difficult to understand and they called him the "riddler" (Ueberweg, 1888a).

Heraclitus's works have not survived intact. However, enough of his writings exist to reconstruct his philosophy. Heraclitus believed that the study of cosmology is required to understand human nature. His great principle is that the world exists in a continuous state of flux. Sometimes change occurs so slowly that humans have the illusion of permanence. However, no matter what the rate, all things change and become something else. To illustrate Heraclitus's philosophy, the ultimate destiny of the Sun can serve as an example. The Sun warms the Earth with daily regularity and has been doing so for countless years. Nevertheless, the Sun is imperceptibly exhausting its nuclear fuel and, at some point in the very distant future, it will begin to collapse into itself and shine no more (Boslough, 1985). The lesson in all of this is that everything changes. To summarize his beliefs, Heraclitus wrote, "You cannot step twice into the same river, for other waters are continually flowing on" and "Everything flows and nothing abides; everything gives way and nothing stays fixed" (Wheelwright, 1959, p. 29).

Heraclitus continued the search for the fundamental unit. Since the World is in constant flux, so also must be the fundamental unit. As representative of continuous change, Heraclitus adopted fire as the fundamental unit. The flickering appearance of a flame serves to represent reality as gathered from these quotes from Heraclitus, "There is an exchange for fire and of fire for all things, as there is wares for gold and gold for wares" and "The transformations of fire are: first, sea; and of sea, half becomes earth, and half becomes lightning-flash" (Wheelwright, 1959, p. 37).

Heraclitus did not allow the process of change to occur haphazardly. Instead, he joined with Anaximander to proclaim that nature results from the activity of opposing forces. Heraclitus said, "Cool things become warm, the warm grows cool;

the moist dries, the parched becomes moist" and "Homer was wrong in saying, 'Would that strife might perish from amongst gods and men.' For if that were to occur, then all things would cease to exist" (Wheelwright, 1959, p. 29). The reason for opposites determining reality is that Heraclitus's concept of God is based upon antagonisms such that "God is day and night, winter and summer, war and peace, satiety and hunger; He takes different forms, just as fire, when it is mixed with spices, is named according to the savor of each" (Martin et al., p. 42).

Human nature also reflects the activity of opposites. Heraclitus attributed to a human both body and soul, the latter drawn from vaporized fire. Humans show the paradox of opposites in many other ways: life and death, male and female, youth and aged, awake and sleep, rational and irrational. This philosophy of opposites illustrates the wisdom found in the myth of Pandora. No matter how painful and sorrowful existence may be, there is always hope because all things come to pass. Finally, Heraclitus's flux principle was important to later Greek philosophers who examined how humans come to have stable knowledge in a world of constant change.

The Philosophy of Stability: The Eleatic School

The town of Colophon, near Ephesus, was the birthplace of Xenophanes (569–490? B.C.) who was of the first to react to Heraclitus's beliefs. Xenophanes apparently travelled to many lands and finally migrated to Elea in Southern Italy to escape the Persians who were conquering Ionia. For his efforts, Xenophanes is considered to be the originator of the Eleatic school of philosophy (Smith, 1956). In challenging Heraclitus, Xenophanes reasoned that, despite change, one fact always remains: the Universe exists. Moreover, he concluded that the Universe is able to have its existence because it is driven by God. Xenophanes accepted the existence of a unitary, impersonal God who has none of the characteristics of the mythical gods. He was sharply critical of polytheistic beliefs found in Greek religion and said: "Homer and Hesiod have ascribed to the gods all things that are shame and a disgrace among men, thefts and adulteries and deceptions of one another" (Rogers, 1932, p. 28). On the contrary, Xenophanes reasoned that, "God is one, supreme among gods and men, and not like mortals in body or mind" (Smith, 1956, p. 14).

The philosophy of stability was strongly supported by Parmenides (circa 475 B.C.) of Elea. He taught that the senses, which indicated to Heraclitus a constantly changing world, actually deceive since change is impossible. In his famous work, *On Nature,* which now only exists in fragments, Parmenides identified thought and being to be the same thing (Martin et al., 1941). If I think of something, it must be real. Since thought reveals existence, the object of my thought must always be. For example, if past, present, and future generations all think of God, God must have eternal existence. Our thoughts are based upon what exists. Perhaps, the best way to understand Parmenides is to image everything to be a single, indivisible atom that always was and always will be. Existence is synonymous with physical being. Existence has no beginning and no end. Existence simply is (Martin et al., 1941).

Metaphysical Pluralism

Is a reconciliation possible between the views of Heraclitus, who maintained that nature is constantly changing, and Parmenides, who did not allow for any change whatsoever? The task of offering a compromise fell to a group of philosophers known as the Pluralists (Empedocles, Anaxagoras, Leucippus, and Democritus). In general, they unified the philosophies of Heraclitus and Parmenides in the following manner. Nature contains several elements which can combine in many ways allowing for the plurality of existing things. However, the fundamental elements themselves might be indestructible and unchangeable. The last of the Pluralists, Leucippus and Democritus, were able to identify more closely than any of their predecessors the fundamental unit of existence.

The first Pluralist was Empedocles (492–432 B.C.), born in Agrigentum, a city in Sicily. He seemed to have had an interesting life as a philosopher, priest, poet, politician, and magician. As a philosopher, Empedocles identified four fundamental elements out of which everything is composed: earth, air, fire, and water. (Note that air, fire, and water were previously acknowledged by Anaximenes, Heraclitus, and Thales, respectively). In agreement with Parmenides, Empedocles taught that these four substances were immutable. As previously mentioned, the four substances combine to make everything else. However, the compounds produced from the four elements are unstable and subject to disintegration. Therefore, Empedocles was able to acknowledge Heraclitus's doctrine of change.

Empedocles called his four substances "roots of all" since they constitute everything physical. Perhaps, inspired by Greek mythology, Empedocles thought that the world experiences cycles of creation and destruction. Love is the enduring force which inspires the four roots to come together. Thus, creation and birth are the products of Love. However, Hate is the opposing natural force causing the roots to separate. Annihilation and death result when Hate predominates (Copleston, 1985a). It is interesting to note that psychoanalytic theories of the twentieth century share with Empedocles the importance of the emotions of love and hate. According to Melanie Klein, how love and hate, which are present at birth, are experienced during the development of the child represents the critical variable determining how the human personality functions (See Chapter 6).

The next Pluralist philosopher was Anaxagoras (500–432 B.C.), born in the Ionian city of Clazomenae. He eventually settled in Athens, having been invited by Pericles to teach the citizens philosophy. Pericles was responsible for the emergence of Athens as the dominant city-state after the defeat of the Persians. However, as he grew older, Pericles's enemies began to show their envy by attacking his friends. Anaxagoras was thrown into jail on the charge of impiety to the gods for teaching that the Sun was really a red-hot stone. With the help of Pericles, Anaxagoras was allowed to leave Athens after promising never to return. He finally settled in Lampsacus, a city far removed from Athens (Copelston, 1985a). This would not be the last time that the Athenians displayed hostility toward their philosophers.

Anaxagoras agreed with Empedocles that everything came from more basic elements. However, the number of primary constituents of matter must be greater than the four supposed by Empedocles. Earth, air, fire, and water themselves must be made from something more primary. Anaxagoras considered the number of fundamental elements, called "seeds," to be infinite. Moreover, Anaxagoras dismissed Love and Hate as the organizing principles of matter. Instead, the seeds are combined to create objects by "Nous" which is identified with intelligence. Therefore, Anaxagoras viewed nature as the product of a supreme intellect that worked through natural causes to give design to all things. The elemental seeds remain inert without the influence of Nous (Ueberweg, 1888a). Although vague about the properties of Nous, Anaxagoras, nevertheless, has been given credit for introducing the determining power of intellect into Greek philosophy.

The work started by Empedocles and Anaxagoras reached a level of major accomplishment with the ideas of Leucippus (circa 440 B.C.) and Democritus (460–370 B.C.), both of whom lived in the remote Ionian city of Abdera. Unfortunately, no direct writings of the two remain and what we know of them is derived from secondary sources such as Aristotle (Rogers, 1932).

Leucippus and Democritus, sharing the intellectual companionship of teacher to student, identified the fundamental units of nature to be "atoms." Leucippus was apparently the author of the atomic theory and Democritus developed it more fully. Atoms are imperceptible, indestructible, and infinite in number and represent individual pieces of the primary substance of the Universe. Atoms only differ in their sizes and shapes. They combine together to make objects and, when an object disintegrates, the atoms scatter but remained unaltered (Martin et al., 1941).

According to Democritus, ". . . only the atoms and the void are real." (Smith, 1956, p. 40). From this belief, Democritus produced very important implications for understanding reality. First, the senses do not give us the atomic structures of existing things. Hence, Parmenides was correct in asserting that the senses deceive. It is the atoms acting upon the sensory apparatus that is initially responsible for consciousness. Atoms are real, not the sensory qualities experienced within the human mind.

Secondly, Democritus, in contrast to Parmenides, believed that empty space existed between celestial objects. Atoms, timeless and eternal, move through space, occasionally collecting together to make the Sun, stars, and planets.

Democritus found it unnecessary to postulate a guiding force allowing the fundamental units to organize. Thus, Empedocles's principles of Love and Hate and Anaxagoras's concept of Nous were abandoned. Instead, atoms obey natural laws that govern the existence of all things, including humans. No mythical forces, no purposive intelligence, no God was needed to account for existence. The activities of the Universe are solely based upon the inherent spins and motions of the countless atoms. Even mental thought is nothing more than the motions of atoms in the material soul (Martin et al., 1941). Thus, Democritus gave a deterministic and materialistic interpretation of reality that would forever influence philosophy and psychology.

Democritus accepted the soul as distinct from the body. Although made from atoms like the body, the soul represents the highest aspects of human existence and its activities should be cultivated. The soul dominates when humans act in moderation and experience happiness through the attainment of knowledge (Martin et al., 1941). Democritus spoke of the interaction between body and soul: "Men in their prayers beg the gods for health, not knowing that this is a thing they have in their own power. Through their incontinence undermining it, they themselves become, because of their passions, the betrayers of their own health." (Smith, 1956, p. 43). The wisdom of this quote is verified in the modern research on psychoimmuniology demonstrating that mental and physical health are harmoniously linked.

Democritus attracted several followers such as the philosopher Epicurus and the Roman poet Lucretius. However, the atomic theory was not without its critics. Aristotle was one of them and asked how it was possible for individual atoms to stay together in a structure. Should they not physically spread apart by their own inherent motion? To this question Democritus had no response, and not until the modern understanding of strong and weak attractive forces holding atoms together could Aristotle's challenge be successfully answered.

Pythagoras and the Mystical Power of Numbers

Pythagoras (582–510 B.C.) stands as a mysterious figure in Greek philosophy. He was born an Ionian in Samos and lived at the time of Anaximenes. Most assuredly, he was conversant with the Milesian search for the fundamental unit of nature. However, Pythagoras believed that Ionian philosophy was misdirected. The most important aspect of existence is not the physical Universe but the soul which Pythagoras studied from the viewpoint of the cult of Orpheus. To escape Ionia, Pythagoras migrated to far away Croton in Southern Italy to establish a religious community in 530 B.C. Eventually, the people of Croton came to despise the community, and Pythagoras was forced to leave in 511 B.C.

The cult of Orpheus taught that a human has a spiritual soul which will live beyond the body; however, the soul is confronted with the major task of freeing itself from the consequences of sin. These beliefs were drawn from the myth of Dionysus that became popular in Greek religion in Pythagoras's time. This myth offered another explanation to Hesiod's for human origins. Essentially, the myth tells of the infant Dionysus, son of Zeus, being murdered and eaten by the nefarious Titans. Zeus, in his anger, strikes down the Titans with lightning bolts. From the smoldering ashes of the Titans, humans arise. But humans have a nature based upon the collision of opposites. Humans are partly good since they are derived from the remnants of a god but also partly evil since they come from the Titans. (Luckily for Dionysus, his heart was saved allowing for his rebirth.) The good part of man is identified with the soul while the evil part is represented by the body (Morford & Lenardon, 1985).

Pythagoras believed, like the Orphic priests, that the soul must suffer for the wickedness of man. Thus, the soul is imprisoned in an imperfect body. Even after death, the soul must reunite with another body. The reincarnation principle became known as the doctrine of the transmigration of souls. Successive reincarnations occur until the soul is finally purified from evil. For Pythagoras, the purification is accomplished by "the cultivation and exercise of the intellect in the pursuit of knowledge and science." (Martin et al., 1941, p. 22) The term PHILOSOPHER, which means lover of wisdom, may have been invented by the Pythagoreans to indicate proper human conduct. Philosophers lead a detached life, not tempted by worldly goods, so as to be free to contemplate the meaning and implications of existence. (Martin et al., 1941)

Contemplation of existence requires mathematics since "all things are numbers" according to Pythagoras (Copleston, 1985a). Aristotle noted in his *Metaphysics* that the Pythagoreans were the first Greeks to study mathematics and apply it to the understanding of the world. The Pythagoreans discovered that musical strings obeyed certain mathematical principles. The vibration rate of a string is inversely proportional to its length. To give pleasant sound, strings on a lyre must have lengths which are ratios of one another. Since music is based upon the harmony of numbers, it was considered valuable for cleansing the soul, a point later developed by Plato and Aristotle (Martin et al. 1941). The Pythagorean society also discovered the squares and cubes of numbers and the famous theorem for determining the length of the hypotenuse in a right-angled triangle. This Pythagorean theorem became very useful in land survey. However, the Pythagoreans also uncovered numbers that caused them great confusion. Numbers, such as the square root of two and pi, were not orderly because they could not be expressed as the ratio of two integers. Hence, these numbers were called "irrational" in that they produced decimals which were endless and followed no regular pattern. The Pythagoreans decided to keep secret the existence of irrational numbers until they could be understood. Nonetheless, a member of the society leaked the existence of these numbers and, for his treason, was murdered (Schneer, 1984).

The Pythagorean society practiced many eccentric habits, such as "not to break bread," "not to step over a crossbar," "not to look in a mirror beside a light," "not to stir a fire with an iron," "not to let swallows share one's roof," "practice silence," "do not eat beans," and many more (Copleston, 1985a; Martin et al., 1941). However, their true importance was to show that mathematics serves as a powerful language for science. In addition, the Pythagoreans raise the possibility that existence is divided into two realms, that of the spiritual and that of the physical. Therefore, one has to be both a philosopher for the immaterial world and a scientist for the material world to understand reality.

The Greek interest in mathematics was generated by the attempt to understand the World, more specifically, the application of numbers. Thus, Euclid, working at the magnificent library in Alexandria, developed geometry as the number system that describes shapes (Devlin, 1994). Geometry, which means earth measurement, has practical applications in land surveying and building. Moreover, the Greeks believed that certain patterns have the innate capacity to elicit from the human an appreciation of beauty. Thus, the Greeks developed the Golden Ratio which roughly computes to 1.618. This number is achieved by taking a line and dividing it into two unequal segments such that the ratio of the complete line to the longer of the two line segments is 1.618. The Greeks used the Golden Ratio in the construction of the Parthenon (Maor, 1994).

With the development of the scientific method, physics required a new type of mathematics to describe motion and change in motion. Thus, in the 17th century, Newton and Leibnitz would independently develop calculus as the mathematical tool that describes motion and change (Devlin, 1994).

Athenian Physics

Plato and Aristotle

Plato (427–347 B.C.) and his most famous student Aristotle (384–322 B.C.) developed the philosophies having the greatest impact upon Western Civilization. However, these two intellectual geniuses often disagreed on fundamental issues. Their sharpest differences concerned human nature and the origins of knowledge which will be discussed in Chapter 5. Also, their inquisitive minds were drawn to the enduring problem of the Universe's origin. Using myth and the earlier philosophers, Plato and Aristotle were able to generate remarkable insights regarding the nature of the world. In the following, the cosmologies of Plato and Aristotle and their implications for human existence will be briefly surveyed.

Plato's Life

In the Golden Age of Pericles, Athens assumed preeminence among the quarrelsome Greek city-states. Plato was born just at the time the supremacy of Athens was being threatened by Sparta and her ally Corinth. Soon the Peloponnesian war would ignite again, eventually leading to the subjugation of Athens by Sparta in 405 B.C. (Wallbank & Taylor, 1960). Thus, Plato developed his philosophy at a tumultuous time and, no doubt, the traumatic events shredding the Greek peninsula markedly affected his philosophical positions. Plato's family was very wealthy and he was able to gain an exceptional education. The profession selected for Plato was politics, befitting a young man of his social order. However, around the age of 20, Plato became attracted to the personality and teachings of Socrates (470–399 B.C.) who wandered around Athens, barefoot and often in a state of ecstasy, giving lectures to the youth. Socrates questioned the merits of the Peloponnesian war. With the ascendancy of Sparta, the Athenian government externalized its anger and directed it to Socrates. He was arrested, given a trial, and convicted of "corrupting the youth." The friends of Socrates arranged for his release in return for his exile from Athens. However, Socrates would have none of this and bravely accepted his death sentence. As reported by Plato in his *Phaedo,* Socrates, surrounded by his grieving followers, drank the poison and reminded his friends and students, "Be of good cheer and say that you are burying my body only" (Durant, 1938, p. 16). The story of Socrates is reminiscent of America's Vietnam experience when leaders such as Bobby Kennedy and Martin Luther King protested the war and, in turn, became victims of the violence that they decried. As the Freudians know well, those who offer hope to some elicit hate in others.

Plato, 28 years old at Socrates's death, was filled with anger and remorse. Plato decided to leave Athens and embarked upon an ambitious journey that took him to Egypt, Sicily, and Italy where he joined a Pythagorean society (Durant, 1938). Finally, Plato returned to Athens at age 40 and opened his famous Academy which might have been the first University and lasted until 529 A.D. (Clagett, 1955). The Pythagorean influence upon Plato is easily recognized by the inscription over the door of the academy, "Let no one ignorant of mathematics enter here" (Bernal, 1972, p. 90). Plato continued to teach in Athens until his death. However, he ventured from the city two more times after the founding of the Academy. In 367 and 361 B.C., Plato was invited to Syracuse so that he could educate its young ruler, Dionysius II. The aim was to train Dionysius to be the philosopher-king, the type of ruler Plato considered to be the ideal. However, to his disappointment, Plato's educational efforts were thwarted by political intrigue and the intellectual inadequacies of his pupil (Bury, 1913). Plato's long life ended in Athens. According to Durant (1938), he was invited to a wedding banquet for one of his pupils and had an enjoyable time. In the morning, he was found dead in a chair, having expired quietly during the night.

Fortunately, most of Plato's writings have survived. The style of his literary work is the dialogue form in which different speakers discuss philosophical and scientific issues. The main character of the dialogues is Socrates who speaks with other characters historically known to have existed. Thus, Plato explored ultimate questions with drama, often mixing comedy and tragedy within his stories. Finally, Plato often resorted to mythology in many of his writings to help confer meaning upon difficult issues (Erdman, 1956).

Plato's Physics

Plato certainly knew of the works of the previously discussed philosophers and many of their ideas were incorporated into his views. From Heraclitus, Plato believed that the physical world revealed by the senses is in a constant state of flux. Nothing is physically permanent. Based upon Parmenides, Plato accepted that immaterial existence, represented by God, soul, and knowledge, remains stable. Thus, the physical world is in a state of flux but the spiritual world of existence and ideas remains fixed. Finally, Plato relied upon the Pythagoreans for their ideas on the immortality of the soul and the importance of mathematics in describing reality. All of these elements were combined into Plato's view of the Universe which was presented principally in his work, the *Timaeus*. Plato also was wise to acknowledge that his theories were only guesses and should be considered only to be tentative.

In his view of the Universe, Plato accepted that physical substances are composed from the four classic roots: earth, air, fire, and water. However, these are not the fundamental units of existence. Instead, earth, air, fire, and water must be composed of something more basic and Plato seems to have accepted the atom as the fundamental unit of nature. In turn, the atom is modeled after geometric triangles. When triangles are given a third dimension, they now become solids, and it is possible to produce distinctive geometric forms based upon combining three-dimensional triangles. The Earth is composed of atoms shaped like cubes; air is made from atoms with the octahedron (pyramidal) shape; fire comes from atoms shaped like the tetrahedron; and water is based upon atoms with the icosahedron shape (Russell, 1972).

Plato was also convinced that the Universe is the result of intelligent planning. Some force with intelligence is necessary to bring the atoms together and construct physical reality. Moreover, the evolution of the Universe is not finished since physical existence still is changing. With the continuous changes taking place, the world will eventually reach its final state of perfection. But who is responsible for giving order to the Universe? Plato's answer is that the Universe follows an ideal pattern contained within the mind of God. God's intellect allows atoms to bind together. Since intelligent design was imposed upon matter by God, the Universe must also have been given a spiritual soul. Only the soul allows for intelligent functioning. Therefore, the order in the world is maintained by its soul, and physical existence can never be understood apart from spiritual existence.

God is portrayed as the master craftsman, or the Demiurge, who formed the objects of the Universe and gave it a spiritual soul. Plato also wondered what existed before the Universe and he retreated to mythology for an answer. What was present before creation was Chaos, a void through which individual atoms freely moved. God's goodness impressed upon Chaos order and the sensible world was made from the pre-existing atoms. Thus, the Universe is a receptacle or container in which God crafted reality (Martin et al., 1941). Plato's description of God differs from the Judeo-Christian tradition. For Plato, God is not the creator of the original Universe (Chaos), which apparently had and will have eternal existence. Instead, God is the supreme intelligence within the Universe directing the activities of the uncreated "chaotic stuff" (Martin et al., 1941, p. 124). Thus, God is not the all-powerful Creator of everything as portrayed in the Judeo-Christian theology.

Plato considered the Earth to be stationary and located in the center of the Universe. Since the circle is the most perfect of geometric forms, Plato, along with the Pythagoreans, placed the Sun, Moon, planets, and stars as points on the surface of spheres which revolved around the Earth. The circular and uniform rotation of the spheres around the Earth accounted for the movement of celestial objects from east to west. Moreover, the sphere was adopted as the carrier of celestial objects since the circle was the most perfect geometric form and the only one God would use in constructing motion within the Universe. However, Plato recognized a problem with this theory as an explanation of planetary motion. Planets do not move with uniform speed across the sky. Sometimes, they even show retrograde motion, initially moving from east to west, then backing up moving from west to east before resuming their westward course. Eudoxus of Cnidos (408–355 B.C.?), a student of Plato, tried to explain the strange motion of the planets by constructing an elaborate model of the Universe in which planetary motion is controlled by multiple spheres turning at different speeds. Eudoxus's theory saved the concentric sphere view of the Universe that would endure to the time of Copernicus (Kuhn, 1957).

Aristotle's Life

Aristotle was born to a privileged family in the Macedonian city of Stageira. His father was the physician to King Amyntas II of Macedonia. There is much debate as to the early years of Aristotle. However, it appears that Aristotle became a pupil of Plato at the Academy in Athens by the year 367 B.C. (Copleston, 1985a). The relationship between Aristotle and Plato lasted 20 years until the latter's death. Unfortunately, bitterness developed between the two near the end of their relationship. As aptly noted by Durant (1938, p. 59), ". . . they were both geniuses; and it is notorious that geniuses accord one another as harmoniously as dynamite with fire."

After Plato's death, Aristotle left Athens and travelled to Atarneus where he received a gift from King Hermias. In appreciation for his education, Hermias gave to Aristotle his niece (or sister) for marriage! Somehow, Aristotle accepted this arrangement and was able to make the marriage successful (Durant, 1938). Next, Aristotle was summoned to the court of King Philip, who became the powerful leader of Macedonia. Philip wanted Aristotle to tutor his son Alexander, the future world-conqueror. The education of the unruly Alexander was a difficult chore for Aristotle and only lasted two years. Nevertheless, each had made an indelible impression on the other, and it was the association to Alexander that ordained both future happiness and doom for Aristotle.

By 335 B.C., Aristotle returned to Athens and founded his own school, the Lyceum. It was the custom of Aristotle to give lectures while walking with his students, and so he became known as the "peripatetic" philosopher. However, Aristotle had as enemies the leaders of Athens who resented the Macedonian influence. Due to his association with Alexander, Aristotle had to endure diatribes directed against him by the great orator Demosthenes. But the philosopher was protected by the power of Alexander and his school prospered. Apparently, Alexander supported the school with money and sent back to Athens exotic plant and animal life found in the conquered lands of Asia (Durant, 1938). With Alexander's financial and material help, Aristotle was able to establish a zoo and botanical garden that were used to study biology at the Lyceum.

In June 323 B.C., the order of the world was shattered when Alexander the Great, who, by the age of 33, had conquered Greece, Egypt, Persia, and India, succumbed to a fever in Babylon. When the news reached Athens, a rebellion against Macedonian rule ensued. Aristotle was charged with crimes and exiled himself from Athens "lest the Athenians should sin against philosophy for a second time" (Copleston, 1985a, p. 268). A year later, Aristotle was dead and one can only guess how much the sadness produced by the events in Athens contributed to his demise. It was no better for Aristotle's enemies. Macedonia quelled the Athenians and Demosthenes was sentenced to death. When he was about to be taken prisoner, the orator committed suicide by poison (Bury, 1913). Durant (1938, p. 106) summarized these turbulent times in the following manner, "Within twelve months Greece had lost her greatest ruler, her greatest orator, and her greatest philosopher. The glory that had been Greece faded now in the dawn of the Roman sun . . ."

Aristotle's Physics

Aristotle's view of reality, found in his works *Metaphysics* and *Physics,* attempted to offer a compromise to the positions previously discussed. The Ionian philosophers of Miletus (Thales, Anaximander, Anaximenes) accepted the permanence of matter and searched for the fundamental element of physical existence. In contrast, the Eleatic school (Xenophanes, Parmenides) and Plato taught that matter is corruptible; only immaterial ideas are permanent. Aristotle combined these two views by assuming that matter is real but is subject to constant change (Clagett, 1955). Thus, material objects are always in a state of becoming something else. There can be no constancy in the terrestrial World. Next, Aristotle considered how change is possible and concluded that material objects change according to an intelligent design. Therefore, the growth of plants and animals, the geological changes taking place on Earth, and everything else that is mutable follow a plan. But where do the plans for change come from? Empedocles considered Love and Hate while Anaxagoras used Nous as the source of change. Aristotle invokes the Unmoved Mover, his conception of God, to be the first source of change in the World. The Unmoved Mover is responsible for all motion in the World. Since Aristotle taught that nothing changes but by design, he is called a teleologist. In other words, a teleologist accepts that purpose guides activity since whatever acts, acts for an end or goal. Digger wasps do not consciously know why they must burrow into the ground to lay their eggs; yet this behavior is purposive since it allows for the survival of the species. Therefore, things that change need not know consciously why they change.

The fundamental problem in Aristotle's account of reality is to explain change or motion. To handle this problem, Aristotle offered in his *Physics* the famous theory of causes (Martin et al., 1941). Change or motion bringing about the existence of objects requires four causes, and, to understand a phenomenon completely, its four causes must be specified. Each object first has a *material* cause which refers to the substance the object is made from. The second cause is called *formal* and refers to the shape of the object. The third cause is the *efficient* cause and explains what operations were necessary to create the object. But the most important cause upon which all the other causes rest is the final cause and refers to the purpose of the creator in making the object.

To illustrate his theory of causes, Aristotle took the example of a sculptor making a statue. The composition of the statue (i.e., marble) is the material cause; the completed appearance or shape of the statue, indicated by the statue's name (i.e., Venus), is the formal cause. The tools and skill of the sculptor in fashioning the statue from the raw material compose the efficient cause. But the purpose the sculptor had in mind for making the statue (i.e., to honor the gods, to make something beautiful) is the final cause. Notice the final cause logically must come first and determines the other causes. Intention is required before any physical action can be initiated. Therefore, Aristotle denied Democritus's thesis that the material world operates only through mechanical forces devoid of any intelligent purpose. Aristotle's theory of causes would eventually be the reason for fierce debates regarding the nature of scientific psychology. In the twentieth century, the Behaviorists, such as John Watson and Clark Hull, would argue that a true science of psychology must concern itself with efficient causes. In other words, scientific psychology should only concern itself with *how* human activity is accomplished. In contrast, Sigmund Freud, William McDougall, and the cognitive psychologists (Miller, Galanter, & Pribram, 1960) have maintained that the final cause or *why* an action is done must also be known for the complete understanding of human behavior.

Since it is the nature of things to change, Aristotle discussed in his *Metaphysics* the concept of *potentiality* to describe what a thing can become. Every object has potentiality. Many students have the potential to become physicians, professors, or artists. However, change is required to move from potentiality to *actuality*. Without the process of change or becoming, an object cannot fulfill its nature. Thus, some students with the necessary talent will not achieve what they could have since the required movements (i.e., studying, self-denial) did not occur. The Aristotelian ideas on potency and act may have inspired Maslow's (1970) conception of the ultimate motivational principle for human behavior, the principle of self-actualization. Also, the potentiality principle is celebrated in the poetic couplet written by John Greenleaf Whittier: "For all sad words of tongue and pen, the saddest are these: 'It might have been!'."

Aristotle also thought about the nature of the Cosmos and further developed the idea of spheres to hold and move heavenly objects (Clagett, 1971; Harrison, 1985). He believed that the Earth was stationary and at the center of the Universe. However, the Moon, each planet, and the stars were attached to separate crystalline spheres. In turn, the machinery of the spheres revolved in a circular (the most perfect motion) orbit around the Earth. To account for the retrograde motion of planets, Aristotle's system needed a total of 54 operating spheres (Harrison, 1985).

The Moon occupies the first sphere above the Earth. Everything below the sphere of the Moon is composed of Empedocles's four elements: earth, air, fire, and water. Each element is characterized by a pair of opposite qualities. Earth is cold and dry; water is cold and wet; air is hot and wet; and fire is hot and dry. In his book, *On Generation and Corruption,* Aristotle explained how elements can be transformed. By adding dryness to air, it becomes fire. The possibility that matter can be transformed will be an important step in the development of Alchemy in the middle ages. All the celestial spheres and the objects that they contain are made from a fifth element, ether. The fifth element is special and cannot be changed or combined with anything else. Thus, Aristotle does away with Democritus's concept of the void through which atoms move. The ether fills everywhere above the Earth.

The elements of the Earth and the ether of the heaven are very different. Terrestrial elements can be combined and changed but ether is the most perfect of elements and cannot be changed. Thus, Aristotle concluded different physical laws are needed to describe the activities on the Earth and in the heavens. Only objects on the Earth are subject to change. Thus, laws showing the connection between potency and act are needed for understanding of earthly events. In contrast, the heavens made of the perfect material ether are indestructible and cannot be modified. Objects possessed of ether have reached their complete actuality and are capable of the most perfect motion, circular rotation. For Aristotle, God is also perfect in the sense that God has reached full potentiality as an intellectual Being. Therefore, God cannot change and is the Unmoved Mover, the ultimate source of all motion in the Universe (Copleston, 1985a).

The Search for Harmony

With the gradual decline of the power of Greece in the last three centuries before Christ, two rival theories attempted to reconcile human nature with the nature of the Universe. Both of these theories were started by philosophers who eventually came to live in Athens. The first theory, called Stoicism, was founded by Zeno of Cyprus (350–258 B.C.). Stoicism searched for harmony between humans and the Universe based upon the premise that an intelligent force pervades all matter. The Stoics shared this opinion with Aristotle. However, Epicureanism, the second theory started by Epicurus (341–270 B.C.), tried to unify human and cosmic natures based upon the atomic theory of Democritus.

Zeno's Life

Not much is known of the individual who started Stoicism (Ueberweg, 1888a). His early life was spent in the city of Citium on Cyprus and he worked as a merchant. The life and ideas of Socrates greatly impressed Zeno and he began to pursue the study of philosophy. About 310 B.C., Zeno started a popular school in Athens which contained a covered promenade (Stoa) that inspired the name of his philosophy. Unlike other philosophers of Athens, Zeno was well respected and was given a public burial following his death.

Stoic Physics

The Stoics thought it was necessary to have the proper understanding of the human's place in the Cosmos. Human existence would be made understandable by knowing the nature of the Universe. The Stoics accepted Aristotle's thesis that cosmic space contains matter, thus rejecting Democritus's concept of the void. However, the Stoics disagreed with Aristotle's claim that the most perfect matter exists in spheres above the Earth. Instead, they taught that matter was the same everywhere. The Stoics also rejected Plato's teaching that physically existing objects participate in an immaterial idea, serving as the ultimate basis of reality. For the Stoics, the only thing that exists is matter (Russell, 1972).

The major problem for Stoic physics was to explain the order in the physical Universe. The Stoics revived the idea from Heraclitus that the fundamental unit of matter is fire. All things have a component of fire in them. For fire represents the force or pneuma that binds all matter together. In other words, the pneuma is spread throughout the entire Universe and penetrates all physical things (Sambursky, 1963). The fire of the Universe also is the intelligent God of the Universe. Thus, God is a rational substance that governs all activities of the Universe. God is the center of the Universe and also will bring an end to it. The Universe was created from fire and it will perish in fire. The end of the Universe will perhaps be followed by another cycle of creation and destruction.

The Stoics concluded that the physical world, driven by the intelligence of the fiery God, must be determined. All things and events are interconnected. There can be no accidents in the Stoic Universe. Since past, present, and future events flow together in a causal chain, the Stoics saw the usefulness of astrology and divination (the art of reading the entrails of animals to foretell the future). The Zodiac and animal parts were considered to be signals for what will happen. However, a Stoic scientist named Posidonius (135–51 B.C.?) was able to notice more reliable connections in nature. Posidonius discovered that ocean tides are related to the phases of the Moon (Russell, 1972). This correlation between earthly and heavenly events was explained as the work of the cosmic force linking all matter together. The term adopted by the Stoics to indicate the presence of the supreme intellectual force giving order to the Universe through the continuity of matter was "sympathy" (Sambursky, 1963, p. 141). Thus, the relationship between the ocean tides and the position of the Moon is evidence of the sympathy that runs through all of nature. Regarding humans, the early Stoics assumed that the soul, which is part of the universal intellectual force, died with the body. However, Posidonius thought that the soul, being made from the cosmic fire, returned to the Cosmos after death. Wicked souls stay near the Earth, but good souls occupy the regions of the stars where they can help mortals through astrology (Russell, 1972).

Zeno stressed that Socrates provided the example of how humans should conduct themselves. Humans should be in conformity with the rule of intellect. When Stoics said, "live according to nature," they meant that humans should live according to reason (Copleston, 1985a, p. 395). When one lives a life of conformity to the rules of nature, virtue is obtained. Virtue for the Stoics was signified in one who was dominated by reason and not by emotion, who was temperate, and who would accept adversity as the Will of God. These characteristics put the human in harmony with the rest of the world. Finally, the Stoics were adamant that the first duty of the human is to serve others. The welfare of the group is more important than the welfare of the individual.

Epicurus's Life

Epicurus was born of Greek heritage on the island of Samos. During his adolescence, he became fond of philosophy and thoroughly studied the doctrines of Democritus which became the foundation of his philosophy. As a young adult, Epicurus was a teacher and eventually moved his school to Athens in 307 B.C. Apparently, Epicurus enjoyed a simple life in Athens. His school consisted of a house and garden and he was called the "garden philosopher." Although Epicurus had a long life in Athens, much of it was spent in misery caused by physical afflictions. Epicurus apparently often wrote about his afflictions to the extent that he might have had a hypochondriacal personality. Nevertheless, Epicurus was widely respected in Athens and displayed a gentle, empathic manner in his interactions with others (Russell, 1972).

Epicurean Physics

Epicurus's view of human nature directed him to accept Democritus's atomic theory of matter. However, important modifications had to be made to the theory. Epicurus began with the belief that everything is made from indestructible atoms.

Since atoms are physical, no spiritual existence is possible. In making these points, Epicurus enunciated the following principles: "Nothing can come from nothing; and the existent cannot become the nonexistent" (Ueberweg, 1888a, p. 206).

If there is no intellectual force to guide matter, how did creation take place? Epicurus answered that atoms originally moved through the void at a constant speed and direction. However, he had to grant certain freedom of action to the atoms. Some of the moving atoms spontaneously changed course, as if free will were operating, to allow for atomic collisions. Our world is the result of atoms clumping together. Since humans are made from atoms that have free movement, humans must also have free will. Thus, Epicurus is a unique philosopher who believed only in material existence but allowed humans to have free choice over behavior. At death, the atoms of the soul, having the properties of air, would scatter from the body (Ueberweg, 1888a).

Epicurus and his Roman follower, the poet Lucretius (95–52 B.C.), used the above view of the Universe to teach that humans should not fear death since the soul will cease to be an entity capable of sensation. Epicurus was trying to combat the opinion that death is followed by punishment, an idea that entered Greek philosophy at the time of Plato. As Russell (1972, p. 248) remarks, "hell was not created by the Christians."

Epicurus accepted the existence of gods. They too were made from atoms but did not concern themselves with matters on Earth (unlike the inhabitants of Mount Olympus). The gods occupy a domain in space and exist in perfect happiness. To be in harmony with the Universe, humans should be like gods. In other words, humans should use their free wills to pursue pleasure and happiness. However, Epicurus pointed out that humans often make decisions for happiness that, instead, produce unwanted sadness. Happiness is best achieved through tranquility which requires the human to make choices that minimize the occurrence of disappointment, sadness, stress, and pain.

The Conclusion of Greek Astrophysics

In 331 B.C., Alexander the Great personally picked the site for the construction of a great city to commemorate his victories. The city was to be built on the shores of the Mediterranean Sea in Egypt and named after himself. The result was the marble city of Alexandria, splendid in every detail and renowned for its 300 foot lighthouse (Pharos), one of the seven wonders of the ancient world. Ironically, Alexander himself did not live long enough to see his city. As Athens lost its beauty and influence, the Greeks began to shift the center of their civilization to the new city. A repository of

Greek knowledge was needed and so the followers of Aristotle built the great Museum in Alexandria to meet this need (Bernal, 1972). The Museum, named for the muses, contained a great library holding the works of the notable Greek authors and a faculty of scholars who were paid to teach. Facilities were also provided for research and creative expression. Indeed, the Museum was very much like a university.

Aristarchus and Eratosthenes

Astronomers at the Museum made remarkable discoveries. For example, Aristarchus, who lived in the third century B.C., concluded that the Sun was the center of the system of known planets. Thus, the Earth, the center of the Aristotelian Universe, was relegated to an orbital plane around the Sun as are all the planets. Thus, Aristarchus was able to anticipate the revolutionary theory of Copernicus nineteen centuries in the future. Aristarchus's own work on the nature of the solar system has unfortunately been lost and we only know of him from the commentaries provided by Archimedes (Clagett, 1971).

Archimedes also had a friend Eratosthenes (276–194 B.C.) who was a librarian at the Museum. Eratosthenes, through the clever use of observation and mathematics, concluded that the Earth was round and proceeded to measure its circumference. Eratosthenes knew that the Sun at its high point in the sky on the day of the summer solstice cast no shadow in the city of Syene (modern Aswan). However, to the north in Alexandria, at the same moment, the Sun cast a shadow of 7.5 degrees. The distance between Syene and Alexandria was walked and found to be 500 miles. Since 7.5 degrees is about 2% of the circumference of a circle, the next step was to let the 500 miles represent 2% of the Earth's circumference. Working the mathematics of proportion, the total circumference of the Earth was estimated to be 25,000 miles, a value very close to the actual one (Clagett, 1971).

Ptolemy

Aristarchus tried to account for the passage of planets in the sky by assuming that they orbit the Sun just as the Earth does. This remarkable insight, however, was criticized. Alexandrian astronomy was dominated by the old Greek idea that the Earth was the center of the Universe. Foremost in propagating this belief was Claudius Ptolemy (A.D. 100–178) who presented his cosmology in a book entitled the *Almagest*. (This title represents a combination of Arabic-Greek words for the "greatest").

Ptolemy's model of the Universe resorted to the use of spheres. The perfect motion of the Universe was circular so all the objects of the Cosmos revolve around the Earth in circular orbits. However, planets, like Mars and Jupiter, seem to stop their motion from east to west across the sky and even reverse course. To explain the problem of retrograde motion, Ptolemy's system required planets to have epicycles. The epicycle appears to have been the invention of two earlier Greek astronomers, Appollonius and Hipparchus, and refers to a planet turning in a small circular orbit as the planet moves in its larger orbit around the Earth (Kuhn, 1957). Thus, the irregular motion of the planets is caused by their positions within the epicycles observed from Earth.

The *Almagest* insured that Aristotle's and Ptolemy's ideas regarding the Universe would predominate through the Middle Ages. In 827, the book was translated from Greek to Arabic and it was considered a holy work among the Muslims. Much later, in the twelfth century, the *Almagest* was translated twice from Arabic and Greek into Latin (Haskins, 1960). The Latin translations became the basis for religious authorities to maintain that the Earth was a special place since it was located in the center of the Universe. The Ptolemaic view of the Universe received no serious challenges until 1543 when Copernicus wrote *On the Revolutions of the Heavenly Spheres* that maintained the Sun is the center of our planetary system.

Contributions of the Greeks

Ptolemy can be considered to be the last great representative of Greek science. During the 800 years between Thales and Ptolemy, the Greeks had made remarkable observations about nature without the aid of much scientific technology. Issues regarding the structure of matter, the nature of the Universe, and the basis of reality still very much concern us. The Greeks can be viewed as being the first to ask systematically the fundamental questions.

The Greeks held that the world is an orderly place that is guided by intelligence. This point is expressed eloquently in Aristotle's theory of the four causes. The operation of the final cause, the most important of the four causes, requires that intelligence and reason guide all existence. The legacy of this Greek view is that science tries to understand the order that governs the activity of existing things. The world is not a cold machine operating in a vacuum of self-contained, deterministic principles, as would be maintained by positivistic thinkers of the 17th and 18th centuries. Instead, the world is structured through the operation of intelligence. In the contemporary sciences of physics and psychology, the operations of an orderly world signifies the importance of "information." Indeed, many in physics and psychology today argue that all systems contain an inherent informational structure which must be deciphered in order to understand any phenomenon.

The Greeks accorded a special place to humans. Thus, in Socrates's teachings, humans are urged to acquire virtue which means that each person should develop traits that aid in the acquisition of what we would call today self-actualization. Change, the hallmark of existence, should move a person from a lesser level of perfection to a higher one. As one grows older, one is expected to become wiser and more understanding of the meaning of things. Finally, the Greek view of rationality impressed the Christian writers of the gospel. In the gospel of Saint John, Christ is the supreme example of *logos* (intellect) that provides the knowledge of how to attain virtue.

As appealing as the Greek view may be, the physicists and philosophers accepting the Newtonian view of the world machine would later argue that final causality does not belong within the domain of scientific explanation. Accordingly, philosophers, such as Francis Bacon (1561–1626), and scientists, such as Pierre LaPlace (1749–1827), removed final causality from scientific explanations. In the positivistic view of science, inferences can only be drawn from direct observations of causal connections. No hidden variables, which lurk within the concept of final causality, can be allowed into science. Nevertheless, the Greek view of reality is so powerful that it has provided the basis for the continuing debate regarding how the paradigms of science should be constructed. This issue will be revisited in Chapter 7.

Given the importance of the Greeks to Western civilization, it is tragic that the central locus for their knowledge, the Library of Alexandria, would not survive (Parsons, 1967). The first major threat to the Library resulted from the assignation between Julius Caesar and Cleopatra. As these two vacationed in Alexandria in 47 B.C., their enemies moved against them. Caesar, with only a small army to protect him, was outnumbered and saved his situation by burning the Alexandrian navy. Unfortunately, some of the burning embers from the ships in the harbor blew into the Library and caused a major blaze. In succeeding centuries, a few Roman emperors made threats against the Library with the most serious one coming from Theodosius about 375. As a Christian emperor of Rome, Theodosius ordered the destruction of paganism within the empire. In Alexandria, the Christian zealots carried out Theodosius's orders by smashing Greek art, sacking the Library, and murdering the Library's last great scholar, a remarkable woman name Hypatia. About 640, the Muslims under Omar conquered Egypt and he apparently ordered the destruction of the Library and all of its contents.

The loss of the Library was an immense tragedy for civilization. For 1000 years, it was the guardian and protector of Greek knowledge. With its destruction went the contributions of numerous ancient scholars for whom no written record remains today. The Library's demolition was a fitting signal for the intellectual darkness that would descend over the West in the first centuries of the Middle Ages. However, the flame of knowledge would eventually spark again.

Buddhism: Reconciling Change with Eternity

About the same time that Heraclitus and Parmenides were arguing about the stability of existence, another individual, thousands of miles away in India, was concerned with the same question. His name was Siddhartha Gautama (560–480 B.C.) who would become known as the Buddha or "enlightened one."

Siddhartha was raised in comfortable surroundings; however, around 530 B.C., he became disturbed about the human condition. Outside the protective boundaries of his wealthy existence, he realized that humans must confront terrible ordeals involving change. The young become old; the healthy become sick; and all pass from life to death. Vowing to understand the mystery of existence, Siddhartha left his family and sought out teachers who could help him to gain understanding. However, disappointed with his teachers, he decided to seek understanding through self contemplation. Eventually, he settled under a fig tree and entered successive states of meditation through which several important insights were gained.

Siddhartha's meditations revealed that all living things are linked in an eternal triangle: all are born; all must suffer: and all must die. Furthermore, reincarnation of the human spirit into another body means that the triangle continues its existence indefinitely. For humans, the quality of each reincarnated existence is controlled by moral behavior. This leads to the Law of Karma (i.e., the Law of Cause and Effect) which indicates that humans determine their own future existences in the current life and the next life by their moral choices.

Siddhartha also contemplated the nature of happiness and drew the following conclusions. First, all humans suffer. Secondly, suffering is tied to the demands of the ego taking more from the world than is correct or possible. Thirdly, by leaving the physical world through meditation, suffering is eliminated. Finally, the method to attain *nirvana,* the state of happiness that is eternal, requires the individual to understand oneself, one's current position in life, and morality. By achieving the state of nirvana, the world of change is replaced by a world of constant contentment.

Hinduism: The Use of Consciousness to Discover Being

The Hindu people of ancient India composed between 600 and 300 B.C. sacred writings known as the *Upanishads*. In these writings, the meaning of reality was probed in the same thoughtful fashion as was being done in Greece. The answer to reality, as discovered in the *Upanishads,* is remarkably similar to Plato's conclusions. The human mind, turning within itself, can discover the ultimate source of reality. For the Hindu writers of the *Upanishads,* as for Plato, the insight into the mystery of reality involves the realization that the physical world is temporary. Behind the screen of material existence stands true reality which can only be explored by the mind, not by the senses. By using meditation, Hinduism teaches that the mind can eventually realize that the source of consciousness and the Creator are one. To appreciate the full meaning of this realization, a lifetime of personal study and reflection is necessary.

The most informative insight into the nature of reality comes from the *Upanishad* known as *Katha.* In this story, a young man named Nachiketas experiences difficulties with his family and is sent away by his father to visit and learn from Death. Death, personified as Yama, impressed by the holiness of Nachiketas, offers to him three gifts. Nachiketas takes, as the first gift, reconciliation with his father and family. For the second gift, Nachiketas chooses fire which symbolizes knowledge, meditation, and practice, all of which are necessary for the attainment of wisdom. For his third gift, Death suggests to Nachiketas that he take riches, power, kingdoms, long life, anything whatever that satisfies the heart! However, Nachiketas wanted for his third gift something that Death could never take back. Nachiketas asked Death to explain the meaning of immortality. Death, pleasantly surprised by Nachiketas's wise choice, then instructs him how to find immortality. Death tells Nachiketas that an enlightened individual does not seek things that will perish (i.e., reclaimed by death). The wise individual must seek that which cannot be destroyed. That which cannot be annihilated is the Spirit of the Universe that pervades all existing things. Regarding Spirit, Death explains that (Griffiths, 1994, p.61):

> No eye can see Him, nor has He a face that can be seen, yet through meditation and through discipline He can be found in the heart. He that finds Him enters immortal life.

Then, Nachiketas departed Death "having learned . . . this knowledge, learned the method of meditation, rose above desire and death, found God, who does the like, finds him." (Griffiths, 1994, p. 62)

The Meaning of Reality: Medieval Views

2

The incredible work begun by the ancients to understand reality was momentarily halted in the West by vast changes taking place in the geopolitical order. The Roman conquerors of Greece realized the significance of that culture and became its caretaker. However, as the Roman Empire weakened and finally fell to the barbarian invaders in the West (476), intellectual activity declined. The Christian Church, headed by the Pope in Rome, assumed responsibility for civilizing the barbarian hordes. Finally, western Europe settled into a Feudal society, dominated by the Roman church. This era is known as the Middle Ages which lasted from the years 500 to 1500. After the Fall of Rome, centuries would be required before concentrated intellectual pursuits would again be noticeable in Europe.

Byzantium and Islam

The Byzantine Empire

The Roman Empire in the East remained and became known as the Byzantine Empire. It was to last to 1453 when conquered by the Turks. The center of Byzantium was Constantinople which was a rich City retaining the classical scholarship that had disappeared in the West. Also, Christian authority, represented by the Patriarch of Constantinople, was a dominant force in the Eastern Empire. However, divisions between the Pope and the Patriarch over authority became critical (Greanakoplos, 1979). In 1054, Pope Leo IX sent emissaries to Constantinople to excommunicate the patriarch for not following the dictates from Rome. However, the event that produced irreconcilable differences between East and West was the Fourth Crusade of 1204. Through political intrigue, this crusade was diverted from its mission to rescue the Holy Lands from the Muslims and eventually sacked Constantinople. The pillage was on an immense scale resulting in the destruction of ancient manuscripts and art. Several other ancient works of art along with Christian relics were taken to the West. Sixty years were required for Constantinople to recover from this terrible ordeal and the burning hatred of the Western "barbarians" fortified the split between Greek and Roman churches that has continued to the present day.

The Islamic Empire

The Muslim faith spread from Arabia to include lands from Spain to Pakistan. Their territorial conquests allowed the Islamic people to learn about the Greek, Roman, and Hindu civilizations (Wallbank and Taylor, 1960). Many important works from these cultures were translated into Arabic by the end of the tenth century.

Not only did the Islamic people become conservators of the ancient knowledge, they also made substantial contributions in the areas of medicine, astronomy, mathematics, literature, philosophy, physics, and chemistry. For example, Alhazen (965–1039) studied human anatomy and found evidence that disagreed with the theories of Ptolemy and Euclid that vision depends upon the eye generating rays. Avicenna (980–1037), in addition to his important contributions to mathematics and medicine, developed a philosophy based upon Aristotle. Also, Aveffoes (1126–1198), using Aristotle, tried to reconcile faith and reason which is the same quest undertaken for Christianity by St. Thomas Aquinas in the thirteenth century. In astronomy, Islamic scholars studied Ptolemy's views and were able to make accurate predictions for celestial events. The Muslims improved upon the astrolabe, a Greek device for charting the location of the stars and Sun and telling time. Islamic astronomy was also touched by astrology and the astrolabe was thought to have mystical significance (Browonski, 1973).

The Christian West was threatened by the power of the Islamic movement, especially as the Muslim tide surged into Spain during the 7th and 8th centuries. Eventually, the expansion of Islam into Europe was checked and Christianity struck back. Through the urging of Pope Urban II, the first of eight crusades was launched in 1095 to rescue the Holy Land from the Muslims (Geanakoplos, 1979). As the most successful of all these efforts, the first crusade was able to capture Jerusalem. However, the crusaders were bent upon savagery and killed thousands of Muslims and Jews in the holy city. The Western presence in the Holy Land would remain until 1291 when the Muslims finally drove the last Christian force from Acre.

The era of the Crusades lasted two centuries and resulted in the deaths of thousands. But the Crusades did bring the West into contact with the superior cultures of Byzantium and Islam. European isolation in science, literature, and economics was about to end. However, bloody contact with the Europeans left the Muslims, like the

Byzantines, with a deep hate and mistrust of the West. Thus, the cultural exchange to the West from the East was not freely given.

The Transmission of Scholarship

An indispensable step rekindling the Western interest in scholarship was the translation of Greek and Islamic manuscripts into Latin (Lindberg, 1978). When the Roman Empire fell in the West, knowledge of the Greek language gradually disappeared. Thus, the West was cut off from the intellectual tradition of the Greeks. Fortunately, not all knowledge was lost in the West since the surviving works of several Roman writers, such as Cicero, Lucretius, and Pliny, represented Greek thought. Also, the Latin translations of Aristotle's works on logic, Plato's *Timeaus,* and Hippocrates's medical works appeared to have weathered the barbarian invasions and were never lost. Nevertheless, the bulk of Greek knowledge had to be reintroduced into the intellectually starved West.

The twelfth century was the time for the intensive work of translation and scholars from Ireland, England, Italy, and Spain were mainly responsible for the effort. In the previous century, the *reconquista* of Spain from the Muslims was successful and a great opportunity was given to translate Islamic writers and Islamic versions of Greek works into Latin. Spain had become a center for Islamic intellectual activity and a repository for many of the Islamic translations of Greek classics. After the return of Spain to Christendom, the city of Toledo attracted many Western scholars for the translation effort. It was there that an Italian, Gerard of Cremona, provided the West with a translation of Ptolemy's *Almagest.*

The other renowned centers in the twelfth century for translations were Italy and Sicily. The translations were mostly done from Greek into Latin. These regions were able to maintain close contact with the Byzantine Empire with the result that many Greek sources became available. Here, James of Venice gave the West the Latin translations of most of Aristotle's important books on physics, metaphysics, and the soul. The Greek version of Ptolemy's *Almagest* was given as a gift from Constantinople to a Sicilian king. This provided the opportunity for Henry Aristippus and Emir Eugene to translate the great work from Greek to Latin, about 15 years before Gerald of Cremona's rendering from Arabic.

As Lindberg (1978) notes, the sustained translation work lasting into the thirteenth century was remarkable for many reasons. First, it was not a coordinated effort. Scholars basically translated what was available and what they were curious about. Secondly, the translation work had to be supported. In this regard, the scholars were being financed by the Church and wealthy nobles. Finally, all matters considered, the translations were of excellent quality with most scholars trying to be faithful to the words in the original sources. The great infusion of knowledge provided by the translations required some time to comprehend, and the West moved quickly to the task so that, by the fourteenth century, the foundation for modern science became established. However, one more ingredient was necessary before the West was ready again to blossom intellectually.

The Rise of Medieval Universities

The return of knowledge to the West helped to spark the development of major centers of learning and scholarship. These places were called Universities drawn from the Latin word *Universitas* meaning a collection of individuals dedicated to a common goal. The first University was established in the eleventh century at Salerno, Italy and became famous for its medical school. In the twelfth century, Paris and Bologna developed Universities that became celebrated for theology and law, respectively. By the end of the twelfth century, at least fourteen major Universities existed in Spain, France, England, and Italy (Strayer & Munro, 1970).

Initially, all Universities required their studies to be done in Latin. Following suggestions concerning education made by Plato in the *Republic,* basic instruction required courses in the seven liberal arts—grammar, logic, rhetoric, arithmetic, geometry, music, and astronomy (Kibre & Siraisi, 1978). Sufficient accomplishment in these courses led to an awarding of a degree, the *bachelor,* requiring about four years of study. Continued study for another three years led to the *Master's* degree which mandated the student to present an original piece of work or *Masterpiece.* Continuing the University for another seven years was necessary to obtain the highest degree, the *Doctor's,* which initially was given in three areas: theology, medicine, and law. The granting of all degrees required the student to submit to a rigorous oral exam, called the disputation, and the higher the degree the more arduous was the disputation. When the disputation was passed, the degree was awarded but not before the student arranged a banquet for the professors composing the disputation committee!

Recognizing their eminence and influence, the Popes of the twelfth and thirteenth centuries became important benefactors of the Universities (Strayer & Munro, 1970). By giving financial support, the Church was able to control the possibility that the Universities might spawn heresies against Christianity. Given the strong involvement of the Church, it is not surprising that many of the early scholars of the Universities were also clergy. For example, Albert the Great (1193–1280) and St. Thomas Aquinas (1225–1274), teachers at Paris, were also members of the Dominican order of priests while Roger Bacon (1214–1294) and William of Occam (1290–1349), teachers at Oxford, belonged to the Franciscan order. Both the Dominicans and the Franciscans (and later the Jesuits) were under the direct authority of the Pope.

Universities were able to regenerate the interest in searching for the answers to the fundamental questions raised by the Greeks. More specifically, it was the return of Aristotle's theories which seemed to provide the focus of intellectual attention. Many scholars became concerned with determining whether Aristotle's explanations were indeed accurate or did they undermine the basic tenets of Christianity. The problem of Aristotle provided the scholars of the Universities the means to develop logical argument and methods of verification that later would be incorporated into the scientific method.

Transition from a Platonic to an Aristotelian World View

Changes in the approach to the acquisition of knowledge in medieval times provided the opportunity for the eventual success of science in the 17th century. Ironically, the major intellectual change involved an acceptance of the growing influence of empiricism, championed in Aristotle's philosophy, by the Christian followers of Plato. William of Conches (1080–1154), an ardent Christian Platonist, offered opinions as to how a merger between the philosophies of Plato and Aristotle should happen for the advancement of knowledge.

In Plato's philosophy, the physical World is a mere shadow of the true World of intellectual ideas. All physical things are copies of ideal and immaterial forms with the most celebrated forms being truth, beauty, and goodness. Moreover, Plato concluded that the intellectual forms are embedded, as innate knowledge, within the human soul and can be discovered by a process of rational introspection. In contrast, Aristotle considered the human mind to be void of knowledge at birth. Therefore, Aristotle approached the acquisition of knowledge from empiricism. The senses discover the real World and present it to the mind. The human mind, with its inherent power to generate concepts, then develops an understanding of the World. However, without sensory inputs, humans have no ideas. The growing influence of Aristotle's empirical approach to knowledge favors the development of science since the promise is made that careful observation of the World is the only reliable basis by which humans can know truth.

William of Conches, born in Normandy, understood that the rise of the University system made possible an empirical approach to knowledge. Moreover, William also intuited that future knowledge systems would be much different from those known in his time. In one of his earlier works, *Philosophia* written in 1125, William admitted that philosophers had inadequate understanding of the physical World and human nature. He warned that rhetoric without evidence is foolish. In other words, those who profess an understanding of things need to provide the reasons for their theories. As William said, "We know many who seek the ornament of words, few the truth of knowledge." (Cadden, 1995, p. 6). William implored his audience to seek, "the true understanding of what exists and is not seen and of what exists and is seen." (Cadden, 1995, p. 6). The Platonic approach is necessary to pursue the former, while the Aristotelian approach satisfies the latter.

The *Philosophia* reviewed the status of scientific knowledge in the twelfth century. William carefully considered the hierarchies of complexity in matter that begin with the four elements (earth, air, fire, and water) and eventuate to the human body. William's description of the human body as the result of an orderly development starting from an embryo and ending with the adult form was a remarkable accommodation to the Aristotelian approach. To support his conclusions about human development, William cited the works of Constantine the African, who had translated several Arabic texts on medicine into Latin (Peters, 1962). By using Constantine's writings, which were based upon empirical research, William broke with the tradition of relying upon Plato's works as reference sources. However, in concluding his treatment of human nature, William remained faithful to the Platonic view that the immaterial soul is responsible for mental operations.

Later in his life, William wrote the *Dragmaticon* which was a further exploration into the realm of science (i.e., natural philosophy). However, part of the *Dragmaticon* served as a social commentary regarding the functions of the new Universities. William and other writers, such as John of Salisbury, warned that students were coming to the Universities with the sole purpose of seeking training in such fields as medicine and law in order to have lucrative incomes. These students really have no interest in knowledge and understanding of ultimate themes. William issued a warning to such students (Cadden, 1995, p. 16):

> And thus, with a wise purse and a foolish mind, they return to their relatives. O
> how easy is wisdom! Any usurer can be wise. O what kind of wisdom is it which
> a thief can steal, a mouse can gnaw, a moth can destroy, rain can wash away,
> fire can consume?

In the 20th century, John Henry Newman (1927/1958) would also write about the true value of a University education. Newman acknowledged that the University is the place where a great wealth of knowledge can be obtained by students. However, the passive filling of a student's memory with arcane facts is not the purpose of a University education. Instead, Newman encourages students to become actively excited by their studies so that the maturation of the intellect can occur since this ". . .

puts the mind above the influences of chance and necessity, above anxiety, suspense, unsettlement, and superstition, which is the lot of many" (Newman, 1927/1958, p 28).

In summary, William of Conches conceded that the Aristotelian method of obtaining knowledge is useful. He acknowledged that the progress of empirical science should be encouraged. However, William urged that the Platonic advancements of the past should not be buried or ignored as natural philosophy continues its march forward. Each new age must be caretakers of the knowledge and wisdom of the previous age.

The Return of Aristotelian Thought

By 1250, many of the important translations of Aristotle's philosophical and scientific works were disseminated throughout the West. In addition, the Islamic commentaries, especially those of Averroes, were receiving wide attention by scholars hungry for understanding of the classical past. However, the rediscovery of Aristotle led to crises in theology, philosophy, and science, all of which were closely bound together in the Middle Ages (Grant, 1971).

From the end of the Roman Empire until the thirteenth century, Christian dogma was interpreted from the positions advocated by Plato. This Platonic influence was provided by St. Augustine (A.D. 354–430) who ruled Christianity in North Africa from his position as bishop of Hippo. Augustine found support for many of the Christian beliefs in Plato's philosophy. More specifically, Plato taught that the human soul was immortal, ultimate truth is known by the soul not by the body, and God is responsible for creation. All of these principles were consistent with Christianity. So important was Plato to the early Christians that some thought of him as a Greek prophet for their faith. Augustine himself is often considered to be the Christian Plato. But the return of Aristotle caused reevaluations in the philosophical foundations of Christianity and of the methods by which knowledge is discovered.

Although Platonic scholars, such as William of Conches, were constructively preparing for the return of Aristotelian methodology, others resisted with a vengeance. The Christian Platonists believed that the proper understanding of what is real is conveyed through signs and symbols. These Christian Platonists of medieval times used the signs and symbols contained in prayer and rituals to contact the spiritual God. Thus, many Christian Platonists became threatened by the empirical approach to knowledge that calls into question beliefs not based upon sensory evidence. As portrayed in Umberto Eco's novel, *The Name of the Rose,* the medieval division between the Platonic and Aristotelian world views was charged with anger, treachery, and resentment.

Christianizing Aristotle: Scholasticism

Many scholars of the Church greeted the return of Aristotle as providing another way to understand Christian faith within a philosophical framework. Interest in Aristotle was high in those who had difficulty accepting Plato's philosophy; and a concerted effort, known as Scholasticism, was undertaken to make Aristotle's ideas the basis for religious belief.

Peter Abelard

Much of the stimulation to seek a new way of understanding was supplied by Peter Abelard (1079–1142). He was born in rugged Brittany in France and eventually went to Paris where he became a major philosopher and theologian (Strayer & Munro, 1970). Abelard was a popular teacher with his students but his critical attacks and pompous style created enmity among his colleagues. His fellow teachers showed little compassion when Abelard was castrated on orders of the canon of Notre Dame. The attack resulted from a love affair between Abelard and the beautiful Heloise who was the canon's niece. To escape embarrassment, both Heloise and Abelard entered the clergy (Strayer & Munro, 1970).

In philosophy, Abelard said that knowledge can be obtained through the rigorous use of logic. In his book, *Sic et Non* (Yes and No), Abelard developed a thinking style which requires the reasoner to list arguments for and against a proposition. As Russell (1972) acknowledges, this book helped to inspire confidence in the human mind's ability to discover truth on its own.

Abelard also used the philosophy of Aristotle in seeking a resolution to one of the most difficult questions for medieval thinkers (Geanakoplos, 1979). This issue concerned whether abstract concepts signify something that exists outside the mind. This issue was called the problem of universals or the problem of "the one and the many." The traditional answer to this question, based upon the philosophies of Plato and Augustine, was Realism which said that humans partake in but do not create abstract ideas. Therefore, abstract ideas, such as truth and beauty, correspond to absolute ideas established by God. There may be many beautiful things but only one absolute concept of beauty. In contrast to Realism, others proposed Nominalism based upon Aristotle's philosophy. In Nominalism, abstract concepts are the product of the human mind and they have no ontological status beyond the rational mind. Nominalism was invading the traditional stance of Realism and could lead to the denial that Christian abstractions, such as the Holy Trinity, have real existence. Unsurprisingly, Nominalism was officially condemned as heresy at the Council of Soissons in 1092.

Abelard proposed Conceptualism as a compromise position to rid Christianity of the Realism-Nominalism debate. In Conceptualism, abstract ideas are assumed to have real existence within the human mind. The human mind has the capability to produce these universal concepts by its own power of comparison. In other words, the human mind notices what is similar among many objects and generates a concept to signify the similarities. The ability of the mind to generate abstract ideas is a thesis taken directly from Aristotle. Abelard acknowledged that God's mind also generates ideas. This last point soothed the Realists since it allows God to establish the reality of all existence.

Saint Thomas Aquinas

Abelard demonstrated that Aristotle's approach was valuable in discovering truth. However, Abelard did not develop a systematic philosophy for Christianity based upon Aristotle. That task became the life work of St. Thomas Aquinas (1225–1274).

Thomas was born into a rich family that lived near Naples, Italy. His family made plans for Thomas to become a cardinal, maybe even Pope. However, Thomas had other goals. He joined the Dominican order of monks who lived in poverty but who were devoted to scholarship. One story says that Thomas's family was so angry with him that they locked him in a room with a young lady in hopes that he would renounce his vow of chastity and leave the Dominicans (Geanakoplos, 1979). Apparently, this tactic failed and Thomas, who would become known as the "angelic doctor," went to Paris to study theology with the leading Aristotelian of the time, Albert the Great (1193–1280).

St. Thomas illustrated the use of logical inquiry, initiated by Abelard, in two great works, *Summa Theologica* and *Summa contra Gentiles*. Thomas considered that humans can know reality and the Universe by one of two ways. The first avenue is through the direct revelation from God. The second method is to use the rational capacity of the human mind to produce knowledge. Following Aristotle, Thomas maintained that the human mind has no innate ideas; however, the power to produce understanding is an inherent ability that is activated by sensory observations of the world. In his works, Thomas showed how the rational mind using its abilities could reason to the great truths of Christianity. However, if a conflict arose between faith and reason, the mind must bow to revelation since human thinking is fallible.

Thomas argued that the presence of the World indicates that God must exist. Falling back to Aristotle's principals of causality, God must be both the final and efficient cause of the Universe. God is the Unmoved Mover who determines how potentiality becomes actuality. Thomas corrected Aristotle with regard to the spirituality of the human soul. Since universal ideas are abstract and not physical, the agency for the knowledge (the soul's mind) must also be immaterial. In agreement with Aristotle, Thomas maintained that the human mind generates its own ideas and does not have them innately as supposed by Plato and Augustine (Ueberweg, 1888a).

Although many Platonic Christians sought to have Thomas's works banned, they would be eventually recognized as great works. To acknowledge their importance, Pope Leo XIII in 1879 wrote an encyclical letter stressing the value of Thomas's writings in understanding the Catholic faith.

The Problem of Aristotle

Not all scholars sought to use Aristotle's philosophy to clarify Christianity. There was also a movement in the Middle Ages to accept a secular version of Aristotle. This movement was encouraged by the Islamic works of Averroes, who supplied his own commentaries on Aristotle's philosophy. Hence, the movement to retain Aristotle in pure form was called Averroism.

Several points in Aristotle's philosophy were seized upon by the Averroists that became inimical to Christian beliefs. For example, Aristotle thought that the World always existed, which is inconsistent with the idea of divine creation. Also, Aristotle's opinion that the individual human soul ceases to exist at death questions personal salvation. The crises stirred by Aristotelian philosophy led to the condemnation of 1277. The condemnation was ordered by Pope John XXI, carried out by Etienne Tempier, Bishop of Paris, and aimed at the University of Paris. In total, 219 propositions derived from Aristotelian philosophy, including some formulated by St. Thomas, were judged to be invalid and belief in any of them was punished by excommunication (Grant, 1971). The effect of the condemnation was to create a split between religion and philosophy. Similar episodes to the condemnation would also foster the later antagonism between religion and science.

Roger Bacon

Compared to the Dominicans, the Franciscan scholars were inclined to challenge orthodoxy; and one of their most outspoken members was Roger Bacon (1214?–1294). He was a supporter of Aristotle's philosophy but cautioned that even Aristotle could be fallible. The true means for securing knowledge was through controlled observation (the experimental method). Mathematics was also assumed to represent the highest form of knowledge obtainable without the aid of revelation.

Bacon claimed that the mind must be free of prejudice and prejudgment in order to be effective in knowledge acquisition. In his famous *Opus Maius,* he listed the human traits that produce stupidity (Wallbank & Taylor, 1960, p. 381):

> There are four principle stumbling blocks to comprehending the truth, which hinder well-nigh every scholar: the example of frail and unworthy authority, long-established custom, and the sense of the ignorant crowd, and the hiding of one's ignorance under the show of wisdom.

Unfortunately, Bacon did not use prudence in attacking his critics. In 1278, he was placed in prison for 14 years and his works were banned. Nevertheless, Bacon represented the coming of the experimental method in which observation, and not authority, dictates what is true.

William of Occam

The developing breach between religion and philosophy was made wider by William of Occam (1290–1349). Born in England, William became a Franciscan priest and teacher at Paris. However, continued debates with the Pope over his authority forced William to seek refuge in Germany under the protection of Lewis of Bavaria. Occam asked Lewis to defend him against their common enemy, the Pope. The force of Occam's words earned for him the title, *Doctor invincibilis,* by his followers (Ueberweg, 1888a). However, the invincible doctor could not escape the ravage of the Black Plague and apparently succumbed to it in 1349.

Occam's solution to the developing hostility between faith and reason was to accept an extreme form of Nominalism. First, he claimed that reason could never prove the truth of any religious or theological dogma. Such ideas must be accepted on the basis of faith alone. Thus, Aquinas's attempt to demonstrate the existence of God through the reasonable analysis of the Universe was rejected by Occam. Nevertheless, Occam believed in God but accepted His existence on the basis of intuition.

Occam also rejected the Realistic position with his famous claim that "entities must not be necessarily multiplied" (Ueberweg, 1888a, p. 462). By this statement, Occam meant that abstract concepts exist only in the human mind and do not have independent existence. Each abstract concept can have many definitions; therefore, absolute truth of any concept cannot be demonstrated. For example, there are many definitions of "beauty"; and, it is gratuitous to assume that an absolute concept of beauty could ever be defined.

Occam also questioned Aristotle's theory of causality. All that the human mind knows with certainty is what is presented to the senses. But sensory experience does not give the causes of things. When the mind searches for reasons, it must make an inference that may be correct or incorrect. There is no way to be absolutely certain what causes an event. The human mind can never know if God is directly responsible for an event or secondary causes bring about an event. This reasoning led to Occam's famous principle of parsimony (also known as Occam's razor). Basically, when many explanations are possible for a phenomenon, always choose the simplest way to explain. In other words, use the explanation that makes the fewest assumptions. Better understanding of reality should occur if parsimony is followed. A current fascination about the planet Mars serves to show how Occam's razor is applied. In 1976, a Viking spacecraft orbiting Mars took a photograph of a curious rock formation, one-and-a-half miles long. Computer enhancement of the photograph revealed that the rock formation has a chiseled appearance of a humanoid face with an expression remindful of the sphinx. For now, Occam's razor suggests that we should consider the appearance of the rock formation to be the product of Martian erosion and not Martian artisans.

Occam was the last of the major medieval philosophers and his ideas became very important as the Middle Ages gave way to the Renaissance. He called his views the *via moderna* approach which replaced the *via antiqua* logic of his predecessors. Occam claimed that whatever is not self-contradictory is possible, but humans can only know with certainty through observation. Thus, Occam stood for empiricism that served to propel the development of science in the fourteenth century (Grant, 1971). Also, the animosity among the clergy seen throughout the Middle Ages would finally express itself as the Protestant Reformation. This religious revolt was led by the Augustinian monk, Martin Luther (1483–1546), who claimed that the Pope had no divine right to rule and could make mistakes in establishing dogma. Luther was excommunicated and the future history of the West would be punctuated with wars involving Catholics against Protestants.

Moses Maimonides

Medieval scholars were caught in an intellectual conflict. Writers, such as Bacon and Occam, argued that the human mind is capable of discovering truth on the basis of observation. However, it was also important that truth conform to religious dogma. The consternation caused by the potential conflict between science and faith not only was an issue for Christians but for Muslims and Jews as well. In an attempt to reconcile Judaism with science, Moses Maimonides (1135–1204), a rabbi and physician who lived in the Islamic world of Spain and North Africa, wrote his *Guide for the Perplexed* (Klein, 1970). In this work, Maimonides sanctioned Aristotelian science as the way to approach the understanding of the physical world. However, the understanding of the spiritual world cannot be done through science. Instead, metaphysics and religion are needed to penetrate the mysteries of immaterial existence. Thus, science and philosophy have separate but complementary missions in the process of understanding reality.

Maimonides believed that the proper understanding of God's teachings in the Bible and Talmud is consistent with scientific law. However, he warned that certain stories in religious writings are allegorical. Literal interpretation of these stories produces a clash between faith and reason. For example, Maimonides considered the story of creation in Genesis to be metaphorical. Creation must be given as a story so that humans, with limited intellects, might have some understanding of the cataclysmic power of God. Maimonides considered the Genesis story to indicate that the World was created and so science must look for an explanation of the World that allows for its coming into existence. Therefore, Maimonides rejected Aristotle's claim that the World had no beginning and is eternal.

Medieval Cosmology

The Middle Ages were characterized by the attempt to use both science and religious dogma for understanding reality. This amalgamation was apparent as scholars tried to explain the Cosmos. Medieval thinkers continued to rely heavily on the Greek theories of the Universe, especially those developed by Aristotle and Ptolemy. These positions fitted the orthodox religious view that the Earth was the center of everything. Moreover, it was necessary to make room in the Universe for the presence of heaven and hell, the dwelling places for the good and the bad. The Florentine poet, Dante Alighieri (1265–1321), provided an entertaining view of reality in his *Divine Comedy* which was based upon medieval knowledge of the Cosmos.

The Divine Comedy

The acceptance of Aristotle's view of the Cosmos was evident in Dante's great epic poem. The story in the *Divine Comedy* centers upon Dante, guided by the Roman poet Virgil, travelling through the regions of heaven and hell. The Earth is conceived of as being in the center of the Universe. Hell is composed of nine concentric spheres or levels inside the Earth and souls are assigned to the various levels of hell according to the degree of sin. The most evil are confined to the ninth level along with Satan. After conversing with the denizens of hell, Dante returns to the surface of the Earth before being guided by an angelic spirit Beatrice (representing a woman that Dante loved in real life). Heaven, existing above the Earth, also has nine concentric spheres.

Each of the planets, the Sun, and the Moon occupies a sphere. Finally, the last sphere, the Empyrean, is the abode of God. As Dante travels through the spheres of Heaven, he is allowed to talk to the spirits living in each of the spheres. Finally, in the Empyrean sphere, Dante enjoys a mystical experience of glimpsing God.

The *Divine Comedy* is an allegory depicting the struggling Earth suspended between heaven and hell. Therefore, humans, owing to their unique position as beings in the center of the Universe, are caught between the forces of good and evil. Dante makes the geocentric view of the Universe, drawn from Aristotle and Ptolemy, consistent with religious doctrines concerning salvation. As Kuhn (1957, p. 113) mentions, "to move the Earth was to break the continuous chain of created being."

Criticisms of Aristotle

Ironically, the Middle Ages produced cosmologists who reasoned that the Aristotelian view of a stationary Earth might be false. For example, Jean Burdian (died about 1350), a student of Occam, considered the possibility that the Greeks, Heraclides and Aristarchus, were correct in assuming that the Earth turns while the heavens remain stationary. However, Burdian could not produce any conclusive evidence that the model of the rotating Earth is superior to Aristotle's immobile Earth. Finally, Burdian dismissed the hypothesis of a rotating Earth with the following argument. If an arrow is shot into the air vertically, it should land somewhere to the west of its launch point if the Earth moves from east to west. Since this does not happen, the Earth appears to be stationary (Grant, 1971). Another thinker, Nicole Oresme (died 1382) rejected Burdian's argument against a rotating Earth. However, Oresme concluded that the stationary Earth was more acceptable in terms of religious belief. The stationary Earth serves "to protect the Christian faith from demonstrations based on human reason, experience, and science" (Grant, 1971, p. 69).

Many of Burdian's and Oresme's reasons would eventually be used by Copernicus to support his view that the Earth moves. However, the Middle Ages concluded with the consensus that the immobile Earth was the center of all and surrounded by eight or nine concentric spheres holding the planets, the Moon, the Sun, the stars, and spiritual beings.

The study of the Cosmos also helped to satisfy the medieval fascination with astrology. With Islamic works on the subject available, people in all stations of life turned to astrology for answers. During the period of the Black Plague (1347–1351), astrologers were consulted for advice on how to escape death. Astrology was also aided by the medieval conception of the Universe that placed spirits in the heavens from where they can influence human behavior. The belief that heavenly events predict earthly events was confirmed by the rise and fall of tides which are influenced by the phases of the Moon. The free-thinking Roger Bacon wondered whether biblical events were predicted by celestial events. Astrology also entered medicine with the fourteenth century belief that certain human illnesses resulted from the conjunction of planets (Talbot, 1978).

The Nature of Motion

Medieval scholars also became concerned with the forces that moved objects. Aristotle's ideas were again referenced for the explanation, and Grant (1971) has provided an excellent review of medieval uses of Aristotle in this regard. Much of the following is drawn from Grant's analysis.

As part of his theory of causality, Aristotle assumed that final causes are ultimately responsible for change or motion. Final causes execute change by controlling efficient causes as in the case of a sculptor wanting to make a statue (final cause) and bringing about its creation through the skilled use of tools (efficient causes). In other words, Aristotle's position claims that whatever moves or changes is moved or changed by another.

When heavy objects are launched skyward, why do they appear to decelerate, stop, and then fall back with increasing speed to Earth? Aristotle guessed that heavy objects must contain the elements earth and/or water. As a result, their natural motion is toward the center of the Earth, representing the geometric center of the Universe. Also, the velocity of the object is directly proportional to its weight and inversely proportional to the density of the medium through which it must pass. Thus, objects fall faster if they weigh more and if they travel through air instead of water. In contrast to heavy objects, light objects, such as fire and the resulting smoke, rise naturally upward. According to Aristotle, the natural resting place for fire is the concave surface of the lunar sphere above the Earth. Finally, Aristotle always considered that motion of an object requires a medium. The region between the Earth and the first sphere of the Moon is filled with objects composed from earth, air, fire, and water. The natural motion in the sublunar region is vertical. Above the lunar sphere, the medium is ether. The natural motion through ether for heavenly objects is circular. Thus, Aristotle concluded that a medium is necessary for motion. Since motion occurs everywhere, there can be no empty space in existence.

As Aristotle's theories on motion continued to be studied, they became more tenuous. Aristotle's doctrine of motion requires the mover to be in constant contact with the moved. Therefore, the planets moving through ether were assumed to be constantly pushed along by spirits. In opposition to this contention, thinkers such as Jean Burdian and Nicole Oresme were wondering whether God might have provided the initial motion to the planets and then allowed them to travel on their own inertia.

Burdian, Oresme, and other scholars at Oxford and Paris began to search for another theory of motion to replace Aristotle's. The result was *impetus theory* which claimed that a force is imparted to an object to keep it in motion. The force was provided by the cause of the motion; however, the imparted force was assumed to be a property held by the moving object. Thus, movers and things moved do not need to be in physical contact. Moreover, impetus given to an object gradually weakens, resulting in the loss of motion. Thus, an arrow shot horizontally is given impetus but eventually slows down and falls to the ground. The impetus theory was not accurate but it was important for Galileo's later work leading to the modern theory of inertia—a body continues in motion in a straight line until an obstacle is encountered (Butterfield, 1957). Medieval observers were gradually learning about the forces of nature.

The Nature of Matter

The West also inherited through translations Aristotle's theory of matter. As reviewed in Chapter 1, Aristotle's theory claimed that all terrestrial things are composed from earth, air, fire, and water. Each of these elements has two characteristics. Earth is dry and cold, air is hot and wet, fire is hot and dry, and water is wet and cold. Aristotle's theory also allows the possibility of transmuting elements. For example, earth could become fire by replacing cold with hot. The possibility of changing elements led several thinkers in the Middle Ages to practice alchemy.

Alchemy was developed in Hellenistic Egypt and in Islamic nations before coming to the attention of Western thinkers (Multhauf, 1978). Roger Bacon thought that any substance could be produced if alchemy could discover how to rearrange elements. Following this advice, Bacon produced in 1242 a formula for gunpowder based upon mixing saltpeter, charcoal, and sulphur (Read, 1957). Moreover, Albert the Great said that base metals could be made into gold and several individuals in the fourteenth century tried to perfect the technique (Redgrove, 1969).

Bacon also agreed with Islamic sources that alchemy allowed for the manufacturing of elixirs and medicines. The classical manuscript on pharmacology, *Materia medica*, written by the Greek Dioscorides in the first century A.D., was amended by Muslim scholars before being translated into Latin. The key discoveries of the alchemists aiding pharmacology were the perfecting of the technique for distilling alcohol and the use of minerals in medicines. Also, alchemy refined the use of acids in the production of colors and paints that was crucial for the development of medieval art (Multhauf, 1978).

The greatest medieval alchemist was Paracelsus (1493–1541). He argued against using alchemy to transmute base metals into gold but maintained that alchemy's significance resided in the creations of medicines based upon combining mercury, sulphur, and salt. Paracelsus inveighed against the notions of the Roman physician Galen who theorized that health was regulated by four body humors (blood, black bile, yellow bile, and phlegm). Since Galen's theory was widely accepted, Paracelsus was denounced by the emerging medical establishment. The fact that Paracelsus engaged in mysticism, magic, and astrology also made him a suspicious character to religious authorities. Nevertheless, Robert Boyle (1627–1691) is credited with starting modern chemistry following upon the work of the medieval alchemists such as Paracelsus (Snyder, 1969).

The Natural and the Supernatural

Medieval thinkers trying to understand reality allowed for the possibility that supernatural forces could influence natural phenomena. As we have discussed, Dante wrote about divine beings existing above the Earth and evil ones existing within its interior. Moreover, astrology, well known in the ancient World, continued to attract attention in the medieval World.

A philosophy of good and evil, which originated with the Persian Mani and became known as Manicheanism, attempted to address the vexing problem of why an all powerful, benevolent God allows evil to occur in the World. Mani's answer was that good and evil are coequal cosmic forces locked in eternal battle. Sometimes good wins; other times evil triumphs. Good and evil imbue the Universe and are recognized as paired opposites. Thus, the Sun is considered good, but the Moon is a sign of evil. The human soul is good, but the human body is evil. Mani was executed in A.D. 276 in attempt to rid the World of his philosophy. Nevertheless, Manicheanism persisted well into the Middle Ages and has remnants that are still with us today.

Another view that persisted into the Middle Ages was Gnosticism which represented an amalgamation of Christianity, Judaism, and paganism (Neill & Schmandt, 1957). Gnosticism, which originated in the first century A.D., expressed the belief that a special type of knowledge (gnosis) must be discovered and practiced in order that salvation may be obtained. Of course, the Gnostics believed that they were in the process of illuminating this knowledge. Gnostic beliefs and practices included magic, secret gestures, and a mystical understanding of existence. The Gnostics also accepted the belief that many supernatural spirits exist, some of which are good and others evil.

The persistence of Gnosticism into the Middle Ages led to the formation of cults. Some of these cults attempted to understand the good, but others were interested in exploring evil. The cults interested in evil believed that whatever is condemned in the Bible should be practiced since it represents the worth of evil. Also, it was thought possible that humans could enter into contracts with the agents of evil, such as Satan and other malevolent beings, through the use of magic and special incantations. The summoning of demons through magic and witchcraft was thought entirely possible by St. Thomas Aquinas.

Religious authorities found it necessary to move against witchcraft. In 1484, Pope Innocent VIII appointed two leading priests of the Inquisition, Jakob Sprenger and Heinrich Kramer, to develop procedures for the apprehending, judging, and sentencing witches. Their work became known as the *Malleus maleficarum* ("Hammer against Witches") and was the inspiration for execution of as many as 300,000 people from 1484 to 1700 (Shumaker, 1972).

Belief also existed in white witchcraft as opposed to black witchcraft that required a liaison with demons. White witches practiced their magic with the aid of beneficent spirits. This type of magic was called "natural" and one commentator, Giambattista della Porta, said that all excellent humans should applaud it. White magic was found acceptable to religious authority, but the great difficulty was to distinguish between white and black witches since the latter could take on the characteristics of the former as part of their deception.

The belief in black and white magic was illustrated in Shakespearean plays. Demons controlled the witches in *MacBeth* while Prospero in *The Tempest* practiced white magic. Christopher Marlowe's famous story of *Dr. Faustus* explores human motives for seeking an alliance with evil. One should not be too hasty in considering that the belief in witchcraft is arcane. Many in the modern world continue to be drawn to both black and white magic and the popularity of such movies as *The Exorcist*, *Rosemary's Baby, The Omen, Poltergeist,* and *Halloween* indicate that medieval ways of thinking still persist.

The Contributions of the Middle Ages

The scholars of the Middle Ages were motivated to seek the understanding of reality. However, much of that era was spent evaluating the theories of the ancient philosophers. Aristotle's works were rediscovered and, while much of his philosophy was accepted without question, it was also apparent that he was wrong on many accounts. Medieval thinkers discovered that careful observation could be used to probe the mysteries of the world. However, these thinkers tended to explain the existence of the world as a teleological manifestation of God. Therefore, views of reality could never stray too far away from invoking the role of the supernatural. Yet, the Middle Ages inspired the Renaissance which would witness the power of science for discovering knowledge.

The Middle Ages can be understood as a time of transition. The old knowledge system, inspired by the rationalistic beliefs of Plato, were giving away the positivistic apprehension of truth, championed in the empirical style of Aristotle. While the Middle Ages explored the value of science in the advancement of knowledge, the importance of spirituality remained manifest. The Stoic commitment to altruism was evident through religion, and people were reminded that the current existence is not the last existence. These sentiments were beautifully expressed in the prayer composed by St. Francis of Assisi (1182–1226):

> Lord, make me an instrument of Your peace.
> Where there is hatred, let me sow love.
> Where there is injury, pardon,
> Where there is doubt, faith,
> Where there is despair, hope,
> Where there is darkness, light,
> and where there is sadness, joy.

> O Divine Master, grant that I may
> not so much seek to be consoled,
> as to console;
> To be understood, as to understand;
> To be loved, as to love;
> For it is in giving that we receive;
> It is in the pardoning that we are pardoned;
> And it is in dying that we are born to
> eternal life.

The Meaning of Reality: Newtonian Views 3

A reasonable starting date for the modern era of science is 1543, the year Copernicus published his *De Revolutionibus Orbium Caelestium (On the Revolutions of the Celestial Spheres)*. Copernicus's effort was an important step in disconnecting science from preconceived, and often erroneous, explanations of the World. In other words, Copernicus started a movement to separate science from both the incorrect theories of Aristotle and from domination by religious authority.

The Copernican Revolution

Copernicus's Life and Work

Nicolaus Copernicus (1473–1543), who latinized his family name Koppernigk, always remained loyal to the Catholic Church in his native Poland. When he was 10 years old, his father died and he was adopted by his uncle, Lucas Watzenrode, who as a bishop in the Church would have major influences upon Copernicus. In 1491, the bishop sent young Copernicus to the University of Cracow, famous for studies in astronomy and mathematics. Copernicus continued his schooling in Italy at the University of Bologna from 1496 to 1500. At Bologna, Copernicus met Domenico Maria de Novara, a brilliant professor of astronomy who officially held to the Ptolemaic view of the heavens while having serious personal doubts about its accuracy. Still not tired of education, Copernicus studied law and medicine at the University of Padua. Finally, in 1506, he returned to Poland with a wealth of knowledge and embarked upon a career as a canon (business manager) for the Frauenburg Cathedral (Armitage, 1957).

Beginning in 1506, Copernicus was apparently developing his system of the heavens while attending to the health needs of his uncle. A short report on the heliocentric view was published in 1512 in a work entitled *Commentariolus*. Bishop Watzenrode also succumbed to his illness in 1512. Following the death of his beloved uncle, Copernicus threw himself into his work and began to make his own observations of the heavens. As his work became known, Copernicus began to receive visits from other astronomers eager to find out more. One such visitor was George Joachim von Lauchen, who called himself by the Latin name Rheticus. He was given permission by Copernicus to publish the new theory in 1540. Church authorities also became interested in the new theory and Cardinal Schonberg pressured Copernicus to publish. Copernicus, now an old man, finally consented to the publication of his work. In the winter of 1543, Copernicus was stricken with a serious illness and then suffered a stroke. On May 24th, an advance copy of *De Revolutionibus* was presented to Copernicus who then died hours later. His task was finished.

In *De Revolutionibus,* there appears a preface, written by Andreas Osiander, one of Copernicus's students and a Lutheran theologian. The preface was careful to state that the heliocentric view of the planetary system was just a hypothesis and should not be taken as fact. However, the reason for suggesting the heliocentric possibility is that the Ptolemaic view cannot explain planetary motion without many burdensome assumptions. Thus, Ptolemy had to resort to complicated epicycles to account for the retrograde motion of the planets.

The purpose of the preface was to assuage the potential strife the new hypothesis might engender. Nonetheless, Copernicus offered that the motion of the planets could be explained by putting the Sun at the center of the heavens. Then, Copernicus correctly placed the order of the planets from the Sun: Mercury, Venus, Earth with its orbiting Moon, Mars, Jupiter, and, lastly Saturn. All the planets moved in circular orbits around the stationary Sun. The shifting of the Sun in the sky during the various seasons of the year was explained by having the Earth tilted to its plane as it travels around the Sun. Night and day result from the Earth turning on its axis from east to west. Copernicus also allowed room in his Universe for places containing spiritual beings and the last orb was saved for the stars which were considered to be fixed and unmoving.

Copernicus's theory did not indicate the true size of the Universe and contained several errors (Butterfield, 1957). For example, Copernicus had the planets moving in circular orbits which would be proven to be incorrect by Kepler. With circular orbits, Copernicus still needed epicycles to account for retrograde motion of the planets. To make matters worse, Copernicus's mathematics did not really have the Sun at the center of the Universe! The Sun was a bit off-center relative to the circular orbit followed by the Earth. However, Copernicus's system was simpler than Ptolemy's for calculating planetary motion and, therefore, preferable on the basis of Occam's razor. Also, by having the Earth rotate every 24 hours, Copernicus removed Ptolemy's unlikely assumption that all the heavenly spheres must turn once each day.

Copernicus was careful not to provoke animosity from religious authorities. He was aware of the tension existing in Christianity following the Protestant Reformation begun by Martin Luther. Catholic authorities initially received Copernicus's work with interest and no reprisals were forthcoming; however, Luther was very critical of the new ideas in astronomy. Luther's associate, Melanchton, and other Protestant leaders, such as Calvin, took up the task of attacking the Copernican system (Kuhn, 1957). The Bible was thoroughly searched for passages that would argue against the proposal that creation was Sun-centered. In 1610, the Catholic Church also launched a vigorous campaign against the Copernican ideas. Catholics, under the pain of excommunication, were instructed not to read or teach the Copernican system unless all references about the heliocentric model were expunged. Religion and science now entered an internecine struggle that eventually forced their separation from one another.

Perfection of the System

The Copernican system also came under scientific scrutiny. Two astronomers in particular looked upon Copernicus's model as flawed but with possibilities of being modified into a more accurate explanation of the heavens. These individuals were Tycho Brahe (1546–1601) and Johannes Kepler (1571–1630).

Tycho Brahe's Life and Work

Brahe was a Danish nobleman with eccentric behaviors. He developed an obsession for studying celestial objects and began to build a special apparatus for naked-eye astronomy (since the telescope had not yet been invented). Two events in particular caught Brahe's attention (Trefil, 1985). In late 1572, a supernova appeared in the Constellation Cassiopeia and shone brightly throughout the next year. Europeans were stunned by the event since Aristotle claimed that the heavens were perfect and could not change. Instead, the new bright star, temporary in existence, showed that the heavens were changeable. Some tried to argue that the bright star had to be in the sublunary sphere just above the Earth and not in the fixed crystalline spheres of the heavens. However, Brahe's measurements indicated that the object was not close to the Earth but had a distance much greater than any known planet. In 1577, the second astronomical event important to Brahe occurred. In that year, he took careful measurements of a comet. The Aristotelian-Ptolemaic view always had trouble explaining the appearance and disappearance of comets from the heavens. Brahe's calculations of the comet's path indicated that it had an elongated orbit that required it to cross several of the supposedly impenetrable spheres. Again, the upper heavens were shown to be changeable.

Brahe's studies led him to conclude that the Aristotelian-Ptolemaic model was incorrect. However, he also was critical of the Copernican system. Eventually, he developed his own system which required some of the planets to orbit the Sun while others moved around the Earth (Butterfield, 1957).

Brahe and the King of Denmark developed a dislike for one another prompting Brahe to leave his native land with his data and settle in Prague. His arrival was celebrated by a lavish banquet given by the rich citizens of Prague. Brahe, already in poor health, drank too much and his bladder burst with fatal consequences. Following his death, all of Brahe's data was entrusted to his recently hired associate, a mathematician named Johannes Kepler.

Johannes Kepler's Life and Work

Johannes Kepler was born in Germany and showed himself to be a brilliant student. It appeared that he was heading toward a career as a Catholic priest but religious strife between Catholics and Protestants troubled his conscience. Upon the completion of his higher education, he turned away from the priesthood and began to teach mathematics, calendar making, and astrology.

Kepler accepted the Copernican system of the world, and, in 1596, published his first major work on the subject called *Cosmographical Mystery* (Kuhn, 1957). Kepler explained in cumbersome mathematical detail how the Sun-centered planetary system could explain the retrograde motion of the planets and why the Moon and the Sun did not show such motion. The book was extremely difficult to read and did not bring any immediate acclaim to Kepler.

After Brahe's death, Kepler became the custodian of the great astronomer's data. It was soon evident to Kepler that no system of mathematical circles could accurately represent the motions of the celestial objects (Kuhn, 1957). Through painstaking trial and error, Kepler finally discovered the geometric figure that serves to represent celestial motion. It was the ellipse! In 1609, the world received Kepler's ideas in a work called *On the Motion of Mars*.

Kepler's Laws of Celestial Motion

Copernicus was correct in making the Sun the center of the planetary system; however, Kepler discovered that planets move in elliptic not circular orbits. Kepler's great advancement in the understanding of the heavens was expressed in three laws.

The first two laws were presented in the 1609 publication and stated the nature of planetary orbits (first law) and the means for calculating the speed of a planet as it moves in orbital swing (second law). In 1619, Kepler published *Harmonies of the World* that contained the third law of planetary motion. The third law expressed the relationship between the time required for one rotation of a planet around the Sun and the length of its orbit.

In addition to his scientific work, Kepler kept a firm belief in God. For Kepler, the mathematical ordering of the World served as an expression of God's intellect. Creation involved the Earth and other planets moving in elliptical orbits around the Sun. The 2,000 year old theory of crystalline spheres operating above the centrally located Earth had to be abandoned. A true revolution in scientific thought was taking place.

The Force That Maintains the Universe

Kepler's theory alluded to gravity as the force from the Sun that regulates planetary motion (Harrison, 1985). However, many thinkers were troubled by how gravity could work. The great philosopher Descartes (1596–1650), falling back to Aristotelian thinking, could not imagine empty space existing between the planets and the Sun. Instead, the whole of space must be filled with fine particles making up the ether. The particles are whipped into whirlpools and the planets are pulled by these vortices around the Sun. Thus, Descartes returned to the Aristotelian position that objects could only influence one another by direct physical contact.

The Ultimate Price

Exciting progress was being made regarding the correct interpretation of the laws that govern the Universe. However, as in the case of Descartes, several thinkers did not believe that empty space separates celestial objects. This error was corrected by Giordano Bruno (1548–1600) who not only defended the possibility of a vacuum in the Universe, but also championed the atomic theory of matter. Bruno's scientific, political, and philosophical views would make him a threat to religious authorities; but he was willing and did pay the ultimate price for his beliefs.

The Life of Giordano Bruno

Bruno was born in Nola, Italy, and showed strong intellectual promise as a youth. He entered the university at Naples and was attracted to Averroism. Despite his unorthodox beliefs, he was ordained a Dominican priest in 1572. Bruno was open to many ideas and he began to teach and explore philosophies forbidden by the Catholic Church. He eventually left the priesthood and fled to Paris and then to Oxford to teach Copernican theory and denounce Aristotle's views of the heavens. After a brief return to Paris, Bruno journeyed to Germany but the stay there was uncomfortable due to his notoriety. Finally, a Venetian nobleman, named Mocenigo, invited Bruno to come back to Italy and be his teacher. Bruno accepted the invitation which was to prove fateful. Mocenigo apparently became angry at Bruno's style of teaching and turned him over to the Inquisition which was interested in his unusual beliefs. Bruno was sent to Rome and remained in custody for eight years. Many attempts were made by the Church to get Bruno to retract his teachings, but he refused, saying he had nothing to take back. The matter was concluded with Bruno being burned at the stake (Singer, 1950). The execution of Bruno served as a strong warning that religious authority was becoming more impatient with individuals who challenged the established order.

Bruno's Beliefs

It was not only Bruno's ideas about the heavens but also his philosophy relating human and cosmic existence that made him a menace to Christian authority (Lerner & Gosselin, 1986). Bruno was an advocate of a world spirit. All things, animate and inanimate, have souls that are in communication with God. Since all humans were in direct spiritual contact with God, Bruno was hoping that this realization would force a change in the political and religious thought. His wish was that the Protestant and Catholic groups would be reunited when they realize their spiritual commonality with God. Bruno imprudently thought that he could convince the Pope of his philosophy which may have been one reason for his unfortunate return to Italy.

Embedded in Bruno's philosophy was a very important extension of the Copernican view of reality. Bruno, in giving homage to God, taught that the Universe is infinite. The Sun may be the center of our system of planets but the Sun is only one of countless stars that inhabit the Cosmos. Bruno also imagined the possibility that other intelligent life existed on planets elsewhere in space. However, such planets would also orbit their central sun.

The existence of an infinite Universe helped to make it easier to reconsider the atomic theory of matter. Aristotle said that the terrestrial elements (earth, air, fire, and water) were inferior to the celestial element (ether). The atomic theory of matter claims that matter everywhere in the Universe is the same which is a more sensible approach if there are multiple Earths and multiple Suns (Kuhn, 1957). However, the atomic theory would not be taken seriously in science until well into the 18th century.

Glimpse of the Universe

Modern physics began with the careful, observational work of Galileo Galilei (1564–1642). Galileo used the newly developed telescope to explore the Sun, Moon, and the planetary system, thus ending naked-eye astronomy. Also, he carefully investigated gravity showing the relationship between time and the rate of fall of an object. Sadly, Galileo, like Bruno, became embroiled in controversies with the Church and was punished by house arrest for supporting the Copernican system.

Galileo's Life and Work

Galileo was born in Pisa, Italy, to parents who appreciated education and the arts. Galileo's university education was spent in Florence and Pisa studying medicine. However, he became more interested in mathematics and made an early important discovery based upon watching a chandelier swing in a church. Galileo curiously noted that the chandelier appeared to take the same time to swing in its arc no matter how long the arc. To repeat the observation, Galileo constructed different pendulums and again discovered that the oscillation periods remained the same despite changes in the length of the arc (Gamow, 1961). Galileo applied the pendulum clock to medicine showing that it can be used to count the number of heart beats over time.

During a brief stay at the University of Pisa (1589–1592) as a professor of mathematics, Galileo began to study the Copernican system. Then, he moved to the University of Padua for the most productive and happy eighteen years of his life. At Padua, Galileo taught mathematics and astronomy. Also, he constructed a laboratory and began to do systematic research. In 1609, Galileo became acquainted with the telescope, invented in Holland, and soon he perfected the instrument. Galileo also realized the military significance of the instrument and informed the Doge of Venice of its existence. Venice was very appreciative of Galileo's work and, since the University of Padua was controlled by Venice, he was rewarded with a major increase in his salary (Segre, 1980a). Galileo turned the telescope skyward and most likely was the first human to see the moons of Jupiter, sunspots, the stars of the Milky Way, the mountains of the Moon, and the phases of Venus. Galileo reported his observations complete with drawings in a work, *Sidereus nuncius* (Starry Messenger).

Aware of his importance, Galileo wanted to live in the most glorious city of the Italian Renaissance, Florence. Abandoning his common-law wife and placing his daughters in a nunnery, Galileo moved to Florence in 1610 against the better advice of his friend Sagredo (Segre, 1980a). Such rash behavior suggests that Galileo may have considered himself to be on a most important mission. The heliocentric view of the planets was correct and must be publicly defended. The Church must be convinced to give up its allegiance to the dead Aristotelian-Ptolemaic system or suffer a worse embarrassment later when the faithful eventually learned the truth from science. Certainly, Galileo was aware of Bruno's fate. But Galileo felt he was on a mission to save the Church (Lerner & Gosselin, 1986).

In 1611, Galileo went to Rome with his data and even convinced the papal astronomers of the validity of his observations. Back in Florence, he continued to press openly for the Copernican system and carried on correspondence advocating that the Bible should not be literally read (De Santillana, 1955). However, Galileo angered those who were supporters of the Aristotelian-Ptolemaic view. Sharp debates occurred in the Church between the representatives of the old system and the Pope's scientists who now leaned toward Copernicanism. Most distressed were the Dominicans, champions of the Aristotelian philosophy of St. Thomas Aquinas. Finally, in 1614, the animosity against Galileo broke loose and he was openly attacked from the pulpit by a Dominican priest, Tommaso Caccini. Galileo sought assurances from Rome that his position was safe. A member of the curia, Cardinal Barberini, assured Galileo that he could continue teaching Copernicanism. However, other powerful forces were moving against Galileo.

In 1616, Galileo met with Cardinal Robert Bellarmine of the Inquisition and was told that he must not "hold or defend" the heliocentric view of the planets (De Santillana, 1955, p. 125). Galileo returned to Florence still a believer in Copericanism but gave up his public support of the position.

In 1623, Galileo was cheered by the election of his friend, Cardinal Barberini, as Pope Urban VIII. Galileo journeyed to Rome to congratulate the new pontiff and, in return, was warmly received. Apparently, Galileo was also given assurances that he could resume his defense of the Copernican system as long as he did not engage in theological debate. In 1632, Galileo published his great book *Dialogo di massimi sistemi del mondo (Dialogue on the Two Great World Systems)*. The format of this work was to have three people debate the Copernican and Aristotelian-Ptolemaic views of the planets. The learned Salviati represents Copernicanism; the dull-witted Simplicio supports the Aristotelian-Ptolemaic position; and Segredo is the wise listener who must decide who is the winner of the debate. The *Dialogue* concludes with no firm decision regarding the better cosmic system; however, it is clear that the Copernican view had the more favorable arguments. However, the manner in which Galileo closed the debate was ill-advised. Simplicio proclaims that the teaching of

Copernicanism, even if it is correct, is a danger to the Church. Apparently, the Pope's benevolence toward Galileo weakened considerably. Suspicions were cast that Galileo was trying to undermine the authority of the Church by defending Copernicanism. Even the emblem of three intertwined dolphins appearing on the title page of the *Dialogue* was interpreted to mean that Galileo might be conspiring with French forces hostile to the papacy (Lerner and Gosselin, 1986).

Near the end of 1632, the Pope designated a special commission to investigate Galileo who was called to Rome to determine whether he broke the 1616 order not to teach or defend Copernicanism. Galileo's trial ended in June, 1633, with a guilty verdict returned. The *Dialogue* was judged to have breached the 1616 order even though the book had been sanctioned by the Church before its publication. The circumstances of the trial were even made more bizarre because Bellarmine, who issued the 1616 order against Galileo, died just before the start of the trial. Bellarmine's testimony was needed to clarify the meaning of the 1616 order. The inquisition found Galileo guilty and he was saved from death because he admitted his Copernican beliefs were "heresies." At 70 years of age, Galileo was sentenced to house arrest in Florence. He was allowed to continue his scientific work and he completed a major treatise on mathematics. Galileo made appeals for his release and they were routinely denied.

On January 8, 1642, Galileo died. In the diary that he kept while under house arrest, Galileo affirmed his belief in Copernicanism and lamented the condition allowing the ignorant to suppress knowledge. But the drama of Galileo was still not over. In 1979, Pope John Paul II, at a commemoration for Einstein, suggested that a review of Galileo's trial was in order with the purpose of granting an exoneration. The Pope also urged that the relationship between science and religion should be clearly defined in order to reduce conflict. In November 1992, the Pope accepted the recommendation that Galileo should be exonerated from the charge of heresy. In doing so, the Pope urged that the battle between science and religion is based upon ignorance of each other's position. The Pope offered the hope that this battle will never occur again.

The Importance of Galileo's Work

Galileo's unfortunate fate has inspired many myths about him as an innocent hero attacked by ignorant authority. However, individuals who carry the message of change must be very careful to diffuse the hostility of the non-believers. Galileo apparently could have averted danger to himself had he stayed at Padua where the authority of the Pope was weak (Segre, 1980a).

Galileo's audacity not withstanding, he also deserves considerable praise for trying to enlighten his generation. Galileo did so by careful experimental work that has earned him the appellation, "Father of Modern Physics." Not only did Galileo explore the heavens with his telescope, but he offered principles to explain motion, which was a difficult problem for medieval thinkers. Galileo's investigations on motion produced a paradoxical conclusion. The speed of fall obtained by an object is determined only by its original height at the time of release. Thus, a baseball and a cannon ball fall at the same rate with the final speed determined by their original heights above the ground. Legend claims that Galileo demonstrated this principle by simultaneously dropping objects of different weights from the Leaning Tower of Pisa and having them hit the ground at the same moment, confounding those who watched.

Galileo's conclusions about motion also must have been bewildering to the Aristotelians of his day. Aristotle's theses that heavier objects fall faster than lighter objects and whatever is moved must always be in contact with its mover were dispelled by Galileo's Laws of Motion. Galileo demonstrated with observational data that the Aristotelian view of the world had to be revised. Apparently, Galileo's enemies thought it would be easier to get rid of the messenger of change than to refute established beliefs.

Galileo's life and work inspired others to take up the cause of science. When the Renaissance reached northern Europe, more tolerance was shown by religion toward science. In Holland, Christian Huygens (1606–1669), whose father corresponded frequently with Galileo, became interested in physics. Huygens used improved telescopes to show that Saturn was ringed, a possibility raised by Galileo. Also, Huygens worked on the development of accurate clocks and was one of the first to consider light to have wave properties (Segre, 1980a).

However, in the year Galileo died (1642), one of the world's greatest geniuses was born. This new Aristotle did more to advance the understanding of the physical world until the arrival of Einstein in the twentieth century. On Christmas Eve, the world received Isaac Newton.

Isaac Newton and the World Machine

Isaac Newton became the great systemizer of knowledge. He clearly showed the power of the human mind for the resolution of the fundamental laws that govern the material World. Newton demonstrated the power of science to produce accurate descriptions of the World. He, more than anyone before him, showed the promise of science for discovery, and his conclusions served to dispel the reliance upon authority for understanding.

Newton's Life

Isaac Newton (1642–1727) was born prematurely in a rural area of England near Woolsthorpe. Newton's father, a farmer, had died three months before Isaac's birth. When he was three years old, his mother remarried and Newton was shipped off to live with his grandmother. At age 11, Newton's stepfather died and he returned to live with his mother and her children by the second marriage. All these traumas and shifts in early life have been considered as eventful in the development of Newton's gloomy, suspicious, and sometimes vicious adult personality (Andrade, 1954; Segre, 1980a).

As a child, Newton was a good student who perhaps was a bit bored by his schoolwork. He became keenly interested in mechanical drawing and made handicrafts such as sundials, kites, doll's furniture, and water-wheels. His mother wanted him to abandon his studies and become a farmer. However, Newton's penchant for books convinced his schoolmaster, Mr. Stokes, that Isaac should go to the University. His mother acquiesced and, in 1661, Newton was off to the famous Trinity College at Cambridge University. Newton was very poor and had to earn his way through school.

Newton graduated from Cambridge in 1665 without showing any particular ability. However, he was scheduled to continue his association with the University as an associate of his major professor, a mathematician named Isaac Barrow. However, in 1665, an extremely deadly plague struck England, and Cambridge University was closed for eighteen months to help control the spread of the pestilence. During this time, Newton returned to his family at Woolsthorpe. Much of the time was spent in quiet, but fruitful, contemplation. In his isolation at Woolsthorpe, Newton drew together the ideas for all his major scientific accomplishments.

Newton, armed with the ideas that would eventually make him famous, returned to Cambridge in 1667 and quickly rose through the professorial ranks. At 26, Newton became Lucasian Professor of Mathematics replacing the retiring Barrow. Newton conducted research and wrote prolifically. However, his suspicious nature made him reluctant to share his findings and ideas. Finally, in 1672, Newton was elected a member of the Royal Society and published his first paper on optics. The paper drew some criticism from members of the Royal Society, such as Robert Hooke, and Newton's fragile self-esteem was severely injured. He reacted bitterly by saying he would never publish again (Segre, 1980a).

Newton might have kept his ideas secret were it not for the astronomer Edmund Halley (1656–1742). Halley was interested in working out the details of Kepler's laws of planetary motion and consulted several members of the Royal Society for help. No breakthroughs in understanding occurred so Halley, in 1684, decided to visit Newton at Cambridge for consultation on the problem. To Halley's surprise, Newton had already worked out the mathematical details of planetary motion based upon the principles of gravity. No one knows how Halley did it, but he convinced Newton to publish his ideas. Newton abided and, in 1687, his *Philosophiae naturalis principia mathematica (Mathematical Principles of Natural Philosophy),* 547 pages long and written in Latin, appeared. The laws which govern activities of the physical World were presented with their mathematical derivations. Great admiration was shown for Newton's work and his fame was now secured.

In 1689, religious conflict surfaced again in England between Roman Catholics and Anglicans. When King James II wanted to staff Cambridge with Catholic professors against the will of the University, Newton was elected a member of Parliament representing the University. Now living in London, Newton developed a friendship with the philosopher John Locke and thought about leaving academe. His plans were sidetracked when his mother died. Newton was deeply attached to his mother and felt depressed at her passing. His grief took on psychotic features, and, by 1692, Newton was in a serious mental crisis. He railed against his friends saying that everyone was deceiving him in his attempts to secure another position outside of the University. By 1696, the intensity of Newton's delusions of persecution declined and he seemed to be in better spirits. Newton's disposition improved when a friend, Charles Montagu, obtained for him the job of Warden of the Mint. In 1699, Newton became the chief officer or Master of the Mint. The world's greatest scientist was now in charge of printing England's money. Newton took his job seriously and successfully redesigned British coinage to keep it safe from counterfeiters and others who tried to shave off the precious metal content of the coins.

Newton held his position at the Mint for the rest of his life but also presided over the development of science in England. In 1703, he was elected President of the Royal Society and remained in that position until his death. In 1704, a year after the death of his scientific enemy, Robert Hooke, Newton published his *Optics* that attempted to explain the nature of light and color based upon his prism experiments done many years earlier.

As Newton aged, his truculent personality led to bitter disagreements with several of his famous contemporaries. Newton and Robert Hooke were often in dispute regarding publications. In addition, Newton and John Flamsteed, the first Royal astronomer at Greenwich, worked together to calculate the orbit of the Moon but became bitter toward one another over time. Newton and Huygens argued at a personal level over the nature of light. However, the most volatile quarrel of Newton's came with Goffried Wilhelm von Leibnitz concerning which of the two should be credited with inventing calculus. Newton implied that Leibnitz plagiarized calculus and, in 1712, the Royal Society published a proceedings of the whole question very much unfavorable to Leibnitz. The judgement of history is that both Newton and Leibnitz independently developed calculus and are given joint credit.

Finally, Newton had a mystical side to his character which contrasts with the precise, logical individual who authored the *Principia*. He quietly studied alchemy and thought that its secrets represented grave dangers to the world (Segre, 1980a). On March 20, 1727, Newton, a life-long bachelor, died. Great honors were paid to him at his funeral and he was interred at Westminster Abbey, reserved as the burial place for the illustrious. A verse from Alexander Pope is a most fitting tribute to Newton's genius:

"Nature and Nature's laws lay hid in night;
God said, Let Newton Be! and all was light."

Newton's Views on Nature

It is only possible to give a brief account of Newton's major contributions to the understanding of reality. His accomplishments were to state the three laws of motion, define the principle of gravity, and develop a workable theory of light. These principles were meant to be universal in that they operated on Earth and in the heavens.

The laws of motion form the basis of classical mechanics in physics and can be briefly stated (Gamow, 1961; Gribben, 1984). The first law, or Law of Inertia, states that a body stays at rest or moves in a straight line with constant velocity, unless outside force is applied. The second law defines momentum or change in motion of an object when an outside force is applied. A body accelerates by the amount determined by the force applied divided by the mass of the object. In other words, force equals mass times acceleration. Newton's third law states that every action produces an equal and opposite reaction. Thus a rocket is forced skyward by the venting of its fuel.

All of the laws of motion were meant to explain gravity. Newton may have been led to think about gravity when, as a youth, he saw an apple fall to the ground. Newton explained the behavior of the apple as due to the attractive power of the Earth. However, the apple also attracts the Earth but loses due to the greater mass of the planet. Every object in the Universe exerts gravitational force due to its mass. More formally, the Law of Gravity states that all material bodies attract each other with a force that is directly proportional to their masses and inversely proportional to the square of the distance between them. With the laws of motion and gravity, Newton derived and quantified Kepler's three principles for planetary orbits. Also, Newton's laws were used to predict the existence of the planet Neptune in 1846 due to the fact that Uranus's orbit was disturbed by the then unknown planet. Similar circumstances led to the discovery of Pluto in 1930 since Uranus's orbit was still being affected by an unknown object. Physics has found proof that, as Newton claimed, the laws of motion and gravity must work the same way everywhere. Thus, Newton's work put an end to the Aristotelian belief that there are two levels of existence (one in the sublunary sphere and the other in celestial spheres). An interesting implication of Newton's work is that the physical World must follow strict determinism. Theoretically, it should be possible to predict with perfect accuracy the location and speed of every particle in the Universe. However, this notion had to be abandoned by the quantum physics of the twentieth century (See chapter 5).

Newton observed white light being broken into a spectrum of colors when passed through a prism. In his desire to hold to the universal action of gravity, Newton proposed that light was composed of corpuscles or particles. When white light passes through a prism, the corpuscles move at different speeds and emerge as separate colors. Also, having light as made up of particles with slight masses also meant that light was subject to the influence of gravity. Newton made an interesting prediction based upon the assumption that light has weight. If light were to pass closely to an immense object, such as the Sun, the light particles would be pulled by the Sun's gravity with the result that the path of the light would be deflected. Modern astronomy has shown that massive objects do bend light rays but to a much larger extent than predicted by Newtonian physics. An alternative explanation for light bending was proposed by Einstein who claimed that gravity disturbs both time and space, producing the change in the light's path. For Newton, space and time are absolute; for Einstein, they are relative.

Newton's Positivism

Newton demonstrated that experimental observation is necessary for accurate conclusions about the physical World. The observational approach to knowledge is called positivism. Newton's view of positivism may be condensed to the following four statements (Burtt, 1952):

1. The human mind is capable of knowing reality through observation.
2. Reality can be mathematically described.
3. Objects occupying physical space are considered to have real existence and can be studied by the methods of observation.
4. Efficient causes (how something is done or made) are used in scientific explanations.

These principles assume that the human mind can reflect reality and does not create it. Moreover, science can only study what takes up physical space. Therefore, the soul and any other immaterial entity cannot be approached by science. Since the physical world obeys laws, the use of mathematics can be used to describe the regularities in nature. Finally, science attempts to answer the question "how" (efficient causality) a phenomenon occurs. Science cannot give the answer "why" (final causality) something happens.

Newton's reliance upon efficient causality as the cardinal principle of explanation in science is especially important. According to the Newtonian view, two events have a causal linkage if event A can be observed to influence event B directly. In other words, for event A to be the cause of event B's activity, there must be in the present time a direct physical connection between the two events. Newton relied upon gravity to provide the basis of efficient causality for all natural phenonemon in the Universe. For example, the ocean tides on Earth are influenced by the Moon. How can this happen if the Moon is 240,000 miles away? The answer, of course, is the Moon's gravity which, in present time, pulls upon the Earth's oceans. To deny that cause and effect operate in the material world through the direct action of physical forces leads to an interesting dilemma. If event A were to influence event B without the intervention of a direct physical connection acting in the present, then "action at a distance" has occurred. The Newtonian view of science dismisses the possibility of action at a distance as did Einstein. However, certain phenomena in quantum physics and psychology (to be indicated later) may indicate that action at a distance is real!

Newton's Personal View of the World and God

Newton, in his *Principia,* agreed with the atomic theory of matter, and he considered atoms to be tiny, indestructible units operating in a purely lawful manner. Since all things in the Universe are made from atoms, all things obey the laws of nature. However, Newton was curious how the laws of nature came to be. His conclusion was that God is the Creator of the laws. These laws operate continuously and regulate all events. In other words, Newton said that God authored the laws of nature. However, once these laws were implemented, God essentially abandoned the Universe and allows the Universe to run on its own internal principles. These beliefs about God and the Universe form the basis of a philosophical-religious position known as Deism.

If God has abandoned the Universe, can miracles occur? Newton and his colleagues addressed this issue (Harrison, 1995). They considered that several events which have been considered to be miraculous are really the results of natural forces at work. A true miracle is an event that violates the laws of nature. In this regard,

Christianity is based upon a series of miracles such as the virgin birth of Christ and Christ's resurrection from the dead. Newton claimed that such miracles are extremely rare and probably no longer occur. In other words, the age of miracles is over. Nevertheless, God can do whatever with the Universe. Therefore, Newton and his colleagues considered that God can time the occurrence of natural causes to allow the occurrence of an event that seems miraculous. For example, the Biblical story describing the parting of the Red Sea which allowed Moses and the Israelites to escape the pursuing Egyptian army might have resulted from a massive earthquake that momentarily shifted the water level just as the Israelites arrived at the Red Sea. The synchronicity of these natural events could have involved the intervention of God. However, such events are not truly miraculous since the laws of nature were not suspended to bring about the event. Thus, Newton continued to believe in the existence of God who, for the most part, allows the Universe to operate according to the mechanical laws of nature that science hopes to discover.

The Return of the Atom

Newton's work clarified how the Universe operates and argued that the laws of nature hold everywhere. But, the nagging question remained into the seventeenth century as to what composed nature. As previously reviewed, Newton allowed the reconsideration of Leucippus and Democritus's atomic theory of matter which had been abandoned in favor of Aristotle's theory of basic elements (earth, air, fire, water, and ether). The individual who prepared the way for the acceptance of the atomic theory was Robert Boyle (1627–1691), one of Newton's contemporaries. Boyle extended positivism to the field of chemistry which eventually freed that science from alchemy and led to a period of sustained experimental work searching for the fundamental units of matter. By 1900, chemistry established the validity of the atomic theory of matter, In the following, a brief review of this dazzling work, showing the existence of atoms, is given beginning with Robert Boyle.

Boyle's Life and Work

Boyle was from an aristocratic background. He was the last son born to the Earl of Cork, Richard Boyle, who amassed a great fortune based upon extensive land-holdings. However, Boyle's mother died when he was four and her loss remained one of the deep regrets of his life. Also, as a youth, he developed a stuttering problem that continued into adulthood and dissuaded him from seeking a public career. Boyle's privileged social position afforded him the opportunity to travel throughout Europe at the time of the English civil war. In fact, Boyle was in Florence when Galileo died. Also, during his stay abroad, he suffered a deep depression as he wrestled with his religious convictions. Boyle always retained a firm belief in God but had difficulty understanding the bitter hatred between the Catholics and Protestants in Britain as each side was trying to control the monarchy (Crowther, 1960).

Following his father's death in 1643, Boyle returned to England and eventually settled with a group of scholars at Oxford University. His stay at Oxford lasted from 1654 to 1668 and was very important in the formation of the Royal Society in 1660. Intellectually, Boyle believed in the views of Francis Bacon (1561–1626). In his famous work, the *Advancement of Learning,* Bacon argued that science would be very successful in ascertaining knowledge if it operated with a correct philosophy. According-ing to Bacon, scientists should make conclusions about nature on the basis of obser-vations and not on the basis of trying to prove a dogma. In other words, Bacon believed in logical induction as the way to establish truth. Careful observation should reveal regularities in nature that may not be discovered if one is guided by preconceived ideas. Bacon was an ardent foe of Descartes's philosophy which placed great emphasis upon reasoning to first principles without the aid of observation.

At Oxford, Boyle hired a young student, Robert Hooke, to construct an air-pump, which allowed for the production of a vacuum. Boyle and Hooke discovered that sound could not be produced in a vacuum and animals could not survive. Eventually, the air pump experiments led to Boyle's famous gas law: At constant temperature, the volume of gas is inversely proportional to the pressure (i.e., if the volume is halved, the pressure is doubled).

In 1661, Boyle produced an important work, called *The Sceptical Chymist,* that revived the atomic theory of matter (Schneer, 1960). Boyle dismissed the Aristotelian doctrine that the basic building blocks of matter were earth, air, fire, water, and ether. Instead, he proposed that these substances were made up of something more basic. Boyle considered that matter must be made up of tiny particles or atoms. Also, atoms can combine together to make the basic elements which were defined as substances that cannot be chemically decomposed into simpler elements (Crowther, 1960).

Boyle and Hooke combined their efforts to produce a theory that tried to show the connection between life forms and inanimate matter (Schneer, 1960). Boyle and Hooke thought that air contained a special essence that allowed for fire. The essence was also carried by the blood and supported the life functions of animals. Boyle and Hooke did not know it, but they were talking about oxygen.

From 1668 to the end of his life, Boyle, who remained a bachelor, moved to his sister's mansion in London. He conducted himself with style and grace and displayed none of the petulance so prominent in Newton's personality. In 1680, Boyle was asked to be president of the Royal Society but refused the honor. By 1687, his health began to decline and his death occurred on December 30, 1691, one week after his sister had died.

Near the end of his life, Boyle published in 1690 an interesting book entitled, *The Christian Virtuoso*. One of the aims of this work was to dispel the growing belief that science and religion were incompatible (Mulligan, 1994). The supporters of science, such as Deists and atheists, were insisting that the human intellect was capable on its own of apprehending the true laws of nature. The human mind needs no help from revelation or divine inspiration. Science should disconnect itself from religion which continues to seek the understanding of the supernatural. Boyle, a masterful contributor to the cause of science, however, rejected the claim that science and religion are mutually antagonistic. While the philosophers Francis Bacon and John Locke were removing theology and religion from science, Boyle maintained the contrary position. Like the philosopher Spinoza, Boyle supported the view that science provides another avenue for the study of God's nature. Going beyond Spinoza, Boyle further argued that revelation and theology are necessary to interpret properly scientific discoveries. Thus, Boyle considered himself to be the Christian virtuoso by supporting the integration of science and theology. Boyle's own words on this task are found in *The Excellence of Theology* (Mulligan, p. 244):

> But neither the fundamental doctrine of Christianity, nor that of the powers and effects of matter and motion, seem to be more than an epicycle . . . of the great and universal system of God's contrivances, and makes but a part of the more general theory of things, knowable by the light of nature, improved by the information of the scriptures; so that both these doctrines, though very general, in respect of the subordinate parts of theology and philosophy, seem to be but members of the universal hypothesis, whose objects I conceive to be nature, counsels, and works of God, as far as they are discoverable by us.

Despite Boyle's efforts, science and theology continued to drift apart. If God has left the Universe alone following its creation, as Newton believed, then God cannot be used to explain how the laws of nature operate. By the eighteenth century, the separation of science and theology was complete as indicated by the following story. The great French astronomer and mathematician, Pierre LaPlace (1749–1827) was asked by Napoleon if God was needed to explain how nature works. LaPlace purportedly replied, "Sire, I had no need of that hypothesis." Even more so than Newton, Laplace was extremely influential in forging the division between science and theology (Taylor & Taylor, 1993). However, for those in the modern age who seek a reconciliation between science and theology, the ideas of Robert Boyle serve as a guide.

The Last Aristotelian Remnant: Phlogiston Theory

Boyle's work on gases was criticized by continental researchers who believed in the existence of phlogiston. Two German chemists, Becher (1635–1682) and Stahl (1660–1734), proposed that objects catch fire because they contain the special element phlogiston. When organic matter burns, phlogiston is released. However, phlogiston theory had one drawback. When metal is burned, the resulting ash weighs more than the original metal. Stahl explained this outcome by assuming that phlogiston has negative weight! In other words, the original metal, because it contained phlogiston, is lighter than the burned residue which is now free of phlogiston. There were serious efforts to capture phlogiston from burning objects in order to build levitation devices (Schneer, 1960).

Chemists trying to capture phlogiston found other gases. For example, Joseph Black, about 1750, discovered carbon dioxide and Joseph Priestly, in 1774, studied a gas that he called dephlogisticated air but was actually oxygen, the substance that Boyle and Hooke's work alluded to. Priestly also concluded that water was actually two gases, two parts hydrogen to one part oxygen. However, it was the work of Antoine-Laurent Lavoisier (1743–1794) who brought down phlogiston theory and the Aristotelian view of matter. By 1783, Lavoisier's experiments showed that the residue resulting from the burning of metal was heavier because oxygen combined with the metal fragments to make oxides. In triumph, Lavoisier highlighted his lectures by burning the works of Becher and Stahl. In 1789, Lavoisier authored the first modern book of chemistry that explained how elements could combine to produce compounds and how compounds could then be broken down into elements. Lavoisier's book listed 23 elements. The Aristotelian notion of earth, air, fire, water, and ether as fundamental elements was forever gone. Unfortunately, Lavoisier was also dispatched by the guillotine near the end of the French Revolution. His crime was being involved with an agency that collected taxes for the monarchy. Lavoisier protested his death by claiming that he was mainly a scientist, but was told that the "Republic had no use for scientists" (Snyder, 1969, p 68).

Dalton's Atomic Theory of Matter

Lavoisier's work was important in dispelling Aristotelian beliefs about matter. But another important step was necessary. This next development led to the postulation that elements in nature are composed of different arrangements of atoms. Our modern views of the structure of matter stem from the pioneering work of John Dalton (1766–1844).

John Dalton was the son of an impoverished Quaker weaver and received little formal education. However, through his natural brilliance, he became an instructor at the New College in Manchester, England. Dalton was inspired toward the atomic theory because of his great admiration for Isaac Newton who considered atoms in the *Principia*. From his experiments with gases completed by 1810, Dalton concluded the following about atoms (Nash, 1957). All matter is made up of atoms that are indivisible. All atoms of an element have the same properties. Atoms of different elements have different weights. Finally, atoms retain their identities in all chemical reactions that produce molecules (combinations of atoms from different elements). The key proposal in Dalton's theory was that atoms have weights. Different elements are composed of atoms of different weights, not shapes as proposed in the ancient Greek views of Leucippus, Democritus, and Plato.

Dalton's atomic theory was not widely accepted at the time of its proposal. One reason for the skepticism was Dalton's inability to give a precise way to calculate atomic weights. However, a French chemist, Joseph Louis Gay-Lussac (1778–1850) made a discovery important for the issue of atomic weights. Gay-Lussac discovered the laws predicting the volume of gases. For example, two volumes of hydrogen combined with one volume of oxygen produce two volumes of water vapor. The volume of a molecular gas is in proportion to the volumes of the elemental gases, being in the case of water 2:1:2. These proportions agreed with Dalton's assumption that atoms can combine together to make compounds. With this evidence, an Italian chemist, Amadeo Avogadro di Quaregna (1776–1856), concluded in 1811 that, at a fixed temperature and pressure, equal volumes of gases have the same number of molecules per unit volume. Slowly, the atomic theory was being accepted and chemists began to classify elements on the basis of their atomic weights. By 1871, the Russian chemist, Dmitri Mendeleyev (1834–1907), produced his periodic table of elements based upon a classification scheme using atomic weights and other properties. As new elements were discovered, they were found to fit nicely into vacant spots purposely left open by Mendeleyev on his chart.

The Physicists and the Atom

Physicists finally entered into the study of the atom. Using gases as their model, a Scot, James Clerk Maxwell (1831–1879), and an Austrian, Ludwig Boltzmann (1844–1906), developed thermodynamics. As a gas is heated, the molecules begin to move faster and the pressure within the gas's container increases. The behavior of the molecules bouncing off the walls of the container can be described by statistical mechanics which Maxwell and Boltzmann developed. The underlying assumption of statistical mechanics is that the molecules of gas are determined in their actions by Newton's principles of motion.

Maxwell, a Cambridge Professor, was also an early contributor to electromagnetic theory. His ideas became important for physicists such as J. J. Thomson (1856–1940) who studied the properties of electricity passed through gases (Segre, 1980b). As the charge is passed through gas, it begins to glow, a phenomenon first observed by Michael Faraday in 1833. What could be responsible for the strange light in the gas? Thomson, who was Maxwell's successor at Cambridge, developed special cathode-ray tubes to isolate electrical activity. By 1897, Thomson's brilliant research had measured the mass of the particle responsible and it was much smaller than an atom. What Thomson had found by his measurements was the existence of electrons, parts of an atom that are responsible for electricity and light emission. Thus, Thomson demonstrated that the atom had parts and is not indivisible as proposed by Dalton.

Strange Properties of Atoms

As the study of the atom progressed in physics and chemistry, amazing discoveries were constantly being made. One of the more interesting discoveries was made accidently by Wilhelm Conrad Rontgen (1845–1923). On the night of November 8, 1895, Rontgen was experimenting with a cathode ray tube in his laboratory at the University of Wurzburg and noticed that a fluorescent screen near the tube began to glow. When electrons are generated and strike a metal object, a secondary radiation is emitted. Rontgen's florescent screen was detecting the presence of the secondary radiation passing out of the tube. Rontgen quickly named the energy "X-rays" for he had no idea what they were (X standing for the unknown). What was more amazing is that the X-rays could pass through a solid object and put an image of the object's internal structure on a photographic plate. The discovery of the X-rays created a public sensation and Rontgen had to personally demonstrate their existence to the German Kaiser. The medical community also quickly realized the value of X-rays for diagnosis. Although Rontgen never really understood that X-rays represent released energy produced by electrons colliding with metal, he was awarded the first Nobel Prize in physics (1902).

Atomic Radiation

In France, Henri Becquerel (1852–1908), physicist and member of the French Academy of Science, became interested in Rontgen's discovery. He began to search for natural elements that might give off X-rays. By a chance observation in 1896, Becquerel discovered that uranium served as a natural source for X-rays.

At the time of Becquerel's work, a young scientist from Poland, Marie Sklodowska Curie (1867–1934), sought advice from her husband, Pierre Curie (1859–1906), as to the topic for her doctoral dissertation (Segre, 1980b). Pierre suggested that Marie investigate the nature of elements that produce X-rays. Marie and Pierre Curie set out on an experimental odyssey that quickly showed X-rays were a natural property of uranium and thorium. Marie Curie used the word "radioactivity" to indicate the unique properties of these elements. Their work also isolated an ore sample that produced much larger outputs of radiation than uranium or thorium. Marie drew the correct conclusion that the ore sample must contain an unknown radioactive element which was named *polonium* for Marie's homeland. By September, 1898, the Curies discovered another more powerful radioactive element *radium* and, by 1902, measured its atomic weight at 225 (close to the actual value). The Curies shared the Nobel Prize in 1903 with Becquerel.

The Curies conducted their research in a crude laboratory since the French government was unwilling to provide better facilities. Since it was unknown that radiation is a health risk, the Curies began to suffer strange ailments. Unhappily, in 1906, Pierre was killed by a carriage in a Paris street. Marie was deeply disturbed by his loss but continued her experimental work. She became a professor at the Sorbonne and was awarded a second Nobel Prize in 1911. Now, the French government cooperated and Marie received generous research facilities. She continued to experiment with radium and encouraged the scientific development of one of her daughters, Irene, who was also destined for a Nobel Prize. Marie established that radium undergoes a decay process over time indicating again that Dalton's idea of atoms being indestructible was incorrect. But the last years for Marie Curie involved physical suffering due to radiation poisoning and she died of aplastic anemia. Over her lifetime, Marie received so much radiation that her experimental notebooks, and even her cookbooks at home, were still contaminated 50 years after their usage (Segre, 1980b).

Rutherford's Atom

Ernest Rutherford (1871–1937) continued the work in radiation that resulted in a useful model for the structure of an atom. Rutherford was born in a rugged region of south New Zealand. He showed considerable intellectual promise as a youth and, in 1894, was awarded a scholarship to study with J. J. Thomson in England. Thomson became very impressed with the genius of his new student. In 1898, Rutherford travelled to McGill University to become a professor of physics. In 1907, he returned to England to take a post at Manchester University and later directed the physics laboratory at Cambridge.

Throughout his career, Rutherford probed the internal structure of atoms by bombarding them with radioactivity. More precisely, Rutherford directed beams of alpha particles (positively charged helium ions) at metal foil and observed the scattering of the particles. Some particles went through the foil, some were deflected to the side, and a very few bounced straight back to their point of origination. In 1911, Rutherford designed a model of an atom that could explain the scattering of the alpha particles. Since like charges repel, an alpha particle was deflected if it was within the vicinity of a positively charged particle in the atom. If an alpha particle were to be on a direct collision course with this positively charged atomic structure, the alpha particles would bounce straight backwards. Thus, Rutherford concluded that the atom must have a center with a positive charge. But to keep the atom electrically neutral, the positive charge of the center must be balanced by negatively charged electrons. Rutherford's calculations indicated that the nucleus of positive charges in the atom must be very small compared to the overall size of the atom.

Rutherford's work indicated that change in atomic structure is the basis of the elements. Therefore, the atom must be made up of parts. Also, atoms seem to contain great amounts of energy required to hold the electrons in position around the nucleus. One of Rutherford's students, Otto Hahn, eventually "smashed" an atom. In 1938, Hahn, working in a laboratory in his native Germany, bombarded uranium with neutrons and found that the element barium resulted. The alchemist dream came true. Atomic structure could be rearranged with the result that different elements appear. Hahn's discovery was made known to physicists outside of Germany by Lise Meiter, a close associate of Hahn, who was forced to escape the Nazis for sanctuary in Sweden. Physicists, such as Fermi, Bohr, Oppenheimer, and Einstein, knew the importance of the discovery. The transmutation of an element through nuclear fission should be accompanied by a tremendous release of energy. The atomic bomb proved the physicists correct (Gammow, 1961).

Rutherford enjoyed great honors for his ingenuity: A winner of Nobel Prizes, knighted for his scientific work, made a Baron, and allowed to be buried close to Newton in Westminster Abbey. However, Rutherford did not solve all the mysteries of the atom. One of the more difficult questions concerned the relationship between electrons and the nucleus. If opposite charges attract, what prevents the negatively charged electrons from falling into the heavier, positively charged nucleus with the result that the atom should collapse? The answer to this question becomes a part of the new, provocative quantum physics of the twentieth century.

Understanding What Is Real

Newton's physics is based upon a fundamental principle that space and time are absolute. In other words, any part of space can be measured by the rules of geometry and we can be certain of the answer. Likewise, time is absolute in that different observers can measure the distance between two events and come to the same conclusion provided that they use valid clocks. Moreover, the classical physics of Newton accepted the principle of efficient causality. Everything that is put into motion is acted upon by another force.

Newton's theory helped to inspire the rational philosophy of Immanuel Kant (1724–1804) who studied how humans have knowledge of the World. Kant agreed with his philosophical enemy, David Hume (1711–1776), that knowledge begins with experience. However, Kant goes beyond Hume by claiming that the human mind must use its innate powers or judgements to understand what is being represented by the senses (Durant, 1938). These innate powers are called the *synthetic a priori* by Kant since they exist as active mental powers ready to interpret experience but not derived from experience. The human mind naturally understands events by referencing them in space and time. All human intellects should be able to arrive at the same judgments about experience because all human intellects share the same *a priori* understanding of space, time, and causality.

The Newtonian view of the World and the Kantian view of the mind were successful allies in explaining physical and mental reality. However, disturbing developments were occurring in physics at the turn of the 20th century. Light phenomena could not be described by Newton's laws. Instead, the experiments with light began to question whether time and even space were absolute. As physics began to recast the meaning of time and space, the implications for contemporary psychology became profound. To explain light energy, modern physics has produced two provocative views of reality: the theory of relativity and quantum theory. These developments have redefined the capabilities of the human mind to know reality. Niels Bohr, one of the founders of quantum theory, has observed, "anyone who is not shocked by quantum theory has not understood it" (Gribben, 1984). The next chapter is devoted to a discussion of modern physics and its implications for the ability of the human mind to understand reality.

Cosmology, Relativity, and the Quantum

4

Newton's view of the World proved adequate for objects that move at relatively slow speeds, such as apples falling from trees, rockets blasting into space, and even planets in their orbits. However, when objects, such as atomic particles, move close to the speed of light, Newton's explanations of motion break down. A new physics is needed to account for light phenomena and the internal activities of atoms while still incorporating the Newtonian laws for slow moving objects. Since the atom is the basic building block of the Universe, unraveling its mysteries would reveal the ultimate basis of reality. In this chapter, the new physics of relativity and quantum theory is reviewed along with the connection between the new physics and the understanding of the Universe (cosmology). The chapter begins with the ideas about reality conceived by the most celebrated scientist since Newton, Albert Einstein.

Einstein's Theories of Reality

Like Newton before him, Einstein formulated his most important theories at an early age. In particular, his most famous scientific contributions were on Brownian movement, the concept of light quantum, the Special Theory of Relativity, and the General Theory of Relativity. But also, Einstein was a public figure who spoke for several movements that were important to him. Thus, his long life was filled with excitement and his legend continues to live on.

Einstein's Life

Albert Einstein (1879–1955) was born in the city of Ulm to a German Jewish family (Segre, 1980b). He did his early schooling in Munich and was an excellent student contrary to some reports that he was intellectually slow as a child (Pais, 1988). Due to business reversals, Einstein's family moved to Milan in 1894 and Albert soon joined them. Apparently, Einstein was growing weary of the German educational system which he despised after several altercations with his teachers (Segre, 1980b).

After a short but pleasant stay in Italy, Einstein eventually entered the Polytechnical Institute in Zurich. He enjoyed Switzerland and later received Swiss citizenship which he retained all his life. At Zurich, Einstein's major professors were H. Minkowski and A. Hurwitz, both distinguished mathematicians. Einstein also spent long hours reading about physics. Upon graduation, no permanent jobs in education were available to him. So Einstein, in 1902, accepted a position in the government patent office in Bern. In 1903, Einstein married a fellow student from the Institute, Meliva Maric (1875–1948). Recently recovered records indicate that Albert and Meliva had a daughter, Lise, out of wedlock, and the details of her life are not known (Pais, 1988). The marriage also produced two sons. Hans Albert (1904–1973) became an engineering professor at the University of California, Berkeley. The other son, Eduard (1910–1965), had a long history of mental illness and died in an institution near Zurich. Divorce ended Einstein's first marriage in 1919, and, in that same year, he wedded his cousin Elsa who was to die in 1936.

The years at the Bern Patent Office were Einstein's happiest. The work was easy which afforded Einstein a great opportunity to develop his ideas. From March to June, 1905, Einstein submitted for publication in the journal *Annalen der Physik* three papers that were to make him famous. The first paper discloses the discovery of the light quanta, the second paper explains Brownian movement, and the third paper presents the Special Theory of Relativity.

The world of physics was excited by Einstein's papers and several notable scientists journeyed to Bern to meet the author. (The Swiss government also noticed Einstein and he was appointed to the University of Bern and then to the University of Zurich.) In 1911, Einstein accepted a position with the University of Prague, but was very unhappy there. In 1912, the itinerant professor took a post at Zurich's Polytechnical Institute, his old school. Just after settling down, Einstein received H. Walther Nernst and Max Planck who presented a generous offer to Einstein to come to Germany. Einstein took one day to accept the offer and moved to the Prussian Academy in Berlin. As World War I broke out, Einstein was busily working on the General Theory of Relativity which was announced in 1915. General Relativity offered the unbelievable proposal that space bends near massive objects. Then, in 1919, a British expedition observing a total eclipse of the Sun confirmed Einstein's prediction that the gravity of the Sun would bend light rays. At this point, the legend of Einstein was created. The London *Times* announced the overthrow of Newtonian ideas and that space is curved. Meanwhile, the situation in Germany was growing more desperate for Einstein. His theories were attacked by anti-Semites and the Nazis. Einstein had already entered the political world of post-war Germany by announcing his support for Zionism and a Jewish homeland. An anti-Einstein organization was formed with the avowed purpose of murdering him (Hawking, 1988). Instead of keeping a low profile, Einstein continued to be vocal for his political and humanitarian causes as Germany moved again toward world war.

With the success of Hitler assured in Germany, Einstein left the country and, after a bit of wandering, settled for the rest of his life at the Institute for Advanced Study at Princeton. The Nazis took possession of Einstein's personal property and a Berlin newspaper happily announced, "Good News from Einstein—He's Not Coming Back" (Hawking, 1988, p. 178). Einstein, worried about the ability of Germany to build the atomic bomb following Hahn's discovery of fission, urged President Roosevelt to commit the United States to the project. In 1952, Einstein was offered the ceremonial position as president of Israel but he declined. On April 18, 1955 Einstein's life came to an end when his aorta ruptured. For over 30 years, he worked on a Grand Unified Theory that would explain how all the forces in nature operate together. He died without completing the task.

The Nature of Light

Einstein's 1905 paper on light explained two difficult problems for physics, black body radiation and the photoelectric effect. By doing so, Einstein established that light behaves simultaneously like a wave and a particle. Before getting to Einstein's paper on the nature of light, some background information is necessary.

Newton, expanding upon Greek ideas, considered light to be made up of particles which could be attracted by gravity. However, Huygens, Newton's scientific foe, thought that light was composed of waves. Moreover, research by Thomas Young (1773–1829) indicated that light was subject to interference effects as predicted by the wave model. Light energy was presumed to transfer through air and the ether in space in a manner similar to the propagation of sound waves. By 1870, James Clerk Maxwell was able to describe both electric and magnetic radiation by wave properties. In 1887, Heinrick Hertz transmitted electromagnetic radiation which is similar to light waves but with longer wavelengths. Hertz started radio communication by using electromagnetic waves (Gribben, 1984).

However, toward the end of the 19th century, experiments with electromagnetic energy began to yield disconcerting results for the wave theory. First, J. J. Thomson and Philipp Lenard (1862–1947) established the photoelectric effect. This effect refers to a condition where light energy strikes a charged metal plate that caused electrons from the metal to be ejected and jump to another opposite charged plate. From Maxwell's laws, it was expected that as more light energy was directed to the metal plate, produced by raising the intensity of the light, the greater would be the velocity of the ejected electrons. However, experiments did not support the prediction. When the amount of light energy was increased for a certain frequency of light, the number of electrons ejected from the metal increased but the speed of the electrons remained constant. However, the speed of the ejected electrons would increase if the color of the light hitting the metal was changed. As the light frequency became shorter (moving the color of the light from red to blue), the greater was the speed of ejection (Gamow, 1961).

While Lenard was trying to understand the photoelectric effect, Max Planck (1858–1947), at the University of Berlin, became mystified by the results on light obtained from his blackbody radiation experiments. Blackbody or cavity radiation is produced by heating a black metal box to increasingly high temperatures while watching an outlet hole. When the box is heated, light streams from the outlet hole. As the box's temperature is raised, the light appears red (long wavelengths) at low temperatures, then successively turns orange, yellow, and finally bluish-white (short wavelengths) at high temperatures. However, the intensity of the emitted light did not follow theoretical predictions. Maxwell's electromagnetic theory hypothesizes that, as the heat of the box is increased, more energy stirs the atomic structure of the box causing greater movement of the electrons. Since electron activity is needed to produce light, the intensity of the light should increase as the temperature of the box is raised. The predicted result was known as the "ultraviolet catastrophe." As the emitted light moves to shorter wavelengths, the brightness of the light should increase tremendously. The intense bluish-white light will then give way to ultraviolet light and eventually to X-rays (which have very short wavelengths) as the temperature of the box becomes extreme.

But the ultraviolet catastrophe did not happen. As the temperature of the box increased, the maximum emitted intensity of the electromagnetic energy shifts to the shorter wavelengths but there was always a cutoff at very short wavelengths preventing the ultraviolet catastrophe. Max Planck wanted to know why.

After months of calculation, Planck came up with a formula to explain blackbody radiation. But he was distressed as to the implications of the formula, for it threatened the theoretical framework of all that is understandable in physics. On December 14, 1900, Planck presented his explanation at a meeting of physicists (Segre, 1980b). Electromagnetic energy which included light is not emitted in a continuous pattern. Instead, it is emitted in discrete packages that Planck called quanta (from Latin meaning "how much"). A quantum of light is produced only when the activating energy crosses a minimal threshold. At long wavelengths, the red region, the energy quanta is much less than at short wavelengths, the blue wavelengths. The failure of the ultraviolet catastrophe to happen is now explicable. The heating of the blackbox cannot produce enough threshold energy to form quanta at short wavelengths. Planck summarized his ideas in his famous equation for the quantum:

$$E = h\nu$$

where E is the energy of the quantum, ν is the frequency of the electromagnetic energy, and h is a universal constant (called Planck's constant). What the formula says is that the amount of energy required to produce a quantum is directly proportional to the frequency (wavelengths) of the electromagnetic energy. X-rays with very short wavelengths have so much energy in them that they can penetrate matter but visible light cannot since it has longer wavelengths and less energy. The understanding of the physical world took a dramatic turn as Einstein explained the nature of the photoelectric effect and blackbody radiation based upon the idea of the quantum.

Einstein's 1905 paper on light was entitled, "On a Heuristic Viewpoint Concerning the Production and Transformation of Light." What Einstein proposed in this paper is a step that Planck was unwilling to take, namely that quanta compose all of electromagnetic energy. Planck's view was that quanta produce electromagnetic energy. If electromagnetic energy is made up of quanta, then light must be corpuscles of energy and not continuous waves. Einstein thought that Planck's formula indicated how much energy is in a quantum of light at a given frequency. Light at a particular frequency is made up of quanta having the same energy level. Raise the frequency of the light, and the energy in the light quantum increases. How is the photoelectric effect now explained? As previously seen, the photoelectric effect shows that the speed of ejection of electrons from a metal plate is controlled by the frequency (wavelength) of the light falling on the plate. The higher the frequency, the greater is the velocity of the ejected electrons. The reason for this effect is that light quanta at high frequencies strike the electrons in the metal with greater force. Thus, the electrons are ejected at higher speeds. Raising the intensity of light while keeping the frequency constant produces more quanta (or photons as they are called today) with the result that more electrons are ejected but at the same speed.

Although the quantum theory connotes that light is made up of corpuscles as Newton proposed, Einstein did not completely abandon the wave properties of light. Light energy was still characterized as having a frequency characteristic of waves. Thus, twentieth century physics had to think of matter as being composed of waves as well as particles. Some physicists have considered that Einstein's 1905 paper establishing the reality of the quantum was his greatest effort (Segre, 1980b). Universal recognition of the quantum theory, with its embedded assumption that matter is both waves and particles, occurred in 1922 when Einstein received the Nobel Prize for his explanation of the photoelectric effect.

Brownian Movement

Einstein's second paper of 1905 was entitled, "On the motions of particles suspended in liquids at rest required by the kinetic theory of heat." Einstein's purpose in this paper was to explain the phenomenon of Brownian Movement based upon the existence of molecules.

In 1827, a Scottish botanist, Robert Brown (1773–1858), discovered that microscopic particles of pollen suspended in water were in constant motion. Einstein wondered what caused the motion and concluded that the pollen was colliding with water molecules. In the second paper, Einstein mathematically presented the mass and number of molecules required to cause the Brownian Movement. The importance of this paper was to establish the authenticity of the atomic theory since atoms compose the molecules producing the Brownian Movement. However, in 1905, many notable German physicists were opposed to the atomic theory even though the British and French were much more receptive. Einstein's second paper served to convince the Germans of the reality of atoms. However, the paper was published too late for Boltzmann. He was one of the few Germans who believed in the existence of atoms since it was required by his kinetic theory of gases. In deep depression coinciding with the failure to get his kinetic theory accepted, Boltzmann in 1906 committed suicide without ever having read Einstein's paper (Gribben, 1984).

Special Theory of Relativity

Einstein's third paper of 1905 was simply called, "On the Electrodynamics of Moving Bodies," but contained a formulation about reality that is incredible but apparently true. The paper claimed that space and time are relative to one another, not absolute as proposed by Newton. The new view came to be known as the Special Theory of Relativity.

The Special Theory was proposed to explain mysterious results from experiments attempting to measure the speed of light. The most famous of such experiments was performed in 1887 by Michelson and Morley. The purpose of the experiment was to determine how the ether affected the speed of light. Since the time of Aristotle, an ether vapor was assumed to fill the Universe. Physics in the nineteenth century accepted this view and the ether was considered to be the medium through which light waves travelled through space. Also, the ether was thought to be motion, streaming from the Sun. When the Earth in its orbit is heading toward the Sun, the ether stream should act like a head-wind. Therefore, a beam of light shot straight into the ether stream should be slowed. Conversely, a beam of light shot at right angles to the ether stream should not be so adversely affected, with little change in speed occurring. Michelson and Morley designed an experiment to test the above reasoning and found a major surprise. The speed of light always remained constant and was not influenced by the origination point of the light beam.

Special Relativity Theory starts with the results of the Michelson-Morley experiment. Einstein concluded, perhaps using Occam's razor, that the ether simply did not exist. Therefore, light travelling in the void of space must have particle properties. Especially important was the further belief that the speed of light always is a constant relative to the observer, being approximately 186,000 miles per second. Therefore, if a traveller were moving away from earth at 185,000 miles per second and a little while later a beam of light was launched from earth on the same flight path as the traveller, the beam of light would pass her at a measured speed of 186,000 miles per second not, as common sense would expect, 1,000 miles per second. The constancy of the speed of light is its unique property. However, this property is difficult to appreciate based upon everyday experience. For example, if you are travelling 55 miles per hour on a freeway, and a car comes up behind you at 65 miles per hour, the other car will eventually pass you at a relative speed of 10 miles per hour, as predicted by Newtonian physics. Also predicted by Newtonian physics is that velocities of two objects in motion should add together to produce a final velocity. Consider that you are riding a motorcycle moving 10 miles per hour on top of an aircraft carrier moving 20 miles per hour. Your speed measured by an observer on the shore would be 30 miles per hour. However, adding velocities together for extremely fast moving objects can never exceed the speed of light. Special Relativity actually incorporates Newton's laws of motion but extends the principles to explain motion for objects operating near the speed of light.

The constancy of the speed of light serves to make the measurement of time relative to the motion of the observer. This is shown by the following hypothetical example. Suppose someone is sitting on a distant hill overlooking railroad tracks and sees lightning bolts strike the tracks simultaneously at the eastern and western horizons. The observer naturally assumes that the lightning strikes were simultaneous events. However, at the same moment, a train is moving on the tracks from west to east near the speed of light. A passenger on the train also notices the lightning strikes but would experience the light in the east as coming first followed by the light in the west. Which observer is correct? According to Einstein, both are correct even though they had different experiences, because time is relative to motion. Thus Newton's claim that time is measured in absolute units and always moves at the same rate from past to present is abolished!

We can all experience the past while staying in the present very simply by looking at the night sky. Stars are at great distances measured in light-years (the distance light travels in a year). Thus, seeing a star located 500 light years away means that the currently visible starlight emanated 500 years ago. Likewise, if that star exploded at this moment, earthlings would not know until 500 years from now. Theoretically, it is possible to experience the future by accelerating near the speed of light. Instead of time being absolute, it would appear to slow down as objects move toward the speed of light. In other words, time is measured differently for objects moving relative to one another. Perhaps this factor from Special Relativity can be realized from the equation for the calculation of velocity:

$$v = \frac{d}{t}$$

where v is velocity, d is distance, and t is time. If a car takes one hour to go 40 miles, it velocity is 40 miles per hour. In the above formula, substitute the speed of light, a constant (c), for velocity so that:

$$c = \frac{d}{t}$$

At the speed (or near the speed) of light, as distance increases, time must decrease (slow) in order for the constancy to hold. The following hypothetical example now becomes possible from Einstein's equations (Boslough, 1985). Suppose an astronaut travels through space at 160,000 miles per second (86% of the speed of light) and is gone for 10 years. The clock on the spaceship would only move at half the speed of an Earth-based clock. Therefore, when the astronaut returned, 20 years will have passed on Earth relative to the 10 years experienced by the traveller who now has jumped to the future. The slowing of time has been experimentally demonstrated by accelerating atomic particles known as muons. At rest, muons decay in about a microsecond. However, in accelerators which hurl muons near the speed of light, these particles have longer lives. Time has been stretched as speed is increased. Einstein, using equations developed by Lorentz, showed how to relate time and space to the relative motion of the observer. The mathematical transformations of space and time insure that the laws of nature remain constant to observers moving at uniform speeds relative to one another.

Einstein published one more brief paper in 1907 as an addendum to Special Relativity that states the equivalency between energy and mass expressed in the famous equation:

$$E = mc^2$$

where E is energy, m is mass, and c is the speed of light. This little equation claims that mass and energy are interchangeable and not separate entities. Also, the energy contained in an object is awesome since the multiplier is the speed of light squared. The energy-mass equivalency was demonstrated by the use of atomic weapons in World War II. In a previous equation leading to $E = mc^2$, Einstein showed that an object gains mass as it accelerates toward the speed of light. However, no object could ever surpass the speed of light since it would need infinite mass.

The ideas that germinated into the Special Theory began when Einstein imagined at sixteen years of age what he would see if he paralleled a beam of light as it travelled through space. About the same time, H. G. Wells published his *Time Machine* trying to explain in fiction what Einstein offered as fact, namely, that time is the fourth dimension and affects the measurement of the other three. However, Einstein was not finished revolutionizing the meaning of reality. He was interested in making the concept of gravity consistent with the Special Relativity. This effort became known as the General Theory of Relativity.

General Theory of Relativity

The General Theory of Relativity attempted to resolve a paradox concerning gravity precipitated by the Special Theory. A hypothetical example serves to indicate the anomaly. Suppose the Sun were to completely disappear at this moment. The force of gravity exerted by the Sun would cease and the Earth would be propelled out of its orbit toward the edge of the solar system. Following the hypothetical catastrophe, another eight minutes would have to pass before the sunlight disappeared since it takes that long for the last rays of light from the Sun to reach the Earth. Thus, the disappearance of the Sun would be communicated to the Earth by the release of gravity before the light of the Sun disappeared from the sky! The difficulty provided by this example is that Special Relativity holds that no action can occur faster than the speed of light. The gravity release of the Earth before the sunlight disappeared would be a contradiction to Special Relativity.

Einstein's solution to the paradox was a marvelous insight. General Relativity dispenses with the notion that gravity is a force that acts instantaneously between objects that might be light-seconds apart. Instead, any object with mass does something amazing to space. Objects with mass bend or curve space, and the more massive the object the greater is the curvature. For example, if a heavy cannon ball were placed upon a mattress, the surface of the mattress would curve inward toward the sunken cannon ball. Apparently, massive objects, such as the Sun, stars, and planets, do the same thing except it is space that is curved. The curvature of space explains the acceleration of an object as it approaches a massive object. In our example, if a small ball were rolled across the mattress, the ball would pick up speed (accelerate) as it fell into the curvature created by the cannon ball. Large objects in space accelerate smaller objects as they enter the warp. As objects accelerate and move closer to the speed of light, a time warp also results. Thus, the Theories of Relativity lead to the view that space is a four-dimensional system with time providing the extra dimension. Accordingly, modern physicists use the term "space-time" to refer to the conditions created by the four dimensions.

Einstein had to resort to non-Euclidean geometry to present the curvature of space. The mathematics allowed the elliptical orbits of planets plotted by Kepler and Newton to be represented as straight lines in space-time. Moreover, General Relativity was tested in two ways. First, Einstein's equations accounted for the deviation in the orbit of Mercury caused by its close approximation to the Sun. Secondly, Einstein's mathematics predicted a much larger bending of light rays than suggested by Newton's theory. Thus, a star situated behind the Sun as viewed from Earth would still be visible because the starlight wraps around the Sun due to the curvature of space. As previously mentioned, the theory was tested during a full eclipse in 1919, and a star near the Sun was noticed to be "out of position" as predicted by Einstein.

The New Cosmology

Einstein's theories were quickly applied to the understanding of the origin and fate of the Universe. Over the last sixty years, the knowledge collected about the nature of the Cosmos has exceeded all of the information gathered since the dawn of civilization. The new cosmology of the 20th century, born from Einstein's work and nurtured by quantum theory, portrays the Universe as a dynamic expanding system whose fate is not yet known and whose laws have resulted from a chance combination of events occurring at the moment known as the Big Bang. How different this treatment is from Aristotle's, who thought that the stars and Earth were fixed in their positions and that rest was the optimal state of any object.

The Expanding Universe

Einstein's General Relativity Theory predicts a Universe that should still be expanding. However, Einstein himself was uncomfortable with this possibility and later added constants to his equations to make the Universe static (Hawking, 1988).

Nevertheless, a Russian mathematician, Alexander Friedman, in 1922, took the original mathematical equations of Relativity Theory and forcefully argued against the inclusion of Einstein's additional terms to make the Universe static. According to Friedman, the Universe is expanding with the consequence that two fates are possible. The Universe will keep expanding forever or the Universe will eventually reach its limit of expansion and then collapse back upon itself. In each scenario, the Universe must now still be expanding. Friedman was correct because, in 1924, Edwin Hubble, using the new 100-inch telescope at Mount Wilson began to observe distant galaxies. By 1929, Hubble had evidence to indicate that the galaxies were still in motion moving away from one another. Furthermore, the more distant the galaxy was from Earth, the faster was its movement away. The expanding Universe was demonstrated by observation and Einstein quietly withdrew his support for a static system.

The Big Bang

Hubble's data suggested that the Universe was expanding, but what was the source of the expansion? This problem caught the imagination of a wonderful scientist by the name of George Gamow (1904–1968). Gamow was born in Russia but eventually immigrated to the United States in 1934. In 1948, he co-authored a paper that suggested the early Universe must have been hot and fiery. Essentially, Gamow took the existing Universe and played it backward in time. Contracting the Universe lead to the conclusion that all its matter, as well as space and time, began when a cataclysmic explosion took place. The euphemism "Big Bang" became the way to express the theory. The "Big Bang" theory quickly met opposition from a British physicist, Fred Hoyle, who advocated a Steady State model of the Universe. In Hoyle's model, the Universe is allowed to expand, but there was no Big Bang that started it. In the Steady State model, as galaxies move away from one another, new matter is created in the receding space. In Hoyle's analysis, the Universe has always existed; therefore, time has always existed. Hoyle preferred this position to the deduction of the Big Bang theory that time was created along with space (Hawking, 1988).

Finding Evidence for the Big Bang

Friendly arguments were made for almost twenty years between the proponents of the Big Bang and Steady State theories. Supporters of the Big Bang theory began to study a suggestion made by Gamow that the Universe might contain a residue of the early explosion in the form of background microwave radiation. The radiation would also have a heat component and Gamow estimated that the Universe might have a temperature as low as five degrees Kelvin.

Two physicists at Princeton University, Robert Dicke and James Peebles, were in the process of studying the microwaves that might be in space when two researchers at nearby Bell Labs made the discovery by accident. The Bell researchers were Arno Penzias and Robert Wilson.

Penzias and Wilson were converting the Bell Labs antenna at Crawford Hill, that had been used as a receiver for communications satellites, to function in experiments for radio astronomy. This particular antenna was especially sensitive and Penzias and Wilson were detecting what they initially considered a lot of background noise with a temperature of three degrees Kelvin. Initially, the researchers thought that the equipment was malfunctioning and even had bird droppings cleaned off the antenna. But the low, steady microwave radiation continued to be registered. In January, 1965, the Bell Labs team met with Dicke and the Princeton team to talk about the meaning of the radiation. Apparently, the Princeton team was convinced that Penzias and Wilson were recording the remnants of the Big Bang. The microwave signals represented the remaining blackbody radiation left over from the time of the superheating created by the Big Bang. In 1978, Penzias and Wilson received the Nobel Prize for their work and Gamow's Big Bang model of the Universe was officially sanctioned.

Complexities for the Big Bang Theory

The Big Bang theory is commendable in that it supplies an explanation for the expanding Universe and why galaxies in general are moving away from one another. However, there are major problems for the supporters of the Big Bang theory to consider. First, there does not appear to be enough known matter in the Universe to explain the effects of gravity. For example, the Andromeda galaxy is 2.5 million light years away from our own Milky Way galaxy. Nevertheless, gravity from our galaxy reaches across vast distances of space to influence Andromeda by slowing its rate of recession (Freedman, 1992). In turn, Andromeda affects the velocity of the Milky Way.

If there is not enough visible matter in the Universe to generate its gravity effects, then other forms of matter may exist that supply the needed mass. In this regard, several cosmologists support the proposal that "dark matter" generates the gravity needed to hold the Universe together. Without the dark matter, the Universe should be expanding at a such a fast rate that all the galaxies would fragment. However, this does not appear to be happening since gravity acts as a force binding the galaxies while the Universe continues to expand. Dark matter is so named because it does not radiate or reflect light. In other words, it is a very special form of matter that cannot be directly detected in telescopes since it is invisible. Dark matter is assumed to form a shroud around each galaxy which thereby increases its gravity strength. However, to date no one has been able to discover the composition of the supposed dark matter.

Another problem for the Big Bang theory is to account for the clustering of galaxies. Ostensibly, the Big Bang theory would expect an even distribution of galaxies throughout the Universe. However, in certain regions of space, such as in the constellation Virgo, great numbers of galaxies lie in near approximation. Therefore, in these locations, unusual fluctuations in the primordial soup of the Universe must have occurred to allow matter to clump together forming many nearby galaxies. Until the questions regarding the existence of dark matter and the uneven spread of the galaxies across the Universe can be answered, the Big Bang theory must be considered as tentative.

Black Holes

Einstein's General Theory of Relativity makes a prediction that has profound consequences for the understanding of reality. His theory allows a collapsed star to become what is now called a "black hole." The theoretical scenario for producing a black hole first requires a sufficiently large star that is exhausting its supply of nuclear fuel. As the star cools, it begins a process of collapse. As the volume of the star decreases, its mass increases and the space-time around the star undergoes severe warping. Finally, the mass of the star collapses to an infinitesimal point, making what is known as a singularity. The gravitational force around the singularity is so strong that space-time is infinitely warped. The light produced from the star is now bent inward and cannot escape. The term, black hole, signifies that light and everything else is forever trapped inside the singularity. Although it is difficult to imagine, there is no time and no space inside the singularity. The boundary region between the singularity and the resumption of space-time is called the event horizon. The search of the heavens for black holes has yielded some favorable data.

The alluring mysteries of the black hole have captivated the attention of the remarkable British physicist, Stephen Hawking. Born on January 8, 1942, exactly 300 years following Galileo's death, Hawking now holds the Lucasian Professorship at Cambridge once occupied by Newton. These coincidences even impress Hawking as he continues on his mission to integrate Relativity Theory with quantum mechanics to make the Grand Unified Theory. However, Hawking labors under extreme physical hardship. While a graduate student at Cambridge, the symptoms of amyotrophic lateral sclerosis (Lou Gehrig's disease) were first noticed. This disorder is incurable and involves the destruction of the motor neurons controlling the muscles. Fortunately, the progression of the disease has been relatively slow. But Hawking is confined to a wheelchair, speaks with the aid of a computer which enunciates his typed messages, and must develop esoteric mathematical equations upon the blackboard in his consciousness. Hawking is racing against time to develop the Grand Unified Theory.

Once Hawking recovered from the psychological trauma of his disease, he and Roger Penrose turned their interests to black holes (Hawking, 1988). Based upon General Relativity Theory, they hypothesized that the Universe began as a singularity which exploded. If black holes do exist, then the implication is that their explosions lead to a never-ending string of Universes being created in dimensions of space unknown to us!

In 1974, Hawking presented evidence based upon quantum physics that black holes could emit radiation at their event horizons. Subatomic particles apparently can be created in pairs out of nothing and then cancel each other's existence. However, if the particle pair were created at the event horizon, one member could be sucked into the black hole allowing the other particle to escape annihilation. "Hawking radiation" is the term now used to describe the theoretical release of energy at the event horizon. If such radiation can be found, it would offer strong support for the real existence of black holes.

As Hawking points out, the true understanding of the Universe must involve quantum physics. Inspired by Einstein's explanation of blackbody radiation, quantum physics attempts to depict the internal structure of the atom, and, in the process, offers an interpretation of reality that strains common sense.

Quantum Physics

In 1905, Einstein established the idea of quanta to explain the nature of light. A young physicist by the name of Niels Bohr also seized the quantum theory to explain how atoms work. Over the years, Einstein and Bohr would engage in a mostly friendly debate about the validity of quantum theory. Ironically, Einstein, as one of the originators of the quantum theory, came to abhor it since quantum theory does not allow a precise account of causality in the determination of atomic activity. Einstein's often used quotation that "God does not play dice with the Universe" was meant to express his annoyance with quantum theory. In contrast, Bohr became one of the major defenders of quantum theory and, in a jocular manner, told Einstein "do not tell God what to do."

Bohr's Life

Niels Bohr (1885–1962) was born in Copenhagen to economically advantaged parents. After completing his doctorate, he ventured to England and studied with J. J. Thomson at Cambridge and then with Rutherford at Manchester. With Rutherford's encouragement, Bohr began to study atomic structure based upon quantum physics. In 1913, he published his first article on the quantum atom. Bohr's ideas caused much debate in physics and his reputation expanded accordingly. In 1919, Bohr returned to Denmark when offered a professorship in physics and proceeded to set up an institute. In 1932, the government invited Bohr and his wife to live in the "House of Honor," a mansion reserved for Denmark's greatest contributor to the arts or sciences. As one of the founders of quantum theory, he travelled extensively and encouraged young physicists to develop their ideas. With the rise to power of the Nazis in neighboring Germany, Bohr helped German scientists to escape. When the Nazis invaded Denmark, it was not surprising that an arrest warrant was issued for Bohr, especially since his mother was Jewish. Fortunately, Bohr was able to escape to Sweden by a harrowing dash in a boat. Eventually, Bohr came to England and then, under great secrecy, was taken to the United States. After the War, Bohr returned to Denmark and lived in splendor. However, he continued to speak out vigorously for international control over nuclear weapons as did his friend Einstein. At Bohr's death, there was genuine feeling of loss, not only by physicists, but by the World community (Segre, 1980b).

In 1994, Pavel Sudoplatov, a former high-ranking official in the Soviet secret police, claimed that Bohr and other prominent scientists, who worked on the *Manhattan Project* that built America's nuclear weapons in World War II, gave away nuclear secrets to the Soviets. According to Sudoplatov, Bohr met with a Soviet agent, Iakov Terletskii, in November 1945. Supposedly, during this meeting which was held in Bohr's Copenhagen office, he supplied the Soviets with vital information about nuclear fission. It is true that such a meeting took place. However, an examination of the information exchanged at the meeting has revealed that Bohr never gave away nuclear secrets (Bethe, Goffried, & Sagdeev, 1995). Instead, Bohr informed the Allied governments that the meeting would take place. The fear was expressed that the Soviets might try to kidnap Bohr. Therefore, Bohr received undercover security for the meeting with Terletskii, reminiscent of a *James Bond* movie plot. Bohr used the meeting to protest to the Soviet official the imprisonment of his friends, the physicists Peter Kapitsa and Lev Landau, who were forced to contribute to the Soviet nuclear weapons program. When the meeting turned to the subject of nuclear bombs, Bohr gave vague answers to Terletskii's questions and the answers did not contain nuclear secrets. Terletskii was no doubt frustrated by Bohr's lack of cooperation. When Terletskii reported the results of his meeting with Bohr, the head of the Soviet secret police, Lavrentii Beria, became so enraged that he described Bohr and America in obscene words. Thus, Beria's own reaction has indicated that Bohr was not a traitor. Most importantly, Bohr's excellent reputation as a person who took seriously the ethical and moral responsibilities of a scientist remains intact.

Bohr's Atom

Bohr's greatest contribution was his 1913 model of the atom based upon quantum principles. At the time that Bohr was formulating his atomic structure, Rutherford's model of the atom was widely accepted. In Rutherford's theory, the atom was considered to be like a planetary system in that electrons were assumed to orbit around a small, but heavy center made up of protons. The electrons were moving at great velocity to keep them from falling into the nucleus. However, electron movement should be accompanied by the propagation of electromagnetic energy and, eventually, the electrons should collapse into the nucleus since their movement liberates energy required to stay in orbit. Thus, Rutherford's model does not allow atoms to have stable existences.

Bohr developed an alternate model of the atom based upon quantum physics in order to resolve the difficulties created by the Rutherford schema. Bohr's insight was to view electrons as belonging to certain quantum orbits. In other words, there were only a fixed number of orbits allowed for electrons. If an electron changed its position, it must do so in jumps (quanta) closer to or farther from the nucleus. Each orbital shell is associated with a certain energy level maintained by the electron. An orbital jump closer to the nucleus frees energy (photons) from the electrons, but, conversely, an orbital jump farther from the nucleus requires the absorption of energy. When an electron jumps past the last orbital shell, the electron is free from the atom which now becomes ionized (charged).

Bohr then tested his model for atomic structure by trying to predict the light emission pattern for the hydrogen atom. Hydrogen is the simplest element, whose atoms have one proton and one electron. When electromagnetic radiation is passed through hydrogen gas, a glow of light appears. It is possible to measure the wavelength of the light spectrum given off by the hydrogen or any other element. Bohr predicted the light spectrum lines for hydrogen in terms of wavelengths. The predictions were based upon Planck's formula in that an electron would jump to an orbit farther from the nucleus or closer to the nucleus in discrete steps. Jumps closer to the nucleus liberate photons making the hydrogen glow. The light glow of hydrogen does not make all colors but only certain colors as if the electrons move in discrete steps. In summary, Bohr offered two important principles about atoms. First, only a discrete number of orbits are allowed to the electron and while the electron stays in its orbit no energy is released. Secondly, radiation in the form of discrete quanta is emitted when an electron jumps from a higher orbit to a lower orbit and radiation is absorbed if the electron jumps from a lower orbit to a higher orbit. The amount of energy emitted or absorbed is determined by the energy differences between the beginning and ending orbits of the electrons (Zeilik & Smith, 1987).

During the 1920s, Bohr continued to develop the idea of the quantum atom and found data supporting his views. He was able to explain the relationship between atomic structure and the elements in the periodic table (Gribben, 1984). Atoms can be classified according to the number of electrons in their orbital shells. If two electrons fill the first level of an electron shell, hydrogen becomes helium. But only two electrons can fill the first orbital shell. The next shell requires the electrons to have more energy but as many as eight electrons can be held in that quantum step. Research has now estimated the number of electrons held by successive shells beyond the first two to be 18, 32, 18, and 8. The existence of electrons in quantum orbits becomes the basis for the modern explanation of chemical reactions.

The Divisible Atom

The ancient Greek view that atoms were tiny bits of indivisible matter did not agree with the outcomes of physical experiments done in the late nineteenth and early twentieth centuries. The models developed by both Rutherford (explored in the last chapter) and by Bohr depicted an atom as made out of parts. The central nucleus contained the parts known as protons and neutrons. Outside the nucleus are found the parts known as the electrons. Moreover, the electrons communicate with the nucleus through the exchange of photons which are also the particles of light. Bohr's atom requires the exchange of photons to keep the atom in balance. Electrons capture photons (absorb light) when they move to higher orbits and give up photons (emit light) when they move to lower orbital shells.

The contemporary model of the atom depicts a structure of mostly empty space. A typical atom is assumed to be 10^{-10} meter in diameter. Within the atom the nucleus takes up a space that has a diameter of 10^{-15} meter. An easier way of understanding these distances within the atom is to assume that the nucleus has a diameter of one centimeter. Then the distance between the center of the nucleus and the last orbital electron shell would be 100 meters. Atoms are so small that it would take 10,000,000 of them to stretch across the thin paper of a postage stamp (Gribbin, 1995).

To understand the nature of atoms, physics in the twentieth century initially focussed upon detailing the properties of the electrons and their associated photons. The scrutiny of the electrons was motivated by the interest in light phenomena generated by Planck and Einstein at the beginning of the century. The explanation of the behavior of light began the field of quantum mechanics. Then, the field of quantum electrodynamics (QED) developed to explain how electrons emit and absorb photons. From the insights gained from QED, particle physics developed to explain the nature of the nucleus with its protons and neutrons. The discoveries have been so dazzling that some have claimed that the end of physics is near. These discoveries about atoms have indicated that nature behaves in very peculiar ways (Feynman, 1985). Let us now review the mysteries uncovered by modern physics.

Quantum Mechanics

Newton was successful in identifying rules for predicting the velocity and acceleration of moving objects. However, the movement of objects inside the atom does not follow the rules of Newtonian mechanics. Instead new rules had to be invented since the experiments on the nature of light began to indicate that movement of objects inside the tiny space of the atom does not follow common sense. The new rules are called quantum mechanics. The task of quantum mechanics is indeed imposing since it must address the seemingly impossible reality that light is both a wave and a particle. Understanding the wave-particle duality of light is crucial for explicating the operations of the atom outside the nucleus since light is assumed to be composed of photons released from electrons.

Light's Dual Personality

The mystery of quantum physics began with experiments assessing the nature of light. As seen earlier in the chapter, the photoelectric effect suggests that light in the form of photons acts like a particle in that photons can dislodge electrons from a metal plate. Therefore, light, as Newton proclaimed, is composed of particles. However, earlier experiments by Thomas Young in 1797 also showed that light acts like a wave. For example, if light is emitted from a source and travels toward a screen containing two small holes, then an interference pattern is seen on a second screen which is set behind the first screen. The interference pattern is composed of a pattern of bright and dark bands. The bright bands result from light waves adding together and the dark bands result from light waves cancelling each other. Nevertheless, using Young's experimental procedure, the particle property of light also can be measured. When the experimenter closes one of the two holes on the first screen, the interference pattern on the second screen disappears and is replaced by a bright spot of light seen on the second screen directly behind the open hole of the first screen. Therefore, light is behaving as a stream of particles.

From the above experiments, the physicist is confronted with the dual nature of light. The wave and particle properties of light are demonstrated in the two and one hole experiments, respectively. Now, consider that the physicist wishes to fool light and measure its particle properties in the two hole experiment. To accomplish this task, the researcher places photon detectors at each of the two holes. Therefore, it should now be possible to count the number of photon particles that enter each hole. In this experiment, light does behave like a particle in that the detectors located at the two holes never record an event simultaneously. Thus, it appears that individual photons remain discrete and are arriving at each of the holes independently. Now the great surprise: when the experimenter looks for the interference effect on the screen, it is NOT found! Richard Feynman's description of this anomaly is most appropriate (1985, p, 81):

> Nature has got it cooked up so that we'll never be able to figure out how She does it: if we put instruments in to find out which way the light goes, we can find out, all right, but the wonderful interference effects disappear. But if we don't have instruments that can tell which way the light goes, the interference effects come back! Very strange, indeed!

The mystery is that light acts both as a wave and a particle dependent upon the conditions of the experimental measurement. When the researcher sets up the experiment to measure the wave properties of light, light behaves as a wave. However, when the researcher looks for the particle properties of light, light accommodates. However, light does not show its wave-particle duality simultaneously.

The Explanation

The beginning of quantum mechanics can be traced to the PhD dissertation of a French physicist, Marquis Louis de Broglie who proposed in 1924 the view that electrons, like photons, have a dual nature. They have properties of matter and properties of waves. Therefore, when electrons move around the nucleus, they create a wave pattern which fits within the orbital shells. De Broglie's work inspired a group of German physicists, notably Erwin Schrodinger (1887–1961), Max Born (1882–1970), and Werner Heisenberg (1901–1976), to reconsider the structure of the atom. They then created the mathematics of quantum mechanics to describe the activities of the wave particle constituents of the atom.

The Shadow of Matter

Schrodinger dispensed with the model of electrons as particles and imaged them to be more like charged clouds of negative energy surrounding the nucleus. He then proceeded to develop the mathematics to describe the wave function of the electron cloud. In contrast, Born wanted to keep the idea that electrons are particles. Born interpreted Schrodinger's wave function to indicate the probability of finding an electron at a particular place within its orbital shell. Born was taking a major step that conflicted with the deterministic view of the world held by Newton. Born was saying that physics could not predict with perfect accuracy the behavior of sub-atomic particles such as electrons. Their positions around the nucleus could be guessed through probabilities but their actual locations could never be known with certainty. Gone forever was Newton's idea that perfect prediction of every event in the Universe was possible if the location, mass, and velocity of every particle were known. Both Schrodinger and Einstein could not tolerate indeterminism in the most perfect of all the sciences and campaigned against the Born interpretation. However, Born's assessment was becoming accepted (Pagels, 1983).

The boldest step of all toward indeterminism was taken by Heisenberg who, in 1926, stated his famous uncertainty principle. Heisenberg clearly indicated that it is impossible to measure subatomic particles without disturbing their positions and velocities. For example, to measure where an electron is, light waves must be sent into the atom. Since the electron moves at great speed, the light sent into the atom should have a very short wave length because the observer must depend upon a bounce of a photon off the electron to indicate where the electron is. Therefore, the position of the electron will be indicated more precisely if we send light impulses into the atom with very little space separating the waves (short wavelengths). However, the shorter the wavelength of light, the more energy in the photon. Therefore, when a photon with high energy collides with an electron, a change in direction and velocity (momentum) of the electron results. In other words, one cannot predict where the electron is going after interacting with a photon. Therefore, Heisenberg's uncertainty principle says that the more accurately one tries to measure the position of an electron, the less accurately will be the prediction as to where the electron is going and vice versa (Gribbin, 1984).

The Copenhagen Interpretation of Reality

Heisenberg's uncertainty principle has implications that carry beyond the internal dynamics of the atom. These extensions were recognized by Bohr who presented his thoughts at a 1927 conference. These views have become known as the "Copenhagen Interpretation." Bohr concluded that it is impossible to predict future events with perfect accuracy since it is impossible to know both position and momentum of atomic structures. If one measures position, then momentum cannot be ascertained accurately. Position measures are based upon matter having corpuscular properties, but momentum measures are sensitive to matter's wave properties. Bohr said that the particle-wave dichotomy is complementary. One has to decide which of the two aspects to study. Knowledge of one aspect does not guarantee knowledge of the other. Position or momentum may be accurately calculated but not both. Since atomic activity, the underlying matrix of reality, can only be assessed by probability, predictions about future events can only be given in terms of maximum likelihood estimates. In other words, all things are possible, a few things are highly probable. Bohr also considered that the presence of an observer, such as an experimenter taking readings from an atom, changes the system. Thus, observers are not passive witnesses to the events of nature. Observers, by their presence or by using measurement devices, must change the phenomenon since the observer is connected to the quantum system (Davies & Brown, 1986). To understand how the parts of a system operate, one must appreciate all the contributors to the system. German Gestalt psychology paralleled the development of German quantum physics by emphasizing for human perception that "the whole is greater than the sum of its parts."

Extension to Quantum Mechanics to the Macro World

No experiment has ever found evidence that is inconsistent with quantum theory's explanations of the atom. However, do quantum principles hold exactly for the macroscopic world? In 1935, Schrodinger created a thought problem to challenge the implications of quantum theory with regard to the understanding of objective reality (Davies & Brown, 1986). The thought problem involves a cat that is placed in a steel chamber along with a "diabolical" device. The device consists of a Geiger counter and a radioactive substance that allows one atom to decay each hour with a probability of .50. When an atom decays, the Geiger counter registers the event and a poisonous gas is released in the box that is fatal to the cat. After one hour is the cat alive or dead? Schrodinger pointed out that quantum mechanics requires the cat to be both alive and dead simultaneously until an observation is made. Without the observation, all states of the system are possible, represented by the wave properties of matter. An observation forces the "wave" to collapse into reality.

The cat-in-the-box paradox has been argued in physics and philosophy since its inception. One way to resolve the paradox is to assert that consciousness is needed to make the world objective. The question becomes, is the cat's awareness sufficient to make the wave collapse into a state of reality, or must a human observer intercede?

Despite such problems as Schrodinger's cat paradox, quantum theory has fueled the development of technology (Segre, 1980b). All of the following are based upon quantum principles: the transistor, the electron microscope, lasers, creation of new atomic elements, genetic engineering, and the superconductor. The perfection of the superconductor, which transmits electricity at virtually zero resistance, should allow the technological revolution to continue. For example, superconductors will permit the creation of small, powerful engines capable of generating gravitational fields. Cars of the future will levitate above the ground as they move.

Einstein's Reaction

The Copenhagen Interpretation grants to the human observer the ability to create reality since the act of perception collapses the wave function of sub-atomic particles into a particular state. Applying this reasoning to atomic experiments, Bohr held to the position that uncertainty was a quantum reality. The presence of the observer looking inside the atom changes the activities of electrons in a way that cannot be predicted with any exactitude. Einstein could not tolerate this explanation of the internal operations of the atom. Instead, he assumed that the uncertainty principle arises from our inability to take precise measures at the quantum level. For Einstein, determinism must hold inside the atom as it apparently holds for the macro world. Therefore, in 1935, the same year Schrodinger proposed the cat-in-the-box thought experiment to illustrate the meaning of the Copenhagen Interpretation of Reality, Einstein counterattacked with a plan of his own.

To embarrass the Copenhagen Interpretation, Einstein, along with two colleagues Boris Podolsky and Nathan Rosen, proposed a thought experiment to show how mad quantum physics had become. The so-called Einstein-Podolsky-Rosen (EPR) experiment required the use of the Universe to make a simultaneous measurement of the position and momentum of a subatomic particle. The main feature of the EPR experiment is to use a particle by proxy to fix the position and momentum of another particle (Davies & Brown, 1986).

The EPR experiment proceeds in the following way. A stationary electron explodes into two photons A and B that are travelling in opposite directions. If the photons are created at the same moment in time, they will have one of two wave properties. The wave property is called polarization and refers to orientation of the light wave. In our experiment, the polarization of the photons is in one of two directions: vertical, which means the light wave is travelling in an up-down motion, or horizontal, which means that the light wave is moving side to side. According to Einstein, if you measured the polarization of photon A and found it to be vertical, then you automatically know the polarization path of photon B without even disturbing it.

In other words, the polarization measure of photon A establishes its momentum and from that information one can infer the momentum of photon B without disturbing it. Likewise, if you measure the position of photon A, you can correctly infer the position of photon B in the opposite direction without again directly contacting photon B. Another critical point made by Einstein refers to the speed of light. If photons A and B have travelled many light years apart, the measurements on photon A cannot simultaneously affect the status of photon B since no signal can travel faster than the speed of light and be in agreement with the Special Theory of Relativity.

Einstein believed that the incompleteness of quantum theory was now exposed. Theoretically, the observer could determine both the momentum and location of photons A and B by successive measures. Furthermore, it should not matter if the observer infers the properties of photon B from the measures taken on photon A and *vice versa*. Bohr's principle of complementarity, claiming that the photons are both waves and particles at the same time and the observer can only measure one of these properties, is shattered.

Bohr did not accept Einstein's description of the EPR experiment. Instead, Bohr claimed that measures on the proxy photon have a direct effect on the other photon. In other words, until an observation is made, the polarization of either photon, hence momentum, is not established. Until an observation is made for the position of either photon, each photon has no location. Einstein claimed that Bohr allowed "action at a distance" meaning that somehow the photons can signal information to one another even faster than the speed of light. This cannot be in a determined world.

Supposedly, Bohr was somewhat amused that Einstein would not accept the Copenhagen Interpretation of Reality. Bohr reminded Einstein that the Theory of Special Relativity claims that space and time are not absolute. Perception of space and time change relative to the observer's speed of motion. The principle of complementarity, the wave-particle nature of matter, is another example of the role of the observer in the construction of reality. Therefore, Bohr asked Einstein why did he fight against an extension of Relativity Theory. Einstein purportedly replied, "A good joke should not be repeated twice" (Herbert, 1985, p. 201).

The EPR Experiment Becomes a Reality

Over the years, until his death, Einstein was troubled by quantum mechanics. He had to admit that quantum theory never failed to give predicted results for experiments involving subatomic structures. Nevertheless, Einstein considered quantum theory to be incomplete since it allowed for action at a distance. Instead, Einstein claimed that hidden variables must operate to determine quantum phenomena and science has not yet discovered those variables.

Bell's Theorem

In 1964, John Bell (1928–1990) was a young physicist who became fascinated with the implications of the EPR experiment regarding the interpretation of reality. Essentially, Bell reanalyzed the EPR experiment and made predictions about the results based upon a local, rather than a non-local, interpretation of reality.

According to classical physics, cause and effect activity means that a direct physical connection is present between two objects. The claim that causality involves a direct physical connection between objects is known as the local interpretation of reality. The local interpretation of reality forms the basis of the deterministic model of the World. Thus, if a physician claims that a virus is causing an illness in a patient, then the virus must be invading the body's cells in the present time so as produce the symptoms of the illness. However, Bohr allowed a non-local interpretation of reality to operate in the EPR experiment. In a non-local interpretation, events A and B are connected together without any direct physical force operating between the events. An example from Herbert (1985, p. 213) serves to illustrate non-local interaction. Suppose a voodoo specialist were to place a pin in a doll representation of an intended victim and then the victim suffered a wound. There would be a connection between the events without any physical contact, hence action at a distance. According to Herbert (1985, p. 214):

> A non-local interaction links up one location with another without crossing space, without decay, and without delay. A non-local interaction is, in short, *unmediated, unmitigated,* and *immediate.*

As Herbert also notes, physicists from the time of Newton to the present abhor action at a distance explanations. Newton (Herbert, 1985, p. 213) stated that the ability for one body to act upon another:

> . . . at a distance through a vacuum without the mediation of anything else . . . is to me so great an absurdity, that I believe that no man, who has in philosophical matters a competent faculty for thinking, can ever fall into.

In agreement with Newton, modern physics appeals to the four fundamental forces (strong nuclear force, weak nuclear force, electromagnetic energy, and gravity) to supply the local control of phenomena.

To investigate whether non-local phenomena could be potentially measured, Bell mathematically studied the possible correlations between the properties of subatomic events when simultaneous measurements are made on each event. Assuming that local causality operates and faster-than-light signalling is impossible, then a strict limit is placed upon a correlation value between any measured property of two events. However, if subatomic events somehow are in instantaneous communication with one another without the presence of a physical force and can signal their status to each other faster than the speed of light, then non-locality exists. In this case, the correlation between the measured properties of two events exceeds the limit of the correlation imposed by Bell's theorem. In other words, Bell's theorem has been violated.

The following may serve to illustrate the logic of Bell's theorem from the field of psychology. Assume that an experiment is being conducted in which the effects of stress upon test performance of identical twins is being measured. The researcher designs the experiment so that two groups of identical twins are tested simultaneously. One group of identical twins is subjected to a major stressor, such as loud noise, while taking the Graduate Record Exam (GRE). The other group takes the GRE in a quiet setting. Now it is expected that the two groups will differ in their performances; however, since identical twins were used, a small positive correlation is still expected between the scores of the two groups. An estimate of this correlation can be based upon prior research using identical twins who simultaneously take exams in separate locations. However, if the correlation is too high, well above expectation, a violation has occurred. It appears that the condition of the twin subjected to the noise affected the condition of the other twin not getting the noise. The high correlation exceeds the limit based upon knowledge of the system.

Tests of Bell's Theorem

Bell's theorem did not attract much attention from physicists when it was first published since it did not seem possible to test the non-locality proposition. Eventually, however, several experiments were done on the theorem and the results support non-locality (Herbert, 1985)! Two of these studies, based upon a design suggested in the EPR thought experiment, are reviewed below.

As summarized by Herbert (1985), the first study of non-locality was done by John Clauser and colleagues at the University of California, Berkeley and published in 1972. Basically, in Clauser's experiment, mercury atoms were excited by electron bombardment to release twin pairs of photons that were emitted in opposite directions of the atomic source. Each photon is independently passed through a light polarizer which has a certain probability of changing the direction of the photon's flight angle. Photon detectors (multipliers) then register whether the light polarizers change the direction of each photon. Knowing how photons should behave if they are independent entities according to Bell's theorem led to the following prediction. If the angles of the light polarizers are 60° out of phase, the twin photons have a 50% chance of landing at the same spot on their respective detector plates. However, the data revealed that Bell's theorem was violated. The actual number of times that the photons hit the same place on the detectors when the polarizers were 60° out of phase was 25%. Therefore, Bell's theorem was violated and non-locality was supported. (It is interesting to note that this experiment was done at the University named for the British philosopher, George Berkeley, who anticipated the Copenhagen Interpretation of Reality by claiming "to be is to be perceived.")

A more intriguing test of Bell's theorem was performed by Alain Aspect and associates at the University of Paris. In this experiment, photons are emitted from calcium atoms excited by a laser light. Again, twin photons are released simultaneously from an atom and travel in opposite directions as in Clauser's experiment. While the photons, moving at the speed of light, were in flight, a switch was activated that determined which of two preset polarizers the photons would travel through. The results indicated that the photon activity violated Bell's theorem when the photons were directed to pass through polarizers 60° out of phase. Since the photons are acting in concert with no known physical force connecting them, non-locality appears to be operating. Moreover, since the switching that determined which polarizer the photons would encounter was done after the photons were released from the atom, it appears that the informational link coordinating the activity of the photons was not constrained by the speed of light.

Within the context of Bohr's Copenhagen Interpretation of Reality, the results of Clauser's and Aspect's experiments suggest that subatomic particles that were once part of a single system (i.e., photons which belonged to an atom) maintain coordinated behavior with action at a distance communication. Moreover, the Copenhagen Interpretation of Reality claims that entities within the atom such as photons and electrons have no established properties until measurements are taken. Until a measurement is taken, a quantum object can exist in all possible probability states simultaneously. In the language of the Copenhagen Interpretation, the act of perception through measurement collapses the probability wave of matter into a definite state which then determines the properties of all remaining members of the quantum system. Therefore, the Copenhagen Interpretation grants to the act of perception the ability to establish reality! Do human observers really have this kind of power to determine reality through perception; or does a real world exist independent of perception? The latter view was favored by the brilliant physicist, David Bohm (1917–1992), who devised an alternative explanation for quantum phenomena that dismisses the Copenhagen Interpretation.

Bohm's Insight

David Bohm reached a high degree of fame as a scientist and a philosopher. However, his resiliency was certainly tested by a political crisis. Born in Pennsylvania, Bohm eventually graduated with a PhD degree in physics from the University of California, Berkeley in 1943. At Berkeley, Bohm was a student of J. Robert Oppenheimer who would become the lead scientist in the development of the atomic bomb. Bohm spent the years 1947 to 1951 at Princeton University where he was able to share his thoughts with Einstein. However, while at Princeton, Bohm came under the scrutiny of Congress's Committee on Un-American Activities. This Committee sought to expose communists in the Federal government by using draconian means. On the grounds of liberty, Bohm would not answer questions about himself or his colleagues. As a result, Bohm was blacklisted and fired by Princeton University. Bohm left the United States and settled at universities in Brazil, Israel, and finally England. Eventually cleared of any wrongdoing, Bohm was allowed to travel in the United States again. However, he adopted England as his home and died of a heart attack in London in 1992. Bohm is remembered, "not only as brilliant and daring but also as extraordinarily honest, gentle, and generous" (Albert, 1994, p. 62).

Bohm's theory of quantum physics originated in 1951 and may be described as an objective model that allows for non-local influences. In other words, Bohm's position assumes that the Universe exists independent of any human perceiver. Therefore, Bohm rejects the Copenhagen Interpretation of Reality. Electrons and photons are real particles that have definite locations and velocities. These members of the atomic family are not in a wave-particle duality until perception collapses the wave function into reality. Returning to Schrodinger's cat-in-the-box thought problem, Bohm claims the positivistic position that the animal is either alive or dead without anyone looking inside the box.

The interesting feature regarding reality is that all bits of atomic structure, such as electrons and photons, are connected together in what Bohm called the quantum potential. This potential refers to a special wave of information that coordinates the activities of the entire system. Moreover, the quantum potential is not composed of one of the four forces of physical energy. Instead, the quantum potential is more like an information blanket coordinating all parts of the system. The special property of the quantum potential is that its influence cannot recede with time or space. Therefore, the quantum potential can instantaneously connect parts of a system together independent of the speed of light. Therefore, Bohm's theory supports non-locality while retaining the notion that the Universe is real.

How does Bohm account for the two-slit light demonstration and experimental tests of the EPR paradox? Regarding the behavior of light, the quantum potential encodes information about the entire system including the nature of the measuring apparatus and the presence of observers. Thus, the activity of the photons is linked together informatively with the other representatives of the system. When photons are passed through two slits in a screen to create an interference pattern on a second screen, the quantum potential links the positions of each photon so that light-dark bands appear on the adjacent screen. Photons quite far way from the slits nevertheless affect the behavior of photons passing through the slits. Putting detectors at each slit removes the interference pattern since the presence of the detectors has supplied new information in the system that has modified the quantum potential. In the experimental tests of the EPR effect, the coordinated activity of the photons is again mediated by the quantum potential which allows a continuous connection between the particles. Therefore, a change in the status of one particle is communicated instantaneously to the other particle without the requirement that relativity operates (i.e., no signal travels faster than the speed of light). Bohm used linear differential equations of motion developed by Schrodinger to describe the activity of the quantum potential.

The Implicate Order

Bohm (1980) was not content to develop the mathematical calculations to describe the outcome of experiments in quantum physics. He was also interested in exploring the meaning of quantum physics for understanding the meaning of reality. Since all existence is potentially tied together in informational networks, Bohm stressed that understanding of any phenomenon requires a holistic approach. In other words, objects can never be understood as independent parts that somehow come together to determine the whole. Instead, each part contributes information to the operation of the whole and is similarly affected by the operations of the other parts. The pattern of activity emerging from the informational exchange among all parts of the system is called by Bohm the implicate order. Interestingly, the implicate order is a restatement of Aristotle's principle of formal causality. For example, an acorn has the potential to assume the form of an oak tree. Somehow contained in the informational system of the small acorn is the recipe to unfold into an imposing tree. To become a tree, the acorn must coordinate the activities of several other types of materials in nature, such as photons, nitrogen, phosphorus, water, oxygen, carbon dioxide, etc. so that the oak tree can form following the informational plan. The implicate order of the acorn potentiates into the oak tree found in the physical world of experience which is called the explicate order by Bohm.

Connections to Psychology

Bohm's emphasis on informational wholes guiding the operations of parts is also the message of the Gestalt psychologists. According to the Gestalt approach, it is necessary to establish the entire set of rules that guides the operation of the human mind in order to understand the meaning of an idea or perception. Bohm also became interested in human consciousness and concluded that Descartes made a tragic mistake in separating mind from matter. Instead, mind and matter are ultimately based upon the same stuff—atoms. In turn, all atomic activity is linked together through quantum potential systems of information. Thus, the human mind tries to understand reality by having the neural atoms make informational contact with the atoms outside the brain.

Bohm, as is the case for many physicists, became fascinated with consciousness. To aid in his understanding of consciousness, Bohm sought the advice of the late Indian philosopher, Jiddhu Krishnamurti. From his American home in Ojai, California, Krishnamurti warned that narcissistic thinking patterns would lead to the ruination of the planet and civilization. Instead, people must realize a sense of community, or wholeness, since they, in the last analysis, all inhabit this tiny planet. Therefore, solving problems requires the coordinated activity of all individuals. Krishnamurti taught in ways reminiscent of Socrates. To understand the importance of one's life, the individual must become aware of the process of thought not its content. Krishnamurti said that it is much more important to know how the activity of thinking works. Freud tried to achieve this level of understanding through psychoanalytic methods. Krishnamurti stressed that mind's understanding of the mind is achieved through meditation which allows the mind to ponder and reflect upon itself. For Bohm, the understanding of consciousness has incalculable consequences since (Bohm, 1980, p. ix):

> ... there is the further question of what is the relationship of thinking to reality. As careful attention shows, thought itself is in an actual process of movement. That is to say, one can feel a sense of flow in the stream of consciousness not dissimilar to the sense of flow in the movement of matter in general. May not thought itself thus be a part of reality as a whole? But then, what could it mean for one part of reality to "know" another, and to what extent would this be possible?

Particle Physics

Particle physics is the branch of science concerned with the structure of the nucleus. As quantum physicists were unraveling the activity of the electrons, others began to probe the structure and function of the atom's central core. Until 1932, atoms were thought to be composed of protons and electrons. However, in that year, James Chadwick (1891–1974), who studied with Rutherford, discovered another particle in the nucleus, the neutron, which was almost as heavy as the proton but without electrical charge. Then physicists began to search for other particles, guided by the lessons learned in quantum physics. The constituents of the atom's nucleus, such as protons, electrons, and neutrons, are held together by forces which may be expressed in quantum terms. The forces that bind the atomic structure together must work at certain energy levels and when one of these energy levels is attained, a particle of matter, representing the nuclear force, is revealed. For example, the Japanese physicist, Hideki Yukawa (1907–) began to speculate in the 1930s about the force that holds the protons and neutrons together and worked out the calculation for a small particle, now called the pion, which accomplishes this nuclear binding.

In atomic accelerators, where protons and neutrons are forced to collide, other particles of energy, too numerous to mention, have been found. Today, the particles making up atoms are classified as either being a "lepton" or a "hadron." Leptons refer to particles, such as electrons and neutrinos, that are light and have weak binding influences within the atom. Hadrons refer to protons and neutrons which are heavy particles capable of strong force interactions. In turn, Hadrons are composed of quarks that combine to form protons and neutrons. It appears now that leptons and quarks are the fundamental units of nature and cannot be broken down into anything more elemental. The search for the fundamental substance of nature, begun by Thales twenty-six centuries ago, has indeed been productive.

The topic of quarks deserves special attention. Quarks, whose existence was proposed by the physicists, Murray Gell-Mann and George Zweig, are pin-point objects measured in energy terms (Riordan, 1992). The term, quark, is derived from a passage in James Joyce's novel, *Finnegan's Wake*. (The relevant passage is, "Three quarks for muster mark.") The evidence for the existence of the quark came from experiments that blasted the atomic nucleus with beams of particles in accelerators. Under this bombardment, the protons and neutrons broke apart into more elemental material. From these observations, Gell-Mann, Zweig, and Yuval Ne'eman developed the mathematics of quark theory and predicted how many different kinds of quarks should exist. Eventually, six quark types have been identified and are called: "up," "down," "strange," "charm," "bottom" (also called "beauty"). After a long search, the last quark, named "top" (also called "truth") was isolated.

The atomic nuclei of ordinary matter are composed of the two lightest quarks, up and down, (with down being slightly heavier). In addition, the quarks carry charges with the up charge set at +2/3 and down charge at –1/3. Combining these quarks gives the familiar proton and neutron configurations. The proton carries a positive charge (+1) and is composed of the following three quarks: up, up, and down. The neutron has a zero charge and is made from the following three quarks: down, down, and up. The charge on the quarks refers to their ability to emit and absorb the gluon particle that is another charge holding the nucleus together. Gluons appear to have properties very much like the photons that interact with electrons (Feynman, 1985). The other quarks do not combine to make up typical atoms. These exotic quarks are revealed after high energy atomic collisions take place in the atom. For example, the charm quark emerges from a collision involving electrons and has a half-life of one trillionth of a second. During this time, the charm quark will travel a distance of a couple of millimeters and then decay into more basic particles (Litke & Schwartz, 1995). However, the eoxtic quarks were all presumed to be present at the moment of the Big Bang explosion that may have started the Universe.

The physical world is held together by four natural forces. Two of these forces, gravity and electromagnetic energy, operate over long distances. The other two forces, strong and weak nuclear forces, act over short distances within atoms. The strong nuclear force holds the quarks together resulting in protons and neutrons. The weak nuclear force allows for radioactive decay and binds together the relatively small particles of the atom. Physicists, such as Steven Weinberg and Stephen Hawking, are trying to combine all the forces in nature into one mathematical model called Grand Unified Theory (GUT). This attempt has proven exceedingly difficult even for Einstein who failed to merge together the principles of electromagneticism and gravity. However, the importance of GUT relates to the understanding of the Universe since several theorists believe that all the particles and forces of nature were once united immediately following the Big Bang (Cohen, 1988).

Antimatter Particles

Paul Dirac (1902–1984) tried to combine Schrodinger's work and Einstein's Special Relativity Theory in order to explain the spinning activity of electrons. However, his computations also yielded another startling possibility: that negative energy and mass may exist. In other words, for every known piece of matter, there may be an anti-matter particle. In order to create anti-matter, collisions between energy sources travelling near the speed of light and atoms are necessary. Nature provides such a high energy source in the form of gamma rays which are the nuclei of hydrogen atoms moving near the speed of light. When gamma rays smash into atoms, electrons are produced. Dirac's equations predicted not just a single electron would result but a pair, a particle with positive energy and an antiparticle with negative energy. In 1933, Carl Anderson found the evidence by watching through a cloud chamber the production of electrons when gamma rays impacted a metal plate. The anti-matter electron was called the positron. In 1955, the antiproton was isolated.

The creation of anti-matter was of major importance for the understanding of the Universe. Dirac showed that it followed from Einstein's $E = mc^2$ formula. With sufficient energy bombarding an atom, new particles come into existence. Matter could be created from nothing as long as sufficient energy was present. Dirac also predicted that the contact with matter and anti-matter leads to their mutual annihilation accompanied by a tremendous release of energy. Matter/anti-matter propulsion systems are now being explored as the means for interplanetary space travel (Forward & Davis, 1988).

Quantum Chaos and Cosmic Order

On first thought, there would appear to be very little to connect quantum mechanics to the understanding of the Universe. Quantum theory tries to explain the internal operations of the atom. What could quantum theory say about something as gigantic as the Universe? However, quantum theory is necessary since it describes how atomic structure was synthesized following the Big Bang. In the last 15 years, the fields of particle physics and quantum theory have unified with cosmology to produce fascinating explanations of the Universe's origin and destiny. Moreover, with the advent of modern particle accelerators, fundamental ideas about the origin of the Universe can be tested in the laboratory. The following represents a synopsis of the current views on how the Universe came to be (Cohen, 1988; Gribben, 1986; Schramm & Steigman, 1988; Zeilik & Smith, 1987).

The Origin and Destiny of the Universe

The zero point in time is represented by an infinitely small, extremely hot singularity that exploded into the creation of space. At the moment of this Big Bang, all the forces of nature were combined into one superforce. However, superforce can only be maintained at temperatures approaching 100 billion degrees Celsius. As the tiny Universe began to cool, superforce began to break down at 10^{-32} second following the Big Bang according to Allan Guth. The dissolution of the superforce produced the release of great amounts of energy that allowed the nascent universe to double its size every 10^{-35} second. Guth calls this rapid expansion the "inflationary stage" of the Universe's development and the principle helps to explain why the background radiation of the Cosmos is so evenly distributed. As the superforce disintegrates, the released energy produces the elementary particles of matter, the leptons and quarks. The inflationary period is over at 10^{-30} second following the Big bang. The supercooling of the Universe commences allowing the creation of vast quantities of both matter and antimatter with the temperature settings favoring slightly more production of matter. The production of matter and antimatter from energy suggested to Guth that the Universe is the ultimate "free lunch." The Universe continues its expansion following inflation but at a much slower rate.

The Universe, still much less than a second old, continues to expand as atomic particles are being created while the superforce symmetry is disappearing. At this point, physicists have taken a bold guess as to the reason why galaxies eventually came to be located in clusters in space and are not uniformly distributed like the background radiation. As the superforce was disintegrating into the present forces of nature, certain regions of space may have been spared. In other words, superforce might have been retained locally as the Universe went through various transition states (Vilenkin, 1987). What would the trapped superforce be like? The answer that comes from physicists, such as Alexander Vilenkin, John Schwarz, and Edward Witten, is that superforce could have the appearance of a immensely long cosmic string. The strings would have tremendous gravitational pull allowing matter to collect together to form galaxies. No one has ever observed a string in space. However, there is a curious phenomenon taking place with regard to galactic motion (Dressler, 1987). About 400 galaxies, including our Milky Way, are converging upon a certain region in the Universe, as if they are being drawn by a "Great Attractor." Such an attractor might be a remaining string that has immense gravitational pull. Schwarz (1985) has proposed that vibrating strings could have created all the atomic particles and ten dimensions of space, four of which (length, width, height, time) are directly known to us.

At 10^{-10} second following the Big Bang, the four fundamental forces in nature (gravity, electromagnetic, strong nuclear force, and weak nuclear force) have separated from the superforce, and quarks now exist to form protons and neutrons. One minute after the Big Bang, the protons, neutrons, and electrons group together to form the simplest atoms. This is called nucleosynthesis and predictions from the Big Bang theory state the lightest elements should have been created first: helium, lithium, and deuterium (an isotope of hydrogen). Astronomical measurements indicate that helium is the most abundant element in the Universe, just as the Big Bang theory states. The heavier elements were then produced inside stars and then ejected into the Universe as stars explode. The first stars required as many as 1 million years following the Big Bang to form and our own Sun and Milky Way galaxy may be relatively young in that they were formed 10 billion years after the Big Bang. Now 15 to 20 billion years after the Big Bang, 100 billion galaxies, each having 100 billion stars, have come into existence. The Universe continues to evolve with its fate uncertain as to whether gravity will pull everything back into a singularity (closed Universe) or whether it will expand forever (open Universe). Astronomical calculations indicate that only 15% of the mass required to close the Universe has been observed. Since the Big Bang theory predicts a closed Universe, astronomers have been searching for the "dark matter" that represents the other 85% of the Universe's mass. The candidates for dark matter are: black holes, nonluminous stars called brown dwarfs, and the enigmatic neutrino particles. If the dark matter cannot be found, then the Universe should expand forever. Imagine Aristotle's astonishment if he were to compare the modern view of the Universe to his own which depicted a stable, Earth-centered Cosmos.

Summary: The Fundamental Units of Matter

The unification of quantum physics, particle physics, and cosmology has been very productive in clarifying the nature of atoms. It is now known that atoms are not the indivisible structures proposed by Democritus. Instead, atoms are composed of more elementary particles. How many such particles exist? Based upon deductions from the Big Bang theory and data from experiments with particle accelerators, twelve fundamental particles, each having a corresponding anti-matter particle are presumed to exist (Schramm & Steigman, 1988). Six of the basic particles are the quarks. Each of the six types of quarks has three varieties based upon their polarizations. Thus, there are thirty-six different types of quarks alone! Six other fundamental particles are the leptons: the electron, muon, tau particle, electron neutrino, the muon neutrino, and the tau neutrino. (Each lepton has an anti-particle.) The quarks and leptons produce atoms and are classified as Fermions, named for the great physicist Enrico Fermi (1901–1954).

In addition, the four forces of nature explain how the elementary particles exist as atoms. However, the four forces of nature are assumed to be mediated by particles. The electromagnetic force results from "photons" which represent light quanta. "Gravitons" are responsible for the gravity force. "Gluons" allow for the strong atomic force that keeps protons and neutrons together in the atom. Finally, the weak atomic force that gives rise to radioactivity is based upon "vector bosons." All of the force particles are classified as Bosons, named for S. N. Bose (1894–1974), an Indian physicist. Imagine the astonishment of Democritus if he were told that his atomic theory was correct but atoms themselves result from more fundamental particles that had their origins within the first second of the Big Bang.

The Future of Physics

Physics has enjoyed immense success in defining nature. Fundamental particles and the forces that hold atoms and the Universe together have been identified. What could be the next step in the development of the science? Currently, theoretical physicists are approaching the future of their field from two directions. The first direction is reductionist by attempting to develop the grand unified theory that will essentially describe the Universe in one mathematical equation. The second approach is to understand the apparent complexity of nature. Both of these approaches are briefly explored.

The Theory of Everything

A handful of physicists are trying to reduce nature to one fundamental equation by searching for the euphemistic "theory of everything (TOE)." Such a theory certainly will not explain everything. However, with regard to physics, the theory of everything attempts to reduce the four forces of nature to one force. In addition, the theory attempts to explain the origin of the most fundamental particles of the atom, namely the electron, photon, and the quark, as arising from a single underlying entity. Physicists, such as Edward Witten and Steven Weinberg, are leading the way in the development of TOE. Weinberg (1992) has written a book for the general public, called *Dreams of a Final Theory,* that attempts to explain how TOE will be constructed. Weinberg offers the opinion in his book that the development of TOE will dispel beliefs in mysticism, miracles, and superstition (Horgan, 1996). TOE is meant to be an impersonal theory that describes the activity of the entire Universe. In the grand scale of the Universe, what happens on the tiny speck of dust, known as Earth, is incidental. However, the laws of nature must work the same way on Earth as they do everywhere in the Universe.

The central concept in TOE is called a "string." These postulated entities are extremely small states of energy that collect in lines which can take the form of shapes. However, a string segment is extremely small, perhaps no more than 10^{-33} centimeter long (Mukerjee, 1996). Therefore, it would take 10^{18} strings laid end to end to match the diameter of a proton! Moreover, strings have the ability to vibrate creating waves of energy and matter. String theory appeals to the duality principle used to describe the nature of light. In other words, there is an exchange between matter and energy. Strings as energy states create the matter from which atoms are built. Strings are required to be extremely small since the matter created from them, such as photons and quarks, are also infinitesimal pin-point objects. The existence of strings puts to an end the search for anything more fundamental. The property of strings gives rise to everything in the physical world.

No one has ever recorded the actual existence of a string. In fact, no known technologies could ever measure a string. Accordingly, string theory is highly mathematical and not well understood even by its advocates. String theory is extremely sophisticated and beyond the scope of experimental testing. Therefore, Horgan (1996, p. 70) has wondered whether the approach is on "shaky ground" since it makes so many assumptions as to remind us of the importance of Occam's principle of parsimony. Eventually, history will tell whether string theory will maturate into Einstein's hope that a grand unified theory can be constructed, a hope which even eluded Einstein during his long lifetime.

Complexity Theory

Another avenue for the future development of physics, and science in general, is to understand how complexity arises within physical systems. Complexity is a difficult concept to define. It refers to the organized pattern of activity shown by a self-contained system. Such systems can be as diverse as the human brain to the economy. Organized systems engage in activity that appears to be chaotic. However, under mathematical analysis, signal patterns, carrying information, can be discerned. For example, the neural activity of the brain appears to be highly random. Nevertheless, a fine grain analysis of the electroencephalogram reveals patterns of activity that are the signatures of the healthy as well as diseased brain. Theorists who support complexity hope that a general set of principles will be identified that control how apparently random activity becomes a pattern. Then, these principles can be used to account for the activity of any self-contained system including the Universe. The human mind appears to search for order in chaos. However, recognizing order is a difficult task. Murray Gell-Mann has "defined superstition as seeing patterns that aren't really there and denial as not seeing patterns that are there" (Johnson, 1995, p 290).

One of the major research facilities for the study of complexity is the Santa Fe Institute. Faculty members at the Institute include Murray Gell-Man and Stuart Kauffman. As we have reviewed, Gell-Mann is one of the developers of the quark theory of matter. Kauffman is a biologist who has argued that the principle of natural selection is not sufficient to account for the development of life on Earth. Instead,

Kauffman has argued that genetic structures contain an inherent self-organizing principle that converges on a relatively few patterns of activity. Without this order generating force, an idea embedded in Leibnitz's theory of the monads, biochemical system would drift into entropy or total chaos as described by the second law of thermodynamics.

Complexity theorists use computer simulations of self-contained systems as the means for finding ordered activity in apparent chaotic behavior. As in the case of TOE, future history will reveal whether complexity theory can deliver on its promise as the vehicle through which all self-contained systems can be understood.

Philosophical and Scientific Origins of Psychology 5

As the previous chapters document, physics has a long and successful history developing explanations for the material world. This effort originated with the Ionian philosophers of ancient Greece who searched for the fundamental unit of nature. Intertwined with the development of physics in the ancient world was the effort to understand human nature. Many of the same Greek philosophers who studied the physical World were also interested in knowing human nature. The major issue regarding humans that divided the Greek philosophers concerned the mind-body problem. Should humans be viewed as a material substance (body) that is governed solely by the laws of physics? Or do humans contain a soul that makes mental life possible and is approachable only from philosophy? In this chapter, the mind-body problem is reviewed with regard to its crucial importance for the development of scientific psychology.

The Ancient Greeks and Human Nature

The Greeks debated the mind-body problem by dividing into opposing camps. The materialists believed in the existence of the body only. Therefore, all mental phenomena are due to the activity of physical systems. However, the dualists accepted the existence of the soul along with the body. The body may operate according to the rules of the physical World, but the soul, as an immaterial entity, exists on a spiritual plane and is subject to different principles.

In the following, the works of Epicurus and the ancient medical practitioners are used to represent early materialism. The dualistic counter-proposal is represented in the philosophies of Plato and Aristotle.

Epicurean Materialism

In their understanding of nature, Leucippus and Democritus postulated the existence of atoms. Every aspect of the World, including its human inhabitants, are physical entities composed of the fundamental units, namely atoms. This monistic tradition was developed into a powerful theory of human nature by Epicurus whose view of the world was explored in Chapter 1. Presently, the Epicurean view of human existence, predicated upon materialism, is given.

Epicurus believed that the human, like everything else, is composed of atoms. The term "soul" is used by Epicurus to indicate the activity of those atoms responsible for cognition and other mental phenomena. At death, the atoms of the soul scatter into the void. If this is human nature, how should humans conduct themselves? The question of ethics became the paramount concern for Epicurus's philosophy.

If humans have but one life to live, how should it be lived? Epicurus's answer was that humans need to exercise prudence to maximize both longevity and happiness. The nostrum for happiness can be summarized by three Latin words: *eudamonia via ataraxia* or "happiness through mental tranquility" (Hibler, 1984). The human should be free as much as possible from worry and conflict. This recipe for the proper life was also followed by Democritus who was called the "laughing philosopher" and by Pyrrho (367?–275 B.C.) who taught that humans should be happy. Pyrrho was the founder of the Sceptical school of philosophy that maintained all sensory and intellectual ideas were unreliable. According to Pyrrho, when humans think too much and try to understand reality, they become unhappy. On the contrary, Epicurus taught that understanding of the World is the condition that brings happiness.

Epicurean philosophy is also associated with the pleasure-pain principle that would be resurrected as an important rule of behavior by Freud, Thornidke, and Skinner in the 20th century. However, Epicurus was careful in defining pleasure. The highest pleasures are intellectual ones, not sensual. Ultimate pleasure is produced when the mind is free of anguish, anxiety, and strong desires. One of the great lessons to be learned in life is to limit one's desires. Epicurus's emphasis on limiting desires and accepting substitutes for desired objects has important implications for psychopathology. In recent years, a personality disorder, called pathological narcissism, has been defined and refers to unhappy individuals who do not know how to satisfy their needs and, therefore, appear to be frivolous (Kernberg, 1975).

Epicurus also warned that pain should be avoided since it is a sign of danger. In fact, one should give up pleasure if it involves the risk of pain or mental torment. Moreover, Epicurus advised individuals to live anonymously, especially if they are wealthy. Epicurus was responding to human jealously that often produces harm to those who have possessions desired by others.

In summary, Epicurus, starting with the premise that all existing things are composed exclusively of atoms, formulated a theory of proper conduct for mortal humans. Unlike some of his later followers who did not apply his doctrines correctly, Epicurus advocated restraint and denial as the means to secure long-term happiness.

Hippocratic Materialism

Hippocrates (460?–370?) is referred to as the "father of medicine," but, unfortunately, not much is known of his personal life. Moreover, debate exists as to what works that survive today on Greek medicine were actually written by Hippocrates. Nevertheless, the surviving works on medicine that follow the Hippocratic style are collectively known as the *Corpus Hippocraticum* (Clagett, 1955).

The Hippocratic writings give a materialistic account of human life. The atomic theory of matter was dismissed in favor of Empedocles's doctrine of four basic elements: earth, air, fire, and water (Smith, 1971). All living bodies are composed of a mixture of fire and water. Also, matter cannot be created or destroyed but undergoes constant change, a position advocated by Heraclitus. The term "soul" was also used by Hippocratic writers, but it is clear that the soul represents a physical entity since it is composed of fire and water. The soul was perceived as the energy source allowing for the maturation of the body (Smith, 1979).

The Hippocratic tradition stressed that nature, not the physician, heals the body. In turn, illnesses were often caused by an imbalance of the body's four humors: blood, phlegm, yellow bile, and black bile. Medical treatment, therefore, was aimed at the restoration of the proper proportions of the four humors. The theory of humors was taken seriously through the seventeenth century.

The Hippocratic physicians based their theories closely upon correlations between observations and outcomes. Thus, overweight people were noted to die more suddenly than thin people. However, thin people were more liable to suffer tuberculosis whereas overweight individuals were more susceptible to epileptic seizures. In fact, the Hippocratic writers tried to combat the popular opinion that epilepsy was due to the forced visitation of a god upon the human. Hence, epilepsy was known as the "sacred disease" (Smith, 1979). However, Hippocratic physicians explained it as a disorder of the brain. Brain dysfunction was considered to be the source of the most serious diseases and responsible for psychological disorders. Although the Hippocratic writers made errors in their explanations, it is still remarkable how many of their observations have proven to be correct. Even the theory of humors has an element of veracity to it. There are fluids of the body that have important physical and mental health consequences. Most notably are the endocrine hormones and the neurotransmitters of the brain.

The traditions initiated by Hippocrates and his followers were continued in Roman times by Galen (130–201). Having rejected the atomic doctrine, Galen utilized the theory of humors to explain health. In turn, each of the four humors was linked to one of Empedocles's fundamental elements (Siegel, 1968). Blood, phlegm, yellow bile, and black bile were derived respectively from air, water, fire, and earth. Thus, Galen used all four elements to describe the humors whereas the Hippocratic writers relied only upon fire and water. Galen also connected personality traits to the dominant humor within the individual. Thus, an excess of blood produces sanguine (cheerful) individuals, too much phlegm is associated with laziness, an abundance of yellow bile links to emotional instability, and the dominance of black bile indicates mental depression. Galen even postulated that intelligence is revealed by the development of cranial bones, a hypothesis that would be developed in the nineteenth century theory of Phrenology.

Thus, ancient writers were able to construct important views of materialistic principles. Epicurean philosophy was derived from the atomic theory of matter, whereas the medical views of human nature were built from the doctrine of four fundamental elements. However, other Greeks were compelled to accept dualism as the essential explanation of human nature. The most prominent dualists were Plato and Aristotle.

Platonic Dualism

Plato saw the physical world as being in a constant state of flux. Yet, Plato accepted the teaching of Socrates that absolute truth exists and can be known by the human mind (Rogers, 1932). How could humans come to have truth if they could not trust their senses? Plato's answer is in his *Theaetetus*. The sensory World gives knowledge of individual objects that are subject to change. On the other hand, abstract knowledge is constant and unchanging so it cannot be derived from sensation. To solve the problem of "universal" or "abstract" knowledge, Plato needed dualism. Abstract knowledge, as found in the principles of mathematics and represented by words such as "truth" and "beauty," requires an immaterial existence since the knowledge itself seems to transcend the ubiquities of the physical world. Abstract knowledge represents ideal forms that the human knows. These ideal forms must reside in the spiritual part of human nature, namely the soul. In other words, immaterial knowledge requires an agency in the human that is also immaterial, the soul. Plato considered that the soul is immortal and undergoes a series of reincarnations until it can be returned to the place of ultimate truth (the World of Ideas). The return to the soul's natural home can only be obtained by good works. In his dualism, Plato represented the soul as imprisoned in the body and, therefore, the soul must exercise great intellectual effort to realize its innate knowledge.

Plato's philosophy is difficult to understand since it rests upon the assumption that the material world, revealed by the senses, is deceiving since the material world is constantly changing. What is truly real cannot change. For Plato what cannot change are ideal forms understood by humans as intellectual ideas. Moreover, these ideas are universal in that all humans who think correctly can begin the process of understanding them. The forms revealed as intellectual ideas are rediscovered in consciousness by the human mind. The human mind does not create the forms since they have an independent existence.

Three forms in particular attracted Plato's attention. These forms are known through the ideas representing beauty, truth, and goodness. Objects experienced with the senses reflect these ideal forms but are not the forms themselves. Beauty is the most recognizable form. What can a sunset, the portrait of the *Mona Lisa,* and a lovely human being have in common? They reflect the ideal form of beauty. By studying these objects, the human mind can discover the meaning of beauty. The form of truth is reflected in knowledge that is infallible. The best example of truth experienced by humans is mathematics. (Please note that two of the quarks were named "beauty" and "truth" by physicists.) Likewise, knowledge systems can be studied as a means for understanding truth. The highest form is goodness and is symbolized in Plato's philosophy by the Sun. Humans experience goodness in the physical world through charitable acts.

According to Plato, humans have a strong urge to rediscover the meaning of the ideal forms since, before the soul was forced into union with the body, it had realized the forms. Once exposed to the physical reflections of the forms through the senses, we seek to know them again. Therefore, the emotion of love becomes the agency by which humans seek a reunification with the ideal. Thus, a pleasing person is wanted since this person is remindful of beauty. However, love, directed only to objects in the physical world, cannot be satisfying. The mistake is to assume that the physical object is the ideal form. It is not; it only represents a vague copy of the ideal form. In time, the human body loses some of its beauty to the process of aging. Thus, love should move the human to seek an reunification with the ideal forms on an intellectual basis. Hence, the term *Platonic* love carries the meaning of possession in a non-physical sense. Finally, the apprehension of the ideal form through love is a transforming experience. For example, if one were to understand the idea of beauty and realize that beauty is reflected in various degrees in all human beings (if we look hard enough to find it), then we would not do violence or harm against one another. Love of true beauty would prevent the violence.

In a poetic fashion, Plato expressed his theory of knowledge in the allegory of the cave found in the *Republic.* Here Socrates, speaking for Plato, compares human knowledge based solely on the senses to someone looking at shadows on a cave wall cast by a fire. The cave dweller believes that the shadows are reality and fails to know the truth. Only by looking at the objects in the bright Sun can the cave dweller come to the truth. However, Plato warned that knowing the truth, given by the light of the intellect, is often frightening and drives many back to their delusional shadows. In his dualism, Plato was a rationalist in that the soul contains innate ideas. The sensory world is an aid in helping the individual rediscover the innate knowledge but is not the basis of that knowledge. For example, there are no perfect circles in reality, but the human is reminded of the mathematical formula for a circle by studying sensory objects having a circular form. The understanding of truth is difficult and requires great effort. The realization of abstract knowledge in the conscious mind requires thinking and introspection as if one were searching for a lost memory. Thinking is a skill that is slowly perfected through vigilant application. Consequently, Plato considered that humans need to be 45 to 50 years old before they can appreciate their full intellectual potential. Also, humans are not all equal in their acumen, and the *Republic* addresses what society must do to maximize the differential abilities of its citizens for the benefit of all.

The union of soul and body is troublesome for the human and causes great internal dissension as the human is pulled between the conflicting sensual and intellectual urges. Plato expressed the difficulty of being human in a famous passage from the *Phaedrus* (Hackforth, 1952, p. 69). Here, Plato compared human nature to a charioteer trying to drive a pair of winged horses. The horse on the right is obedient and follows the commands of the charioteer. However, the horse on the left is disobedient and causes the charioteer great difficulty in trying to steer the team. Thus human nature has elements of the rational (the right horse) and the irrational (the left horse). The decision process (charioteer) often has difficulties in choosing between opposing demands. Plato's analogy of the charioteer and his horses has been compared to Freud's analysis of personality requiring id (left horse), ego (charioteer), and superego (right horse). Also, Freudian theory came into agreement with Plato regarding dreams. Plato considered that the "beast" in humans is released during dreams; and the more hostile and unstable is the individual, the more psychotic are the dreams.

Aristotle's Dualism

Aristotle, who contributed many theories about physics and biology, considered human nature from a dualistic viewpoint. Like Plato, Aristotle was curious about the origin of human knowledge. Unlike Plato's rationalistic interpretation of the mind, Aristotle developed dualism incorporating an empirical formula. Whereas Plato held that abstract ideas were innate (rationalism), Aristotle said that all knowledge must be acquired through experience (empiricism). Additionally, Aristotle was more optimistic about human nature than Plato. The soul was claimed to be a prisoner in the body by Plato; however, for Aristotle, the soul-body union is the defining property of human nature.

In his theory of knowledge, presented mainly in *De Anima*, Aristotle accepted the real existence of physical objects (whereas Plato considered them to be crude representations of ideal forms). Aristotle's human soul contains an agency, called the active intellect, that has the power to produce universal (abstract) ideas. The initial step in knowledge acquisition involves experience allowing the senses to register specific events from the external world. The sensory knowledge is placed in a mental agency called the common sense. There, the active intellect seizes the sensory contents and uses its power of abstraction to produce an universal idea. Thus, from experiences with specific objects, the mind can find what is common among them and generates the general or universal idea through the power of abstraction. For example, from sensory contact with objects that have bark, a trunk, branches, and leaves, the mind produces a universal idea called "tree."

Aristotle required a strong interaction between the body and soul to produce knowledge. Without the sensory data provided by the body, the mental process cannot produce generalizations. In other words, Aristotle maintained that the power to know is innate (abstraction); however, knowledge itself is dependent upon first having sensory experiences. The way knowledge is obtained indicated to Aristotle that the union of soul and body was natural and necessary.

The soul is the basis of life and gives meaning to material objects. Anything that is alive has soul according to Aristotle. However, souls differ in their levels of perfection. Plants have souls with one major function, nutrition. In other words, the plant soul has life sustaining abilities. The animal soul includes the nutritive function, but also supplies perceptive and locomotive ones. The human soul is more perfect in that it contains the functions of the animal soul in addition to having thinking ability. All functions of the soul are corruptible at death except one, the ability to think. The thinking component of the human soul continues to exist after death, but the animal and plant souls completely perish (Russell, 1972).

Dualism in the Middle Ages

The Greeks explored many possible ways to represent human nature. However, in the Middle Ages, only the dualistic position, with its religious significance, was sanctioned. Nevertheless, thinkers were divided as to whether rationalism or empiricism better explained how human knowledge is obtained. Early, in the Middle Ages, Plato's rationalism was embraced by St. Augustine (354–430). The later Middle Ages allowed for the return of Aristotle's empiricism through the efforts of St. Thomas Aquinas (1225–1274).

The Dualism of St. Augustine

Following the advent of Christianity, a patristic period, lasting 400 years, occurred in which several apologists adopted Platonic doctrines to give philosophical meaning to the new faith (Martin et al., 1941). One of these writers was Origen (185–253) who made several important doctrinal statements. All knowledge comes to humans from God which is consistent with Plato's belief in absolute truth. Moreover, the teachings of Christ represent the Word of God and the means for the discovery of truth. The patristic period was completed with the monumental works of St. Augustine whose opinions were to remain dominant for 1,000 years.

Joining with Plato, Augustine said that the human soul is immortal and that contemplation is necessary to discover truth. The discovery of truth leads to the better understanding of God, the original source of all knowledge. In turn, having truth is the necessary condition for human happiness. However, Augustine had to reinterpret certain aspects of Plato's philosophy to make it consistent with Christianity. For example, the belief in reincarnation must be denied. Instead, the soul will again be reunited with its body to enjoy eternal reward or damnation. Moreover, souls do not exist before the body as Plato thought, but the soul is created at the moment it is united with the body.

Augustine, in an interesting manner, reevaluated Plato's doctrine of human free will. According to Augustine, the first humans, Adam and Eve, had free will, but they lost it due to their sin against God. Therefore, all the descendants of Adam and Eve are inclined toward evil and have no agency of free will. Only by the intervention of God, through Christ, can humans be saved. However, God's free will decides who will be saved and who will be condemned. Thus Augustine came to accept the doctrine of predestination.

The Dualism of St. Thomas Aquinas

The philosophy of Aristotle was developed by Scholastic writers and, as indicated in Chapter 2, the greatest Scholastic was St. Thomas Aquinas (Ueberweg, 1888a). Following Aristotelian thinking, Thomas argued that human nature is a composite of soul and body. Furthermore, the soul contains the mind with its power of abstraction and the will for making decisions. However, the mind is devoid of any innate ideas and must synthesize the sensory images through reasoning to produce knowledge. The mind generates its own knowledge once activated by sensory experiences.

Thomas also introduced changes in the Aristotelian position. Returning to Augustine, Thomas said that the soul was created at the moment it was united with the body. Moreover, the soul, with its mind and will, is entirely immortal, not just the rational part as claimed by Aristotle. Thomas made an interesting observation that the mind has no direct knowledge regarding how its operations are performed. In other words, humans have no direct knowledge of how cognition and memory operate.

In his analysis of the will, Thomas clarified how human choice operates. He accepted that the will is free to choose in the order of exercise. However, at a higher level, the will is determined. In this regard, the will is forced to seek a perceived good. Stating Thomas's doctrine in another way, humans are free to choose the means to secure a perceived good but the pursuit of the good is determined. In turn, the good is whatever makes humans happy. Unfortunately, there are no guarantees that a course of action chosen by an individual produces the desired effect. History and mythology are filled with examples showing that the attainment of wanted goals has unwittingly led to the destruction of the individual. Also, Thomas stressed that the mind and will are complementary. The mind proposes to the will the means to obtain a desired goal. Then, the will selects which of the various means will be most useful in securing the desired end. The mind and will, belonging to the spiritual soul, have as their respective objects ultimate truth and ultimate happiness. In Thomas's Christian dogma, the mind and will obtain their true end states through a union with God. However, if the will chooses means to secure an end through immoral acts, sin is committed. Unlike Augustine's reliance on predestination, Thomas claimed that human beings are personally responsible for their own salvation or damnation.

Thomas also developed a theory of emotions that was based upon an interaction between soul and body. Emotion itself is a bodily process, but the type of emotion experienced serves as a measure regarding the human's success in securing happiness. Love and hate are the fundamental emotions from which all other emotions are derived. Love represents the urge to be united with a desired object. Hate is the emotion that generates disgust for whatever blocks attainment of a desired object. Therefore, a person feels love when an object is experienced that is wanted. From love, the emotion of hope is felt as the person strives to have the desired object. If this object proves difficult to secure, the emotions of despair and anger are felt. However, if the desired object is finally obtained, the emotion of joy is registered. In Thomas's philosophy, hate is an useful emotion in that it tries to keep humans from situations that cause sadness. In other words, we hate what makes us unhappy. If what makes us sad is approaching, the emotions of aversion, daring, fear, and anger are felt. These emotions serve to warn the individual to take action against the impending doom. However, if we experience what is not wanted, the emotion of sadness is felt. Keeping with Thomas's emphasis upon ultimates, the greatest happiness is experiencing a permanent union with God, but the greatest sadness involves the perpetual loss of God. Applying Thomas's theory of emotions to current times, the level of depression in American society is extremely high. There is a 20% chance that an adult in America will experience sometime in life a debilitating form of depression that should require professional help. Much of this epidemic of depression is related to devastating losses of loved objects producing, in Thomas's terms, the attendant sadness. Perhaps in the remediation of depression, it is important to replace the lost objects with ones that are able to sustain joy.

The Cartesian Compromise

The Dualism of Rene Descartes

Although Augustine and Thomas differed regarding how knowledge is obtained and whether the will is free, both vigorously supported a strong dualism. Mental processes occur in the spiritual soul and, therefore, must be studied as part of philosophy. Science cannot reach to the highest level of human psychology. But science should be useful in ascertaining the principles by which the physical body operates. The differential roles of philosophy and science in the explanation of human nature were advanced by Rene Descartes (1596–1650).

This great seventeenth century philosopher undertook an analysis of human nature by first dismissing all previous explanations. In his *Meditations,* Descartes reproduced his own rational proofs indicating that all the following exist: thinking beings, God, the human soul, innate ideas, and the material world (Ueberweg, 1888b). Descartes's reasoning starts with the notion that humans can doubt the existence of all premises except one. The act of doubting distinctly shows that thinking exists. If thinking exists, then so must the thinker. This leads to Descartes's famous epithet: *cognito, ergo sum* ("I think, therefore I am"). In other words, the conscious activity associated with thinking is the hallmark of human existence.

Descartes also explored how truth is discovered. When thinking leads to clear and precise understanding of a topic, truth is apprehended. For example, humans can think about a being having absolute perfection. According to Descartes, this supposition leads to a clear and distinct impression that God exists. Since the idea of God, as a perfect Being, cannot be derived from an imperfect world, this supposition must be innate, supplied to the mind by God directly. Also, the thinking process indicates the presence of a spiritual soul. Thinking itself cannot be localized within any part of the body; and, therefore, thinking requires an immaterial agency.

Descartes also developed a criterion for ascertaining truth. When thinking leads to ideas that are "clear and distinct," such ideas must be true (Ueberweg, 1888b, p. 50). Since God is a perfect Being and responsible for all knowledge, God cannot deceive. When humans use their thinking minds correctly, true ideas, authored by God, are consciously realized. However, when humans error in the search for truth, it is due to a premature commitment to a judgment about reality that has not been rationally evaluated. Obviously, Descartes was aware of the human penchant to base beliefs on emotional, not rational, convictions. Furthermore, Descartes indicated that mathematics and his own work on analytic geometry illustrate how the proper use of thinking uncovers the innate truth placed in the human mind by God. Since animals and plants do not display rationality, they do not have the spiritual soul. Thus, Descartes limited the soul to humans, whereas Aristotle and Aquinas assumed that all living beings have souls with differential qualities.

If the major property of the spiritual substance is the conscious activity of thinking, then the identifying attribute of material substance is extension (Coppleston, 1985b). In other words, the material world, including the human body, exists because such objects occupy space. As seen in Chapter 3, Descartes's reliance upon extension being the defining principle for matter required him to postulate the existence of ether filling celestial space. The physically existing body is considered to be a machine subject to the laws of science. Evidence was accumulating, such as William Harvey's work on the circulation of blood and neurological work explaining reflex activity, to indicate that bodily activity was governed by physical laws.

With the distinction between soul and body established, Descartes addressed the fundamental issue of how substances having different realms of existence can interact. He recognized that mutual influences exist between the soul and body. The body presents sensory images and registers emotions that enter into the awareness of the soul. Also, Descartes realized that the senses distort the world and reason must be used to correct faulty perceptions. Finally, Descartes proposed that the soul must penetrate the complete bodily substance. However, the soul seems to have a special relationship with the brain. Here the reciprocal influences of soul and body are exchanged. Descartes guessed that the pineal gland, buried deep within the cerebrum, might be the primary location for the soul-body interface. Descartes never explained how the soul-body interaction takes place in the brain.

Descartes also made an important observation about the mind which provides a formidable obstacle for any future development of a scientific psychology. In his doctrine of Subjectivism, Descartes noted that a human being can only know with certainty one's own conscious states. One human has no direct contact with another human's mind. Therefore, making the study of consciousness the subject matter of a science of psychology is problematic since consciousness cannot be observed. Instead, consciousness is personal and every human has to assume that others have consciousness.

Finally, in his *Discourse on Method,* Descartes offered useful advice regarding the attainment of true knowledge. The following four rules guide the establishment of true knowledge:

a. Accept nothing as true which is not clearly recognized as true.
b. Divide each of the difficulties which has to be examined into as many parts as possible. Study the individual parts.
c. Study simple things first before moving to more complicated matters; and
d. Review what one has considered to be true in an attempt to detect previously hidden sources of error.

Significance of Descartes's Philosophy

Although a devout Catholic, Descartes developed his dualism purely from a philosophical and not religious viewpoint. He understood the necessity of science as providing the explanations for the material world. Certainly, the study of the human body falls within the domain of biology, chemistry, and physics. However, these sciences cannot reach the other side of human existence, the conscious mind. Its powers convinced Descartes that humans also have an immaterial component to their existence.

Descartes's position has provoked much interest since its inception. It grants to science a limited role in understanding human nature. Science must concern itself with the specification of bodily processes. However, science is useless in studying the spiritual soul. Therefore, philosophy must be used to understand the soul. However, as science continued to enjoy great success, other thinkers began to doubt the accuracy of Descartes's assessment. The search for the proper understanding of human nature continued.

One of the major questions unanswered by Descartes's dualistic philosophy refers to the exact nature of the soul-body interaction. In other words, how is it possible for a spiritual soul to interconnect with a material body? Thus the soul and body are in two entirely different realms of existence. Many of the following philosophers were inspired by the dilemma left behind by Descartes to develop alternative positions. Thus, Spinoza developed one-substance theory; Leibnitz and Kant expanded upon the doctrine of psychophysical parallelism. Finally, Hobbes advocated materialism, a position that would most easily accommodate psychology as a branch of science consistent with the Newtonian view of nature. The following contains an exploration of the views of these important philosophers whose ideas will help to define the province of psychology.

The Unity of the Mental and the Physical

Often individuals, being victims of injustice and the prejudices of other human beings, are filled with hate and despair. But, this is not always the case. In the history of philosophy, Baruch Spinoza (1634–1677) is an exemplary figure of supreme patience and perseverance who conducted himself with Socratic dignity despite being the target of hatred and disgust by those who could not tolerate his thoughts. Spinoza was born in Amsterdam to a Jewish family whose ancestors left Spain to avoid religious bigotry (Ueberweg, 1888b). At age 22, his philosophy came under suspicion from both the Jews and Christians. He was apparently offered a bribe to stop his philosophizing or face excommunication from the Jewish faith. After this sad ceremony and an assassination attempt upon his life, Spinoza withdrew from society and changed his first name from Baruch to Benedict. He earned his living by making lenses for telescopes and sought little in terms of prestige or glory. However, as his philosophical ideas were disseminated, many were eager to learn from him and he became a celebrated recluse. Spinoza had an early death, succumbing to tuberculosis.

All Is God

Spinoza taught that God is the totality of everything. In other words, God is Nature (Coppleston, 1985b; Durant, 1938). In his work, *Ethics,* Spinoza offered the reasoning for this unique conclusion. If God were separate from the Universe, He would thus be limited. But God is infinite with no boundaries or imperfections placed upon His existence. Therefore, God and the eternal Universe must be one. Spinoza's doctrine is called pantheistic monism in that only one substance exists which is God Who is in everything. Moreover, there are two attributes to the Godly substance of the Universe: mind and matter. Spinoza's unique approach was to start his philosophy with the unassailable assumption that God exists. On the contrary, Aristotle, Aquinas, and Descartes began with human perception and then reasoned to the existence of God.

All finite beings share in the existence of God which indicates that all beings participate in the attributes of God. With this assumption, Spinoza is ready to explain human nature. Since humans are part of the One Substance that exists, they have the attributes of that Substance: mind and matter. The operation or mode of the mind is to think, and the mode of matter is extension (filling space). Thus, the human being is one substance with two attributes. This principle may become clearer by the comparison to the nature of light. As seen in Chapter 4, modern physics must assign both wave and particle properties to physical existence. Light has one underlying reality but it has two attributes or properties.

The inherent connection between mind and matter answers the great dilemma of Cartesian dualism, how the body and soul interact. For Spinoza, this is a pseudo question. Since mind and matter are two aspects of one thing, no explanation of interaction is needed. Humans are not a union of two distinct entities, body and soul. Dualism is rejected and replaced by a special kind of monism claiming that humans are one substance with attributes for thinking and occupying space.

Another way of expressing Spinoza's belief is that mental states must be accompanied by a physical manifestation. The thinking ability is a natural property of matter. If humans are one substance with two attributes, so is everything else. All existence must have consciousness. As seen in Chapter 2, Bruno, about 50 years before Spinoza was born, also concluded that consciousness must be everywhere.

Given this conception of reality, how should humans live? Spinoza adopted the Stoic position that the activity of reason is the highest human virtue. Therefore, anything that compromises the ability to reason is considered a vice. For example, a society that keeps its citizens ignorant is corrupt. Regarding the individual, the pure pursuit of pleasure, wealth, and/or social position, at the expense of reason, are tragedies inflicted upon the human spirit. Human nature is especially blessed with the agency of reason; therefore, the development of the intellect should be the primary motive of human existence. Reason is of ultimate importance because it allows understanding. Since God is the intelligence of the Universe, humans connect to God through reason and understanding.

Since the Universe follows definite rules, it is important to explain phenomena, including human behavior, through the use of efficient causality. Due to his emphasis upon efficient causality, Spinoza has been accused of denigrating human free will. In reality, Spinoza allows for human free choice to operate, but it must operate within the confines of human nature. Since human nature is determined, efficient causality is primary to final causality. Humans cannot act outside their nature. For example, we cannot breathe in water with our lungs, as do fish with their gills. We cannot fly with the flapping of our arms, as do birds with their wings. We cannot do these things because there are limits imposed upon our nature by outside forces. Moreover, humans cannot defeat the limitations placed upon our natures with the use of intention, the basis of final causality. In other words, we may desire to breath like fish and fly like birds, but these desires cannot overcome our natural limitations. However, humans are free to act within the constraints of their nature. Therefore, Spinoza does not completely do away with the operation of final causality. According to Spinoza, humans should intentionally pursue activities that fulfill their nature. The highest of these activities is the use of reason to understand causes for events. Thus, humans should be allowed to expand their intellectual understanding of any phenomena.

Moreover, society should help insure individual self-preservation so that the attainment of the greatest amount of knowledge can be achieved. Lastly, the acquisition of knowledge is an effort of the entire society. Government has the duty to encourage cooperation, not competition, among humans so that the collective knowledge and wisdom of the society is incremented in larger steps. When government seeks retribution against individuals for seeking knowledge, disasters loom for the society. Thus, the punishment of Galileo, who used his intellect to advance the human understanding of the Universe, was an egregious act. For this reason alone, totalitarian governments are doomed to failure. Thus, Spinoza concluded that the optimal social contract between government and society is represented by democracy (Pitts, 1986).

Spinoza also referred to the ideas of Epicurus in trying to understand human nature. Epicurus said that pleasure is the absence of pain. Spinoza added to the hedonic doctrine by defining pleasure as a transition to a higher state of perfection and pain as a transition to a lower state of perfection. In order to reach to higher levels of perfection, humans must sustain their lives. The conscious component of self-preservation is desire. All emotions, in turn, are derived from the desire to have pleasure and to avoid pain. Humans love that which produces pleasure and hate that which leads to pain. However, Spinoza warns that it is easy to fall into servitude to the emotions when one searches for happiness and cannot find it. Ultimate happiness is found in reason. When reason produces knowledge of the causes for outcomes, the domination of emotions in one's psychic life ceases. For example, Spinoza himself was the victim of hatred and intolerance. Yet, he did not return the hate to others because he believed that knowledge of the causes for human behavior allowed him to understand his situation. The accumulation of knowledge is the highest of all human virtues since it ultimately leads to the understanding of God. In this sense, Spinoza adopts a theory of knowledge close to Plato's position. Moreover, knowledge reduces uncertainty and allows the human to experience tranquil emotions. In other words, knowledge and understanding grant happiness. Finally, Spinoza wondered what happens to the human substance at death. As knowledge grows in a human, there is an intuition regarding immortality. The individual human mind will be returned back to the eternal Mind of the Universe which is God.

It is difficult not to notice interesting parallels between the lives and works of Benedict Spinoza and David Bohm. As explored in the last chapter, the physicist Bohm was politically persecuted in his young adulthood as was the philosopher Spinoza. Bohm, like Spinoza, eventually found sufficient political safety to develop theories containing the cardinal principle that the Universe is coordinated in its activity. In this regard, Bohm developed the idea of the implicate order of information guiding all events and Spinoza found the mind of God in all things.

Significance of Spinoza's Philosophy

As seen in Chapter 4, some modern researchers acknowledge the possibility that many dimensions of reality exist and that black holes may implode into a number of countless Universes. All this is possible in Spinoza's system since the majesty of all that exists is God Who has no boundaries. Stephen Hawking is trying to demonstrate that the Universe always existed and that the Big Bang is just one incident in a never ceasing chain of events. Hawking assumes that the eternal nature of the Universe obviously shows that it was not created. If Hawking succeeds, he will have found Spinoza's God.

Spinoza's philosophy also grants a major role to science in the study of human nature and theology. The material and mental attributes of human existence obey laws. Therefore, the physical sciences and the science of psychology should be valuable in discovering the causes pertinent to the body and mind. In addition, since one substance exists, the laws of physics and psychology can be unified. Of course, knowledge about the one substance is really providing knowledge about God. Therefore, all science is an extension of theology.

The Doctrine of Psychophysical Parallelism

German philosophers, cognizant of Descartes's dilemma, approached the problem of human nature through the development of psychophysical parallelism. This position acknowledges the existence of the mental and physical aspects of humanity, but does now allow an interaction between them. Instead, the mental and the physical mirror each other's activities. In this philosophy of human nature, the mental can never be reduced to the physical. Therefore, the understanding of the human requires how the mind-body parallelism operates. The first great German philosopher to take up the task of explaining psychophysical parallelism was Gottfried Wilhelm von Leibnitz.

Leibnitz's Theory of Harmony and Monads

Leibnitz (1646–1716) lived during the wonderful days that witnessed the development of Newtonian physics and the removal of philosophy and science from religious prejudice. As a great intellectual prodigy, Leibnitz attempted to synthesize a view of human nature that was both philosophically and scientifically consistent. Unfortunately, Leibnitz scattered his writings on human nature, and their understanding is very arduous. Nevertheless, his major ideas appeared in the *Monadology,* written two years before his death. In this work, Leibnitz explained that both the mental and the physical exist but never interact (Coppleston, 1985b; Popper & Eccles, 1977).

Descartes located the interaction between the mind and the body in the pineal gland. Other writers, such as Nicolas de Malebranche (1638–1715), who agreed with dualism but disliked Descartes's explanation of soul-body interaction, developed the doctrine of Occasionalism. This position explains soul-body interaction by appealing to God's direct intervention allowing the mind to influence the body and vice versa. Spinoza replaced dualism with a position that claimed both the mind and body are essentially two properties of the same substance. Leibnitz dismissed all of these positions, but selectively borrowed from them to develop his own explanation.

Leibnitz departed from Spinoza's doctrine of one substance. Instead, there are many substances that compose nature. Moveover, Democritus was almost correct in postulating atoms as the units of existence. The real units are what Leibnitz called *monads*. These monads are small bits of spiritual existence and represent true reality. The human being, as every object composed of parts, is an assemblage of monads. In turn, each monad is a spiritual entity, a point in space. When monads congregate to compose an entity, such as a human, the accumulation of monads has the *appearance* of physical existence. The physical world, including the human body, is the result of perceiving a vast collection of monads. Thus, Leibnitz differs with Spinoza by assuming that the physical world is just a shadow of the spiritual world, an idea that can be traced to Pythagoras and Plato. God, for Leibnitz, is the ultimate Monad who created all the other ones. In creating monads, God gave all of them perception but differing degrees of consciousness and mentality. By perception, Leibnitz means that monads internally respond to changes in other monads, existing inside and outside the body. Thus, monads are coordinated to mirror what is called "physical reality." However, only a few types of monads can have their perceptions reflected in consciousness. The animal monad has perception, consciousness, and memory. The human monad has perception, consciousness, memory, and rational thought. In addition, the human monad is blessed with innate ideas initially existing in the unconscious.

Every entity is a collection of monads, however, only one of the monads is allowed to dominate. In other words, what is called the human soul is the dominant monad in the entire collection of monads. However, the dominant monad does not always have clear perceptions and must develop thinking to discover the truth. Thinking allows the recovery of mathematics and logic which are innate forms of knowledge used by the mind for understanding.

How did this arrangement of monads come into existence? Leibnitz appeals to the wisdom of God who pre-established the harmony existing among the monads. God gave monads their properties and their abilities to reflect each other's activity. For the human, the dominant monad is the soul and the others make up the appearance of a body. The relationship between soul and body is like two clocks that keep the same time without directly influencing one another. The harmony between the clocks (soul and body) is pre-established by God. In this harmony, souls act according to desires and apperceptions (changes in consciousness) which is the basis of final causality; however, bodies follow the laws of motion, such as those described by Galileo, Kepler, and Newton, allowing the explanation of their activity in terms of efficient causes. The pre-established harmony between the soul and body eliminates any need for special explanations for soul-body interaction as Descartes attempted. Since the coordination between efficient and final causality was pre-ordained by God, the world is inherently moving in efficient steps toward the final end established by God. Accordingly, Leibnitz concluded that this must be the best of all possible worlds, since it is ordained by God.

Leibnitz offered an extremely important opinion that the mind operates according to its own internal principles. Mental activity is organized by the mind, not by the sensations experienced in the mind. By emphasizing the innate abilities of the mind, Leibnitz was resisting the empirical philosophy being developed by the British. For example, John Locke maintained that nothing is in the mind that first was not in the senses. Leibnitz's reply was that nothing is in the mind before sensation except the mind. In agreement with Plato, Leibnitz acknowledged that sensations help to kindle the thinking process leading to the discovery of innate ideas. Leibnitz referred to *petites perceptions* as the state of nascent knowledge as one passes from sensation to understanding.

There is no doubt that Leibnitz's views are difficult to understand. In his philosophy, the soul and body cannot interact. The soul results from the activity of a special monad within the human being. The body results from a collection of monads of lesser quality than the soul monad. Due to the intervention of God, the soul monad and the body monads are coordinated in their activities. Leibnitz characterized the difference in the activities of the soul-monad and body-monads in the following way (Frost, 1942, p. 271), "Soul acts according to the laws of final causes, by means of desire . . . Bodies act according to the laws of efficient causes or motions. And the two realms are in harmony with one another." Leibnitz (Tomlin, 1963, p. 164) also wrote that "bodies act as if there is no soul, and souls act as if there were no bodies, and both act as if each influenced the other." However, for Leibnitz, there is no interaction, only harmony of operation imposed by God.

The Nature of Evil

Granted that this is the best of all possible worlds, Leibnitz took on the challenge of explaining why evil and pain pervade human existence. If God, the Creator, is all good and benevolent, how can evil exist? Leibnitz gave the answer in his book, *Theodicy* (Latzer, 1994). According to Leibnitz, evil exists since anything created is by definition imperfect. It is impossible for God, Who is all-perfect, to create God. Therefore, the created monads must be less than perfect. In turn, imperfection leads to evil.

Leibnitz defined three types of evil. The first is called *metaphysical* evil and refers to the imperfections that exist in created beings. It is the metaphysical evil that leads to the remaining two. The second kind of evil is called *physical* and consists of the conscious feeling of suffering. Only those beings with the capability of feeling pain and suffering are subject to physical evil. The last type of evil is *moral* and is the basis of sin. In this type of evil, the soul uses its free will to transgress against divine law. Moral evil can only be done by rational beings. Leibnitz does not hold God responsible for any type of evil since creation carries with it the burden of imperfection. Evil results from the inherent limitations of created beings. Interestingly, Leibnitz found a way out of the evil in the World. God, through Jesus Christ, was able to teach how to defeat evil. But in doing so, God too suffered through the death of Christ. Thus, the activity of God showing how to remove the highest type of evil, the moral evil, insured that this is the best of all possible worlds.

"Copernican Revolution in Philosophy"

While Descartes, Spinoza, and Leibnitz relied on rationalism to approach the understanding of human nature, the British philosophers of that era were strongly committed to empiricism. British Empiricists, such as John Locke (1632–1704) and David Hume (1711–1776), claimed that all knowledge is derived from the senses; there are no innate ideas. Moreover, Hume explored the limits of human knowledge from the empirical standpoint and concluded that there is no way to prove the validity of any human idea. Hume represented the mind as a collection of associated sensations. The ideas in the mind are all reducible to how the sensations are experienced. The mind has no innate knowledge and no natural ability to discern truth. The only activity that the mind does well is to associate events through contiguity, contrast, and similarity. Therefore, it is impossible to claim anything with certainty, such as causality and morality. The reply to Hume's scepticism came from the German philosopher, Immanual Kant (1724–1804), who proclaimed that he was awakened from his intellectual slumbers by reading Hume. Kant became so excited by his work that he called it a "Copernican revolution" for philosophy. This revolution attempted to synthesize rationalism and empiricism in order to develop a philosophy that truly characterizes human nature (Durant, 1938).

Kant was a professor of philosophy at the Prussian University of Koningsburg. He was well known for following a strict daily routine, arising, eating, and walking at the same times each day. In fact, the citizens of Koningsburg checked their watches for accuracy every afternoon at 3:30 when Kant ventured out for his daily sojourn. He was filled with unusual obsessions such as never talking while outside for fear of contracting an infection. He always planned his actions very carefully, sometimes hesitating too long. He waited to propose marriage to his love and she wedded another. In old age, Kant slipped into senility and died quietly (Durant, 1938).

In his philosophy, Kant developed a comprehensive theory of knowledge. The mind contains innate mental abilities that organize and give meaning to sensations experienced by the body. All this is explained by Kant in his monumental work, the *Critique of Pure Reason*. The mind, as a separately existing entity, must make judgments about the physical world. Therefore, Kant agrees with the psychophysical parallelism of Leibnitz. There is a physical world, called noumena, that is known indirectly. What humans know directly are the mental states, called phenomena, that serve to represent physical reality. Since the mental aspect of human existence is independent of the physical aspect, the understanding of the immaterial mental operations, "things in themselves" according to Kant, is the province of philosophy (Coppleston, 1985b; Rogers, 1932).

The mind starts with sensory information but must use innate judgmental capacities to produce ideas representing reality. These mental judgments involved in the conscious construction of reality are called "synthetic *a priori*." "Synthetic" refers to the judgments leading to new knowledge and *"a priori"* expresses the innate and universal abilities of the mind to generate knowledge. These abilities exist independently of experience and include the following powers: casual inference, understanding of unity, affirmation and negation, logic, contingency relations, space and time perception.

In addition to innate capacities, the mind has innate ideas about God, morality, and mathematics. The innate knowledge of moral principles is called the "categorical imperative" and is indicated by an awareness of what is righteous and contentious behavior. Humans may know what is morally right but carry out immoral acts. This situation was Kant's argument for the existence of free will.

Although Kant did not offer any hope for the development of scientific psychology, nevertheless, his claim that the mind is an active participant in the construction of reality has been acknowledged by many scientific psychologists (Robinson, 1981).

His influence is seen in the theories of Wundt, Piaget, the Gestalt psychologists, and the modern cognitive psychologists. However, the Kantian conception of the mind is in basic disagreement with Einstein's theories of relativity. Kant held that judgments about space and time were innate mental powers not affected by experience. However, as Einstein explained, judgments about space and time are very much affected by experiential conditions. What appear to be simultaneous occurrences to one observer can be successive events to another witness based upon their motion relative to one another.

The Materialistic Rebuttal to Dualism and Parallelism

The immaterial aspect to human existence, found in the works of several dualistic and parallelist philosophers reviewed above, was challenged by a rekindling of materialism. One of the first to renew the cause of materialism was the British philosopher, Thomas Hobbes, who expanded upon the doctrines first considered by Epicurus. Following Hobbes, several others, such as Julien de la Mettrie, Franz Joseph Gall, Hermann von Helmholtz, Alexander Bain, and Herbert Spencer resorted to biological science as providing the basis for the acceptance of materialism. The major thrust of the materialists carried to the twentieth century and allowed for the ready acceptance of materialism into scientific views of psychology represented by Psychoanalysis and Behaviorism.

The Materialism of Hobbes

Thomas Hobbes (1588–1679) witnessed the bloody spectacle of the English civil war as Catholics and Protestants battled for control of the government. Profoundly affected by the human potential for treachery and destructiveness, he published the *Leviathan* that attempted to formulate the type of government needed to curb the aggressive tendencies in human nature. In this work, Hobbes also expanded upon the materialistic doctrine of human existence (Coppleston, 1985b; Robinson, 1981).

Hobbes noted, along with Spinoza, that self-preservation is the strongest human desire and leads to human destructiveness. Humans are in a natural state of war with each other. Therefore, a benevolent monarch, who has absolute power, is needed to govern the masses of humanity. The leader must represent the needs of the multitude and insure individual safety. Originally, the leader is selected by the masses, but, once selected, can never be removed since anarchy and chaos would result. The social contract is irrevocable.

Hobbes also believed that human behavior and institutions are governed by laws that are just as natural as those of Kepler that describe planetary motion. In other words, the motions of humans are not random, not guided by free will, but are determined by efficient causality. Humans are just physical bodies capable of motion. Once the laws of bodily motion are known, the need to have a soul to move the body is unnecessary.

Hobbes supported a strong empirical position for knowledge. Humans learn by experience and do not have innate knowledge. The contiguity of events becomes the basis of ideas, dreams result form bodily agitation, perception results from objects producing agitation in the brain. When the human engages in behavior, it is governed by the pursuit of pleasure and the avoidance of pain. All human activity is lawful and obeys the Epicurean pleasure-pain principle. In reading Hobbes, the impression is created that his cynicism led to the conclusion that humans did not deserve to have a soul.

Hobbes had a major influence upon the development of British philosophy. He is considered to be the forerunner of British Empiricism that produced a series of thinkers such as John Locke (1632–1704), David Hume (1711–1776), and John Stuart Mill (1806–1873). British Empiricism was strongly opposed to the doctrine of innate ideas and concentrated on the experiential basis of human knowledge. British Empiricism, born from the materialism of Hobbes, was to be a victim of the materialism offered by Darwinism.

L'Homme Machine

The French philosophers of the eighteenth century argued for a reorganization of institutions to combat societal ills. They were reformers who were committed to the doctrine of social change. For example, Voltaire (1694–1778), heavily influenced by Newton and Locke, said that humans cannot depend upon institutions to present the truth. Instead, truth is discovered through observations of the world. However, Voltaire would not venture to the conclusion that there is no God as indicated by his famous statement, "If God did not exist, it would be necessary to invent Him; but all nature cries out that He does exist" (Ueberweg, 1888b, p. 125).

However, other French writers, such as Julien Offray de la Mettrie (1709–1751), supported a comprehensive materialism. La Mettrie wrote *L'Homme Machine (The Human Machine)* as an attack upon Descartes's dualism. Trained as a medical doctor, La Mettrie noted that physical sickness was accompanied by changes in mental function. Therefore, the mental faculties must really be bodily functions. Also a supporter of empiricism, La Mettrie proposed that education develops mental faculties and even apes could learn to talk if they were properly trained. Finally, he supported a strong hedonistic principle as the sovereign determining human behavior. Humans are like robots programmed to pursue pleasure and avoid pain.

The Reliance of Materialism upon Biology

The disposition toward materialism in understanding human nature was greatly strengthened by two major developments in biological science. The first discovery involved craniometry and its companion phrenology which attempted to correlate mental powers with the individual's physiognomy. Craniometry and phrenology, although mostly wrong in detail, inspired research on the brain that continues to the present day. The other movement was the Darwinian theory of evolution that stresses the continuity between all living forms. Still a controversial issue, Darwinism, nevertheless, was used as a major starting point for the development of scientific psychology. In the following, a brief treatment of these two biological movements relative to their importance to psychology is presented.

Craniometry and Phrenology

The doctrine of craniometry was created by Franz Joseph Gall (1758–1828). The basis of craniometry was the materialistic belief that the brain is totally responsible for all mental processes. Furthermore, Gall proposed that it was possible to chart differences in mental abilities by carefully measuring the shape of the head. Without doubt, Gall became the most notorious scientist of the early nineteenth century. He was praised as the one who finally rescued the study of human nature from the philosophers. To others, he was a dangerous enemy to humanity and religion who wanted to degrade the spiritual side of existence.

Gall's Life

Gall was born in Tiefenbronn, Germany to a family of devout Roman Catholics of Italian ancestry. Although his parents wanted him to enter the priesthood, Gall pursued medical training in Strassbourg and then Vienna where he received his degree in 1785. He developed a successful medical practice and treated several famous statesmen such as Metternich (Ackerknecht, 1956).

Around 1792, Gall began to develop his doctrines that mental abilities were controlled by specific organs of the brain and that skull shape might serve to indicate mental aptitude. Gall's interest in craniometry started in his youth when he concluded that students with prominent eyes have strong memory abilities (Spurzheim, 1908). Gall began to give public lectures and demonstrations of craniometry that purported to show the connection between brain and mental development. His intent was to establish the validity of "organology" that the brain is responsible for all the mental operations. Moreover, the brain anatomy and development are directly indicated by the size and shape of the skull. As expected, these opinions were not popular with religious and civil authorities who were perturbed by the materialistic intent of Gall's message. Thus, the Austrian Emperor, Francis I, ordered Gall to leave Vienna. Accordingly, Gall, now joined by his colleague, Johann Gaspar Spurzheim (1776–1832), traveled throughout Western Europe for two years giving lectures and demonstrations as well as collecting head measurements from individuals in all stations in life ranging from the insane to professors. At last, Gall and Spurzheim settled in Paris and Gall received French citizenship in 1819. Napoleon attempted to silence Gall, but after the demise of the dictator, Gall was free to develop his theory. Between 1810 and 1819, Gall published several volumes of his major work, the *Anatomy and Physiology of the Nervous System in General and of the Brain in Particular.* Gall included Spurzheim as a co-author on the initial volumes, but the two became estranged before the completion of the work. Gall entered retirement and the very organ of his study was later to cause his death. Gall's controversial life, adorned with two marriages and many assignations, ended in 1825 due to the effects of a cerebral stroke. He left specific instructions that his skull be preserved and added to his vast collection of human heads. His brain was to be dissected so that his personality and mental traits could be measured more completely. The examining group concluded that Gall was extroverted, creative, strongly motivated, but with average memory ability.

Meanwhile, Spurzheim began to popularize craniometry and his efforts attracted a large audience in France, Britain, and the United States. By 1820, craniometry became known as phrenology largely through the efforts of Spurzheim. In 1832, he visited America to teach and demonstrate the new science. However, Spurzheim died suddenly in Boston but phrenology continued to be advanced with great success through the efforts of the Englishman George Combe (1788–1858).

Principles of Craniometry and Phrenology

Gall was an avid admirer of Francis Bacon's philosophy which taught that truth is discovered through observation. He was interested in exploring whether observations of the human brain and skull could lead to reliable estimates of human mental functions. Thus, Gall became the one of the first to promote mental testing. He concluded from his work that separate organs of the brain are responsible for all mental faculties, emotions, and perceptions. He supported his theory by careful dissection of the brain and made genuine discoveries about its organization. However, he also concluded that the size of a particular brain structure directly indicates the quality of the resulting mental process. Large brain development is revealed externally by swellings (bumps) on the skull. The measurement of the skull should predict the level of various psychological competencies.

Gall advocated that each mental ability is located in a specific brain organ. Gall supported his assertions through careful brain studies. His dissections yielded evidence that imbeciles have reduced amounts of cortical tissue. In addition, insanity was often indicated by abnormal development of the brain. Also, Gall found that damage to the brain through accident or disease predicts changes in cognition and emotionality. However, Gall's assertion that brain function is indicated by skull development proved to be a theoretical embarrassment.

Spurzheim appropriated Gall's ideas and invented the term "phrenology." By the time Spurzheim was finished with Gall's ideas, thirty-seven mental traits and abilities, ranging from amativeness (sexual passion) to the understanding of time and causality, were attached to locations on the skull. Spurzheim demonstrated how skull examinations indicated the mental and personality traits of the individual. He also applied phrenology to ideas about educational and penal reform and the proper treatment of children.

Importance of Gall's Work

Gall was instrumental in stimulating brain research. His theories sparked controversy that could only be settled by the investigation of the central nervous system. Partial vindication for Gall's ideas occurred in 1861 when Paul Broca discovered the "speech center" localized in the left frontal lobe. Ten years later, Gustav Fritsch and Eduard Hitzig, using electrical stimulation of the brain, located its sensory and motor centers. Disagreement with Gall's localization theory motivated the great neuroanatomist, Pierre Flourens (1794–1867), to study the holistic properties of the brain necessary for intelligence, perception, and movement.

Gall's accomplishments were tarnished by the controversy surrounding phrenology. Unlike another Viennese physician 100 years later, Gall allowed his work to be abridged by others. In contrast, Sigmund Freud (the other physician) retained despotic control over the development of his psychoanalytic theory and designated his daughter, Anna, to be the guardian of the movement after his death. Gall had no Anna; instead, Spurzheim proselytized and offered sensational claims for phrenology. But Spurzheim had his admirers such as Horace Mann, Queen Victoria, and Walt Whitman (Young, 1971). Others soundly denounced phrenology as a charade with no scientific validation. Eventually, both Catholic and Protestant clergy spoke against phrenology as a materialistic doctrine threatening the human soul. But phrenology was a popular subject, especially in the eastern part of America, through the first decade of the twentieth century.

The waning of phrenology was encouraged by the emergence of another biological doctrine that also supported a materialistic interpretation of human existence. The biological successor to phrenology was a new evolutionary theory by Charles Darwin. Darwinism attracted the interest of many including philosophers, scientists, politicians, theologians, educators, and eventually those who would create American experimental psychology.

Darwinistic Evolutionary Theory

In the nineteenth century, Charles Darwin (1809–1882) revolutionized the field of biology as Einstein would physics in the twentieth century. Darwin gave a new interpretation to the old problem regarding the origin of species. Exploration of the Earth had revealed a rich diversity of plant and animal life. How did all these life forms come into existence? Darwin's answer was evolution through a natural selection process. Moreover, Darwin's theory gave a clear interpretation of human nature strictly from a materialistic viewpoint.

Darwin's Life

The productive and controversial life of Charles Darwin began on February 12, 1809, a birthday shared with Abraham Lincoln. In his youth, Darwin had to survive the early death of his mother and the harsh criticism of his father. Darwin's initial university training was in medicine, his father's profession. Not surprisingly, Darwin quickly tired of his medical studies at Edinburgh University. His disappointed father then sent him to Cambridge University for ecclesiastical studies with the hope that his son would become a clergyman in the Church of England. In 1831, Darwin graduated from Cambridge without distinction and a disinterest in the ministry.

However, in that year, Darwin received the opportunity that would eventually lead to his fame. One of his Cambridge professors, John Stevens Henslow, arranged to have Darwin be the naturalist aboard H. M. S. *Beagle* which was about to embark upon a five year mission to study flora and fauna around the World. Darwin's father opposed the trip and only relented after Josiah Wedgwood II, son of the famous potter of English bone china and Darwin's uncle, interceded. The voyage of the *Beagle,* which gave Darwin the opportunity to make his critical scientific observations, began on December 27, 1831.

Soon after his return to England, Darwin married his first cousin, Emma Wedgwood, and they became the parents of ten children, three of whom died in infancy. Also, Darwin's mental and physical health began to deteriorate and he moved to a country estate, fifteen miles from London. The speculations regarding why Darwin's health was to remain poor all of his long life range from a chronic viral infection contracted during the *Beagle's* journey (De Beer, 1971) to a lifelong depression, partly induced by the burden of being the author of evolutionary theory (Gruber & Barrett, 1974).

Darwin formulated his evolutionary theory in 1838 and coincidentally began to have terrifying dreams of being hanged and decapitated. Darwin mentioned that discussing his evolutionary theory was "like confessing murder" (Gruber & Barrett, 1974, p. 43). Under mental stress due to the anxiety generated by his theory, Darwin refrained from publishing it and gave instructions to his wife that the theory should only be released after his death. Darwin was very aware of the great debate and personal attacks that the theory would engender.

In 1856, Charles Lyell urged Darwin to publish and he reluctantly began to write a book. Darwin's efforts lagged until he received a letter in 1858 from another naturalist, Alfred Russel Wallace. The letter astonished Darwin for Wallace was communicating an exciting new theory that was essentially Darwin's own view of evolution! Instead of engaging in tactics to sabotage Wallace, Darwin was gracious in allowing both his theory and Wallace's to be presented officially to the Linnean Society on July 1, 1858. In 1859, Darwin's book, *Origin of Species through Natural Selection,* was finally released. Darwin's fear concerning the debate his theory would provoke proved correct. His ideas were denounced as atheistic and materialistic by the clergy and were challenged on their scientific merits by other biologists. However, Darwinism had several able supporters led by Thomas Henry Huxley, Asa Gray, Joseph Dalton Hooker, Francis Galton, and Herbert Spencer.

Darwin himself rode out the controversy safely tucked away at his country estate. Eventually, he succumbed to heart failure and was buried in Westminster Abbey, a paradoxical situation given the opposition to his ideas from religion. His long life was filled with international awards for his scientific genius, but the one country that failed to honor him officially was England which indicates the political power of the Anglican church. Nevertheless, no other theory in the modern age so changed the way that humans look at themselves than did the theory of evolution through natural selection.

Darwin's Preliminary Observations

Just before the voyage of the *Beagle,* Darwin began to read Lyell's *Principles of Geology* which offered a new explanation for the development of the Earth. Until Lyell's work appeared, it was a common belief in geology that the planet is only affected by major catastrophes and, in between such events, plant and animal life remain stable. Catastrophes can occur (such as the recent hypothesis by physicist Louis Alvarez that the Earth's collision with comets changed the climate enough to kill the dinosaurs); however, the Earth is also subject to constant geological changes produced by volcanos, earthquakes, and weather. The continuous modification of the Earth by natural forces was the principal tenet of Lyell's alternative to catastrophism. During the *Beagle's* voyage, Darwin made many geological observations that confirmed Lyell's thesis. Darwin was also impressed with the gradations in species from their extinct ancestors to their existing forms. Apparently, life forms must change to meet the inevitable modifications of the planet. It was on the Galapagos Islands that Darwin made his most stunning discoveries regarding the ability of finches to adapt to specific ecological niches. Some finches ate seeds and others insects and the bills of the finches were consistent with their eating habits. Thus, Darwin witnessed the harmony existing between the environment and the structure of living forms. (De Beer, 1971).

Competition and Adaptation to the Environment

After his return to England, Darwin jotted down his observations and suppositions in his *Notebook on Transmutation of Species.* He was sure that evolution of species was controlled by adaptation to the environment. Some species were more successful than others in adaptation, and those that were not successful become extinct. But how did the process of adaptation occur? The insight for solving the riddle of evolution began in September 1838, when Darwin read Thomas Robert Malthus's controversial work, *Essay on the Principles of Population* (Gruber & Barrett, 1974).

Malthus opposed the utopian views of society that were being proposed by Romantic writers. Instead, as a curator of a poor church, Malthus was witness to the plight of the underprivileged as they struggled for existence. Malthus sounded a warning that continues to be a serious problem for today. The human ability to procreate is geometric to the arithmetical growth of the food supply. Without the checks provided by natural disasters, war, and birth control, the human population will grow to a point where it cannot be maintained by the planet. Thus, competitive pressures are placed upon humans for their survival, welfare, and happiness.

Darwin incubated Malthus's work and, sometime in 1842, the insight for evolution was fully realized. Based upon what Malthus had written, Darwin understood that each species produces more progeny than survive. Many young of every species die prematurely through a variety of causes. Those that live become the procreators and pass their valuable characteristics for survival to their offspring. Thus, the environment naturally selects those who will survive and those who will perish. The ones that survive pass along numerous characteristics and the ones that are useful come to predominate in the phenotype of the species. Since the environment constantly changes, the process of evolution is never finished.

Ironically, Alfred Russel Wallace, in 1844, had read Malthus's book. While recovering from a malaria-type disease in southeast Asia in 1858, Wallace remembered the competition principle as he tried to understand evolution. Independently, he drew the same conclusion about evolution as Darwin did.

Theory of Evolution through Natural Selection

In 1859, the *Origin of Species* was published and offered the following principles explaining evolution (Darwin, 1859/1963).

1. All existing vegetable and animal life forms are descended from earlier and generally more simple life forms.
2. Variation in species is produced because the environment and the use and disuse of organs lead to changes in structure that are inherited.
3. In the struggle for survival, the fittest win because they succeed in adapting themselves to the environment.
4. Differentiation within a species is the result of sexual selection allowing the fittest to procreate.
5. Some variations in species seem to happen spontaneously (now recognized as genetic mutation).

The central problem for the evolutionary theory was to explain how variation enters into the system. The laws of genetic transmission were not yet understood in 1859, and Darwin had to rely upon the controversial view of Jean-Baptiste de Lamarck (1744–1829) to explain inheritance. Lamarck's theory of the inheritance of acquired characteristics proposed that the activity of an animal increases the development of certain organs and structures. In turn, what is acquired by an animal during its life can be passed to its offspring through inheritance. Never satisfied with the Lamarckian theory, Darwin added amendments to it in 1863. Called pangenesis, Darwin's explanation of inheritance is reminiscent of Leibnitz's monad theory. Pangenesis claimed that the body produces self-representative hereditary units that enter the blood stream and unite with the reproductive cells making possible the inheritance of acquired characteristics. Near the end of the nineteenth century, the German physiologist August Weismann proposed that chromosomes are the basis of inheritance. The theory of evolution now had its genetic mechanism.

The Campaign for Darwinism

The supporters of Darwinism faced formidable opposition who were supporters of creationism. The creationists included religious authorities and many respected scientists. Therefore, it is amazing that Darwinism, within twelve years after the publication of the *Origin of Species,* became recognized as the most important scientific theory of the nineteenth century (Caudill, 1994). The march to victory for Darwinism was led by two very capable biologists, Thomas Henry Huxley and Joseph Dalton Hooker. However, the leader of the war against the opposition was Darwin himself. Tucked safely away at his country estate in the village of Downe, Darwin rarely engaged the opposition directly. Instead, he remained in close personal communication with Huxley and Hooker who skillfully argued the case for natural selection.

At his estate, Darwin continued to do research (Milner, 1996). He built a greenhouse and studied pollination in orchids as well as tropic movements of vines. He also experimented with barnacles to learn the secrets for classifying species. He explored inheritance factors by raising pigeons and talking with the local farmers regarding the breeding of animals. Darwin also took long walks on his "thinking path" as he pondered the meaning of evolution. Although he was limited to working just a few hours a day due to his strange illness, he was able to complete several books in addition to the *Origin of Species.* By the time Darwin's *Expression of Emotions in Man and Animals* (1872) was published, natural selection had become the dominant paradigm for evolutionary biology.

Darwin seized upon an interesting strategy to win the battle against the creationists. Darwin's plan was twofold: win the support from the public for natural selection and try to convince the younger biologists that the theory was valid (Caudill, 1994). To keep the public's attention, Darwin wrote articles for the popular press regarding gardening and animal domestication. Darwin assigned to his two loyal followers, Huxley and Hooker, the task of also enlightening the public and challenging the opposition within the scientific community. In 1861, the Darwinists started a new journal, *Natural History Review,* that was aimed at convincing the scientific establishment. Huxley wrote several articles for the journal and fought openly with the scientific critics of Darwinism, such as Sir Richard Owen, who was a renowned anatomist and director of the British Museum. Huxley personally detested Owen and was most eager to embarrass him. Also, Huxley, motivated by strong dislike of formal religion, had public debates with members of the clergy. Huxley's acerbic manner regarding the opposition earned him the nickname "Darwin's bulldog" (Caudill, 1994). Huxley could not accept creationism as the explanation of life. Nor could he accept the then prevalent Spinozan notion that science would discover God's design for the Universe. Huxley fought passionately in public and in scientific circles for Darwin's materialistic view that life forms are the product of natural selection. Hooker's role was to present evidence and arguments in favor of Darwinism within the scientific community. Hooker was a polished speaker and not given to the pith and demagoguery of Huxley. The measure of Hooker's success within the scientific community is indicated by his election in 1868 to the presidency of the prestigious British Association for the Advancement of Science. Hooker was the first Darwinist elected to this position indicating that the war with the creationists had been essentially won. As the scientific battles subsided, Hooker joined with Darwin and Huxley in explaining natural selection to the public. The campaign for natural selection was not confined to England. In the United States, the Harvard biologist, Asa Gray, fought hard for the understanding of natural selection by both the scientific community and the public.

Darwin and his allies changed forever how science is to be conducted within democratic societies. Before Darwin, scientists were not especially interested in explaining their work to the public since the funding of science was done by rich benefactors or authoritarian governments. (Note that Galileo did not take his arguments for Copernicanism to the people but to the Vatican.) However, the public's access to information dramatically increased in the last half of the nineteenth century with the emergence of education and the print media. In England and the United States, which had built strong traditions of democracy, the support of science depends upon the good will of the voting public. Therefore, scientists must now keep the public informed as to the merits of their efforts. Scientists, whether they relished the task, were forced to become politicians. As a contemporary example of this role for scientists, the National Aeronautics and Space Administration (NASA), in August 1996, released findings to the public indicating that a rock from Mars, which had landed on Earth millions of years ago, bore evidence of bacteria-like life forms. The public's excitement following the announcement that Mars might have harbored life certainly allows Congressional appropriation bills for space exploration to pass more easily.

Darwin, Huxley, and Hooker were exemplary politicians for natural selection who not only convinced the younger biologists, but also the general public. To sustain the victory, the philosopher-author Herbert Spencer then took on the task of explaining the importance of natural selection to sympathetic audiences in England and the United States.

Impact upon Biology

The course of biology was profoundly influenced when evolutionary theory was combined with the principles of genetic inheritance first observed by the Moravian monk Gregor Mendel (1822–1884). Mendel, working in obscurity, demonstrated with pea plants that the inheritance of physical characteristics is subject to statistical laws. Combining Mendel's work with Darwin's has brought about the grand synthesis for twentieth century biology. Sir Ronald Fisher, in 1930, showed that Mendelian laws of inheritance and the mechanisms of chromosomal meiosis could be combined to explain the occurrence of structural mutations required for the evolutionary changes in plants and animals. Then, in the stunning discovery of 1953, Francis Crick and James Watson constructed the model of genes and chromosomes from the molecular structure of deoxyribonucleic acid (DNA). Life is based upon the atoms of carbon, nitrogen, oxygen, and hydrogen forming sugars and phosphates that compose the spiraled double helix arrangement of the DNA molecule.

Knowledge of genetic mechanisms has several practical applications. Through genetic engineering, bacteria have been modified to produce human growth hormone which is necessary for the treatment of several maladies. Currently, ways are being devised to take cells from the body, alter the genes, and replace them back into the body as a means of eliminating inherited diseases such as cystic fibrosis, sickle cell anemia, Huntington's chorea, and some forms of carcinoma (Roberts, 1988).

Knowledge of inheritance has also been useful in deciphering human evolution. In 1973, Donald Johanson and his colleagues digging in Africa, discovered 47% of a skeleton from a female member of *Australopithecus afarensis,* the earliest human ancestor to diverge from apes. The skeleton was dubbed "Lucy," inspired by music from the Beatles that had been playing at the time of the discovery. Lucy's bones are thought to be between 3 and 4 million years old. The oldest bones for modern humans, *Homo sapiens sapiens,* are about 120,000 years old. Relying upon the rate of mutation that takes place in the DNA of mitochondria, it is estimated that the common human ancestor to everyone who is currently alive walked in Africa about 200,000 years ago (Cann, 1987).

Impact upon Psychology

Herbert Spencer (1820–1903), self-taught author of many works, began to apply the evolutionary doctrine to psychology and sociology. In his work, *Principles of Psychology,* Spencer argued that the evolution of mental abilities is tied to the evolution of the brain. Animals and humans have their mental abilities through the development of the nervous system. So effective were the arguments of Spencer and others that British Empiricism, with its emphasis on the mind being blank at birth, was abandoned. Humans are born with innate potentials and the most important mental capacity, according to Spencer, was intelligence. Spencer also coined the term, "survival of the fittest," to indicate that adaptation to the environment is the major challenge of life. For humans, their advantage in adapting to the environment resides in the well-developed brain.

Darwin's brilliant but autocratic cousin, Francis Galton (1822–1911), attempted to show that human intelligence and achievement is inherited. In his *Hereditary Genius,* he said traits tend to be perpetuated within families. He further proposed that intelligence is a trait that is normally distributed in the population. Galton and his students began to develop statistics, involving correlation, to indicate the strength of inherited tendencies. In 1884, he opened his "anthrometric laboratory" to measure intelligence through sensory-motor skills. Although Galton's tests are now considered to be poor measures of intelligence, he must be credited as the forerunner to modern mental testing.

Evolutionary theory accepts a continuity between humans and animals in terms of mental and physical functions. Therefore, Descartes's argument that humans are unique was dismissed. Instead, the study of animals was expected to produce understanding of how both mental and physical abilities evolved. Darwin's handpicked successor, George Romanes (1848–1894), supported the study of animals as a means to learn about the origins of human capabilities. Moreover, animals were assumed to have in varying degrees the mental characteristics of humans including consciousness. However, there is no direct way to sense an animal's or a human's mind. Therefore, mental activity must be carefully inferred from behavior. Romanes was accused of being overly anthropomorphic in his explanations of animal behavior. Therefore, another British evolutionist, C. Lloyd Morgan (1852–1936), reinstated Occam's razor for the study of the animal mind. In trying to infer mental states from behavior, always use the simplest explanation, staying away from the use of higher mental processes when lower ones will suffice.

The evolutionary doctrine was the pillar for many of the movements in twentieth century psychology. The first American school of psychology, Functionalism, was fully committed to the view that human mental traits were shaped by the survival imperative. Psychoanalytic theory acknowledges evolutionary theory by the proposal that the core of human personality is driven by inherited functions. Developmental psychology, spearheaded by Jean Piaget, is based upon the premise that the mental growth of children follows a genetic blueprint.

Impact upon Society and Philosophy

The new evolutionary movement led to Social Darwinism, strongly advocated by Herbert Spencer. In Social Darwinism, the state is considered as analogous to an organism whose survival depends upon adaptation to changing world conditions. The society can only be as strong as its individual members. Social Darwinism attracted the attention of many since it seems to be relevant to the great economic changes that occurred in the last half of the nineteenth century.

Countries were moving from a monetary system based upon agriculture to one based upon manufacturing. The industrial revolution fueled by the advancement of technology placed great stresses upon the individual members of society to cope with change. For those who could adapt to the rapid changes, great rewards awaited.

Exactly how Social Darwinism was to be applied differed among various commentators. Herbert Spencer considered that the main duty of the state was to insure the maximum freedom for the ablest in the society. Such individuals through their collective efforts move society forward and should be freed from burdens of over-taxation and government restrictions. Also, the government should not be involved in social welfare programs since it diverts resources from the strong to the weak. However, Spencer did not oppose private donations to charity.

The German philosopher, Friedrich Nietzsche (1844–1900), favored the "superman" instead of Plato's philosopher-king as the head of a state. Nietzsche considered the fittest person to rule was an individual with supreme will power to attain authority by any means. Socialism, Christianity, and democracy were attacked by him for aiding the weak at the expense of the strong. For Nietzsche, war is justified if it insures that the fittest nation survives.

In the United States, the application of Social Darwinism was tempered. A view emerged that education of the citizenry was necessary to allow the country to compete successfully in the world. Thus, America after the Civil War expanded the education system allowing the number of high schools to go from only 100 in 1860 to 6,000 by 1900 (Williams, Current, & Freidel, 1961). The gospel of wealth doctrine was also popular in America. The gospel of wealth allows individuals to acquire fortunes, but they are expected to use some of their resources for the benefit of society. Thus, captains of industry, such as John D. Rockefeller and Andrew Carnegie, created foundations to aid worthy societal programs.

American philosophers William James (1842–1910), Charles Peirce (1839–1914), and John Dewey (1859–1952) were stimulated by evolutionary theory to create pragmatic philosophy. In pragmatism, the emphasis is upon judging the merits of one's ideas and society's institutions on the basis of their ability to produce desired outcomes. Therefore, the test of truth is determined by consequences. If an idea or institution brings about a desired change, then truth is established. There is no absolute truth in pragmatism; instead, truth is relative and determined by what works.

Natural Selection in Modern Science

Biologists, geologists, and paleontologists have retraced the history of life on Earth. From these efforts, some have concluded that natural selection may just be one principle among many that determine the biosphere. Darwin considered that life becomes more complex as it continues its evolutionary development forward in time. However, there is substantial evidence that the movement of life toward complexity has not been a smooth process (Levinton, 1992). From the geological record of our planet, it appears that evolution took a momentous leap forward about 600 million years ago during the Cambrian period. What happened at that time was the sudden appearance of several body designs for multicelled organisms. These basic "blueprints" for the construction of animal bodies have not changed in the succeeding 600 million years. Therefore, evolution seems to proceed in quantum leaps not in slow progressive steps. The body blueprints that came into existence 600 million years ago are familiar in the present day. The simplest blueprint is for a body to have two layers of tissue and a radial design (i.e., jellyfish and anemones). A slightly more complicated design involves three layers of tissue arranged in a bilateral symmetry (i.e., flatworms). The still more complicated design involves three tissue layers with a cavity in the middle tissue. All twenty-six existing phyla of animals follow one of these three basic designs. Before the explosion of different life forms 600 million years ago, the geological record suggests that the previous 3 billion years of biological development on Earth was relatively quiet. Thus, modern evolutionary biology is confronted with two major questions. First, what caused the "big bang" of animal development 600 million years ago, and why have no other major body plans developed over the succeeding millennia?

Another fantastic occurrence has been revealed by the geological record. Roughly 250 million years ago, during the Permian period, a mass extinction of life took place (Erwin, 1996). It is estimated that 90% of all ocean species, 67% of the reptiles and amphibian types, and 30% of insect orders perished. This is the only time that insects were subject to mass destruction. The devastation that occurred in the Permian period overwhelms the smaller mass extinction that eliminated the dinosaurs and other species about 65 million years ago. What caused this enormous upheaval in the biosphere 250 million years ago? Could it happen again? There is no firm answer as to what caused the Permian mass extinction, only a possible scenario. The suggestion is that an unusual series of events produced the calamity. During the Permian period, all land masses of Earth were linked together to form one giant continent known as Pangaea. The Earth was experiencing a busy time of volcanic activity. Also, the sea water around Pangaea suddenly began to lose its supply of oxygen. While the oxygen diminished in the oceans, carbon dioxide increased in the atmosphere due to vulcanism. The concatenation of these events made the biosphere so unstable that life forms died in abundant numbers. Several millions years were to pass before the biosphere recovered. The mass extinction of 250 million years ago and the elimination of the great reptiles 65 million years ago by a comet hitting the Earth certainly indicate that chance events can also contribute to evolution. For example, without the disappearance of the dinosaurs and other species, would the mammals of the present era have ever emerged? The role of chance in the operation of complex systems means that knowledge of the beginning conditions for any phenomenon does not guarantee the ability to predict with absolute certainty any end state.

As reviewed in the last chapter, scientists at the Santa Fe Institute are trying to discover the rules that govern the behavior of any complex system. The evolution of life is one of the complex systems studied by the Institute (Ruthen, 1993). Although the specification of the rules by which complexity operates is far from complete, the scientists at the Institute have made some interesting observations. First, all systems start from a simple basis that grows more complex. The complexity results from the interaction of processes that govern the system, allowing it to adapt to its environmental conditions. Eventually, the complexity will lead to entropy or disorder, as described by the second law of thermodynamics, due to the failure of a critical interaction to function. For example, Earth is composed from the elements who had their origins in the explosion of stars. The simple elements, such as hydrogen and helium, combined to make the more complicated elements such as carbon and oxygen. Physics has had spectacular success in explaining the rules by which matter congeals. However, the systems that compose the Earth will eventually reach as state of disorder due to a critical failure that looms billions of years in the future. The one critical interaction involves the Earth-Sun connection. Any event that is catastrophic for the Sun will produce the demise of the Earth. Eventually, over the course of billions of years, the Sun will gradually die as its burns its nuclear fuel. The death of the Sun brings about the death of the Earth. On a more immediate level, complexity theory may generate insights relevant for the social sciences. Complexity theory suggests that those individuals or countries that become too dependent on the connection to a critical process are liable for disorder. For example, the person who bases his/her happiness upon the existence of another is susceptible to catastrophe if the other person were to fail to act in the expected manner.

Human Nature at the Advent of Scientific Psychology

Throughout a span of 2,300 years, the question of human nature has been studied with no agreement reached. The dualism of Plato and Descartes affirmed two realms of existence, one physical (body) and the other immaterial (soul). Spinoza offered an alternative suggesting that one substance exists with two irreducible modes of being, mental and material. Leibnitz and Kant forged the doctrine of psychophysical parallelism claiming that mind and matter are separate but have correlated activities. Bishop George Berkeley (1685–1753) resorted to idealism that said only mental reality exists with the physical world being an illusion. Berkeley's slogan was, "to be is to be perceived." In other words, to exist, one must be the subject of another's perception (Russel, 1972). Berkeley's position is similar to the Copenhagen Interpretation of Reality, drawn from quantum physics, which claims the stability of the material world is imposed by perceivers and does not exist otherwise. However, the biology of the nineteenth century brought back strongly the materialism of Democritus and Epicurus. Human mental powers are solely the product of the brain argued Gall and Spencer.

The last half of the nineteenth century also witnessed the emergence of scientific psychology in Germany through the work of Gustav Fechner (1801–1887) and Wilhelm Wundt (1832–1920). This first experimental psychology was based upon the doctrine of psychophysical parallelism which is not surprising given its long philosophical tradition in Germany. Therefore, the first psychology made no attempt to reduce the mental to the physical. However, the evolutionary doctrine, with its philosophical commitment to materialism, soon invaded scientific psychology. Would Darwinism speed the progress toward the development of a successful science? The next chapter explores the maturation of scientific psychology.

Contemporary Models of Psychology

6

Wilhelm Wundt established the first laboratory for research in psychology at Leipzig, Germany, in 1879. He also proposed a paradigm for experimental psychology to follow. The new science is to be concerned with the analysis of consciousness as its primary subject matter (Wundt, 1910/1973). The task of researchers is to reduce consciousness to more elemental states of sensations, images (memories), and feelings. Psychologists should also establish the combination rules showing how the psychic elements merge to form various conscious states. Wundt's paradigm has interesting parallels to physics. Physicists search for the fundamental elements of matter and are concerned with the rules permitting elements to form compounds. Likewise, the research psychologist should discover the fundamental elements of the mind and show how they come together to form the compounds, known as conscious states. The paradigm articulated for experimental psychology eventually became known as Structuralism and included a commitment to psychophysical parallelism regarding human nature (Boring, 1950; Watson, 1971). Therefore, the elements of consciousness are analogous or parallel to the elements of matter; however, consciousness cannot be reduced to processes of the brain. One of Wundt's students, Edward Branford Titchener (1867–1927), moved to the United States but was unsuccessful in getting Structuralism established since American psychologists were inclined toward Functionalism, a paradigm committed to Darwinism.

Wundt's approach to experimental psychology also was greeted with resistance in Germany. The Wurzburg group, led by Oswald Kulpe (1862–1915), wanted psychology to study mental processes and not just mental contents. Kulpe's approach was known as Act Psychology which pioneered the study of thinking and problem solving. The most serious German threat to Wundt's approach came from the Gestalt psychologists, Max Wertheimer (1880–1943), Kurt Koffka (1886–1941), and Wolfgang Kohler (1887–1966). The Gestalt psychologists vigorously opposed Wundt's contention that mental phenomena can be analyzed in terms of sensations, images, and feelings. Instead, consciousness is based upon the innate ability of the mind to organize sensory experiences. Once produced, conscious experience exists as a separate entity from its elemental origins. The Gestalt psychologists were heavily dependent upon Kant's philosophy which stresses that innate processes (categories) construct mental reality. Gestalt psychology began with the demonstration of the "phi phenomenon" in 1912 which is the illusion of moving lights as seen on a theater marquee. The phi phenomena is created when the flicker rate between successive flashes of two lights reaches a certain value. The two lights now appear to be one light that jumps back and forth in space. The Gestalt psychologists explained that the mind must be creating the illusion out of the sensory experiences and the analysis of the conscious experience back into elemental states cannot reveal why the illusion takes place. Therefore, the Gestalt psychologists concluded that the whole experience of consciousness is greater than the sum of its parts. This became the slogan for Gestalt psychology (Heidbreger, 1933). The holistic nature of mental activity is also revealed in thinking. In a famous series of experiments with apes, Kohler (1925) discovered sudden solutions (insight) often occur in problem solving. Again, the phenomenology of the mind indicates that its internal processes use sensations to construct a representation of reality.

The great failure of all of German psychology was its disinterest in Darwinism. The commitment to psychophysical parallelism kept the German psychologists from exploring the ramifications of Darwinism for the study of human mentality. Instead, others who were interested in fostering the new experimental psychology included Darwinism. The first American paradigm for experimental psychology, Functionalism, had a strong Darwinian character. However, Functionalism was modified into Behaviorism to establish a rigorous experimental science. Behaviorism was followed by the articulation of psychobiology and cognitive psychology. In Europe, Darwinism became a cornerstone of Psychoanalysis. In the following, these historical movements producing the modern science of psychology are reviewed. The chapter begins with an introduction to the person most responsible for the emergence of scientific psychology in the United States.

The Remarkable William James

William James (1842–1910), more so than any other thinker before or since, envisioned the hope of experimental psychology. His brilliant insights into human nature still elicit acclaim and respect. Although James is credited with the founding of American psychology, he also became disillusioned by the character of the new science and finished his career as a philosopher. The involvement of William James in the articulation of American psychology is explored below.

The Development of William James

James was born into a wealthy family that included his brother, Henry Jr., who became a renowned novelist. James's father, Henry Sr., strongly believed in the value of education. Thus, the children were afforded the luxury of private schools and frequent trips to Europe to meet famous scientific and literary people. From an early age, William showed a strong natural talent for drawing (Leary, 1992). At age eighteen, he entered into an apprenticeship with the famous American painter, William Morris Hunt. However, Henry Sr. was very unhappy about the career choice his son had made. For reasons that are still unclear, William abandoned his artistic ambitions and, in 1861, entered the Lawrence Scientific School at Harvard University where he studied chemistry and biology. William then attended Harvard's medical school and graduated in 1869. Interestingly, during a trip to Germany in 1867, William encountered the writings of Wundt who was trying to establish psychology as a laboratory science.

After his graduation from medical school, William James suffered an episode of major depression, an affliction he would experience in various degrees all of his life. While in this deep depression, he had the opportunity to study an essay on free will written by Charles Renouvier (1815–1913). The essay inspired James to resist the thoughts of suicide that came with the depression. Moreover, from Renouvier's essay, James discovered the importance of the will in shaping the human experience. James used his will power in order to fight off the depression. This battle convinced James of the will to believe. Aided by the palliative effects of Renouvier's essay, James's mood improved as he began his mission to start American psychology. In 1872, James joined the faculty of Harvard University and soon established a laboratory for research in psychology. In 1878, with the laboratory functioning, James began a twelve year task of writing the definitive statement for the new science. Finally, in 1890, the *Principles of Psychology* was published and received wide acclaim. Even today, this two-volume book is considered worthwhile reading for its penetrating analysis of scientific psychology.

In 1943, the journal *Psychological Review* printed a retrospective on the 50 years of psychology since the publication of the *Principles*. One of the contributors to the retrospective, Gordon Allport, summarized from James's *Principles* six basic issues the science of psychology must address. These issues are:

1. How does consciousness relate to the neural activity of the brain?
2. Can the methods of research used in the natural sciences be effectively employed to study mental phenomena?

3. How does the sense of self remain intact as a person moves through the various experiences of life?

4. Is behavior determined through the rigid natural laws discovered by physicists or do humans really enjoy a free will?

5. Are the laws of association sufficient to explain how learning, memory, and consciousness function?

6. How do all the factors that govern the formation of personality work to produce the unique individual?

Although James had opinions regarding each of the above questions, no precise answers to any of them have ever been formulated. Thus, the *Principles of Psychology,* more than a 100 years old, still provides psychology with fundamental challenges.

James was very concerned about how humans seek knowledge. He became convinced that human understanding of any topic is best achieved through the use of an appropriate metaphor or analogy. For example, in chapter nine of the *Principles,* James spoke of consciousness as a "stream." In addition, James was fond of using metaphors drawn from Darwinism to express his philosophical ideas. Leary (1992, p. 156) has summarized James's commitment to natural selection by noting that:

> The ultimate metaphors that founded and framed his psychological thinking, and that came to undergird his philosophical pragmatism, pluralism, and radical empiricism, were the Darwinian metaphors of variation, selection, and function. All psychological states and actions, according to James, are products of spontaneous variation and selection in terms of their consequential utility.

Let us examine briefly James's various theoretical contributions.

Pluralism

James noted in the *Principles* (vol 2, p. 312) that philosophy is often frustrating because it cannot give precise answers to fundamental questions. However, James saw value in the confused state of philosophy. The contradictions in philosophy are symptomatic of the human condition. We live in a buzzing world of ideas. Thus, it is not philosophy's fault that it cannot produce a coherent theory to settle a major issue. Accordingly, humans must admit to a *pluralism* of ideas that fills our minds. Pluralism should be used to our advantage. By acknowledging different possibilities, the mind does not become "frozen" as it tries to attain understanding. If a person becomes too rigid and stubborn with regard to an issue, the acquisition of knowledge languishes. This is why James preferred empiricism to rationalism. The hallmark of empiricism is to have the mind experience in order that it can appreciate and judge alternatives. A closed mind is doomed to a world of few possibilities; an open mind is rejoiced by constant discovery. This should be the lesson that philosophy teaches to all. James (1907/1991, p. 58) summarized the importance of pluralism by writing:

> What our intellect really aims at is neither variety nor unity taken singly, but totality. In this, acquaintance with reality's diversities is as important as understanding their connection.

James (1902/1958) indicated the value of pluralism in his work, *The Varieties of Religious Experience.* This book was based upon a series of lectures James gave at the University of Edinburgh in 1901–1902. In *Varieties,* James presented several concrete examples of the importance of religious beliefs in people's lives and then provided philosophical interpretations for various religious experiences. Healthy religious experiences are those that create a sense of well-being. On this topic, James (1902/1958, p. 53) wrote:

> And here religion comes to our rescue and takes our fate into her hands. There is a state of mind, known to religious men, but to no others, in which the will to assert ourselves and hold our own has been displaced by a willingness to close our mouths and be as nothing in the floods and water-spouts of God. In this state of mind, what we most dreaded has become the habitation of our safety, and the hour of our moral death has turned into a spiritual birthday. The time for tension in our soul is over, and that of happy relaxation, of calm deep breathing, of an eternal present, with no discordant future to be anxious about, has arrived. Fear is not held in abeyance as if by mere morality, it is positively expunged and washed away.

Whatever religious experience can create the sense of well being and freedom from fear is valuable and positive.

Mental Toughness

Human consciousness is the arbitrator of what is accepted as true. In turn, the operations of consciousness are related to character traits. Thus, James (1907/1991, pp. 8–9) introduced his famous distinction between the "tender-minded" and the "tough-minded." Tender-minded people believe in established principles (i.e., rationalistic) and are described as intellectual, idealistic, optimistic, religious, non-deterministic, and dogmatic. In contrast, tough-minded people are guided by observable facts (i.e., empiricistic) and are described as materialistic, sensationalistic, pessimistic, fatalistic, pluralistic, and sceptical. James also remarked that a given individual might be a mixture of tender- and tough-mindedness. However, the propensity for being tough-minded carries the advantage of being open to all possible experiences.

Pragmatism

Near the end of his life, James (1907/1991) wrote a treatise on the nature of truth entitled *Pragmatism*. In this work, James confronted the problems created by competing ideas. Which of the many versions of truth is valid? To solve the problem, James adopted pragmatism, a view defined earlier by the philosopher Charles Peirce, to indicate how to validate the truth value of ideas. The method is very simple. Ideas are said to be true if they produce desired consequences. In other words, ideas must be tested by actions. If ideas produce desired consequences for the individual, that person's ideas are true. Nothing is left out of pragmatism. Even philosophical ideas are judged to be true if they produce beneficial effects for the believer. Therefore, pragmatism tests truth by finding out whether there is agreement between ideas and their practical consequences. James (1907/1991, p. 94) expressed this sentiment in the following way:

> To "agree" in the widest sense with a reality *can only mean to be guided either straight up or to it or into its surroundings, or to be put into such workings touch with it as to handle either it or something connected with it better than if we disagreed.* Better either intellectually or practically! And often agreement will only mean the negative fact that nothing contradictory from the quarter of that reality comes to interfere with the way in which our ideas guide us elsewhere. To copy a reality is far from being essential. The essential thing is the process of being guided. Any idea that helps us to deal, whether practically or intellectually, with either the reality or its belongings, that doesn't entangle our progress in frustrations, that fits, in fact, and adapts our life to the reality's whole setting, will agree sufficiently to meet the requirement. It will hold true of that reality.

From the above passage, James metaphorically makes use of Darwin's natural selection principle to illustrate pragmatism. Ideas are true to the extent that they help an individual to adapt to the environment. Finally, according to pragmatism, an absolute truth would have to be a belief for which no experience could ever contradict. From pragmatism's perspective, very few, if any, absolute truths have been discovered.

Radical Empiricism

In the last year of his life, James (1912/1976) published a work entitled, *Essays in Radical Empiricism*. The *Essays* attempted to defend a special kind of empiricism that James believed was necessary for the science of psychology. Radical empiricism acknowledges the importance of individual experiences. What matters the most for the human mind is how it interprets reality starting with sensory inputs. Whereas the traditional empirical doctrine, as stated by John Locke, stresses the importance of sensory inputs being the source of ideas, radical empiricism moves another step in emphasizing that the individual interpretation of sensory inputs is the critical experience. Thus, two people can have the same sensory input but end up with highly different interpretations of the same event. Moreover, as a radical empiricist, James called upon the science of psychology to study all phenomena that can be experienced and interpreted by the human mind. In other words, the science of psychology should investigate the entire range of human experience and determine the reliability and validity of any conscious report. As Taylor mentioned (1994, p. 354), radical empiricism is pluralistic since it affirms that many ways exist for interpreting reality. In addition, radical empiricism is pragmatic since interpretations of reality are made in order to help the individual cope in the world. It is ironic that a year after the publication of the *Essays,* John Watson (1913) defined Behaviorism as the paradigm for scientific psychology. Behaviorism took away from scientific psychology what James would consider its most powerful approach, namely radical empiricism. It was the movement away from radical empiricism that troubled James the most about the character of the emergent scientific psychology in America.

The James-Hall Controversy

In 1892, one of James's early students, G. Stanley Hall (1844–1924), seized upon a way to advance his career. In July of that year, Hall brought together a group of foremost psychologists in order to form the American Psychological Association (APA). However, for reasons that are not publicly known, William James did not attend the meeting (Taylor, 1994). Not surprisingly, Hall was elected the first president of APA.

Hall was already thirty-four years old when he received his doctorate degree in psychology from Harvard University. From 1878 onward, Hall seems to have engaged James in a battle as to which one would be the most influential psychologist in America. Although James praised Hall in the preface to the *Principles of Psychology* as one who helped to formulate the contents of the book, Hall was not so generous. For Hall was growing suspicious of James's interest in pluralism and radical empiricism. Specifically, Hall openly criticized James for his association with the American Society for Psychical Research and for having an interest in the French work on psychopathology. At times, James would retaliate as when he criticized Hall's studies of hypnosis (Taylor, 1994).

It was impossible to keep James from being a prominent part of the APA. Accordingly, James was elected the third president of the APA in 1894 during the time of his conflict with Hall. Thus, James's presidential address was highly anticipated since it would allow him to comment on the progress of scientific psychology. James's address, entitled "The Knowing of Things Together" started with his famous distinction regarding the two ways to acquire information. The first way, called "knowledge about" is indirect and based upon secondary sources; the second way, called "acquaintance with" is based upon direct experience. James illustrated the distinction by asking his audience about their knowledge of tigers in India. Reading about this topic grants the learner "knowledge about" tigers in India. However, if a person has gone to India and experienced the tigers, then that individual has "acquaintance with" knowledge that is very vivid and clear compared to knowledge based upon reading about tigers in India.

After James explained the distinction between the two ways of knowing, he surprised his audience by announcing his apparent abandonment of the new experimental psychology that he helped to create. James stated that he was leaving psychology since he no longer could agree with his earlier advice for the new science. In the *Principles,* James had said that psychology, as an independent science, needs no recourse to philosophy. However, in his presidential address, James claimed that it was undesirable and even impossible to keep philosophy out of "psychology-books" (Taylor, 1994, p. 53). In well-measured words, James explained that he was giving up the attempt to bring radical empiricism to psychology. James said (Taylor, 1994, p. 53):

> My intention was a good one, and a natural science infinitely more complete than the psychologies we now possess could be written without abandoning its terms. Like all authors, I have, therefore, been surprised that this child of my genius should not be more admired by others—should, in fact, have been generally either misunderstood or despised. But do not fear that on this occasion I am either going to defend or to re-explain the bantling. I am going to make things more harmonious by simply giving it up.

Even though James in effect withdrew from psychology, his differences with Hall continued. They publicly argued as to which of the two should be credited with starting the first laboratory for psychological research in the United States. (James did.) In addition, James, along with his friends Morton Prince and James Jackson Putnam, were becoming fascinated with Janet's work in Paris regarding psychopathology and psychotherapy. Janet discovered that dissociation could produce the multiple personality disorder. Not to be outdone, Hall also became interested in psychopathology. He cleverly planned and executed the now-famous 1909 conference held at Clark University that brought Freud and Jung to the United States to present their work. One could only wonder what William James, already with a failing heart, was thinking while listening to Freud at Hall's conference.

Tribute to William James

On August 26, 1910, James died at his summer home in New Hampshire. He was instantly proclaimed as America's greatest psychologist and preeminent philosopher (Myers, 1986). James lived his professional life in the manner he wanted psychology to follow. Later, the great mathematician-philosopher Alfred North Whitehead indicated the source of James's greatness. According to Whitehead, James authored theories so inventive that they were not made obsolete by theoretical developments in other sciences, especially physics (i.e., Einstein's Relativity Theories and Bohr's Copenhagen Interpretation). Despite the richness of James's approach, American psychology, in its early days, could not resist the temptation to define a positivistic paradigm that restricted the subjects that could be studied. Three years after James's death, the young John Watson published a paper announcing that behavior, not consciousness, is the proper subject matter of experimental psychology. With Behaviorism, Watson proclaimed, psychology could achieve the true status of a science.

Wundt's Influence upon American Psychology

The last decade of the nineteenth century witnessed the impressive development of scientific psychology in the United States. By 1900, forty-two laboratories for research had been established in American Universities. With the emergence of the scientific basis of American psychology, an interesting drama was unfolding involving the direction American psychology should take. Should the new American psychology be a strictly laboratory science consistent with Wundt's approach, or should psychology develop an interest in applied research, consistent with the Darwinian emphasis?

Wundt must be honored as the person who promoted psychology as a laboratory science. Wundt's hope was that careful research analysis would reveal how the mind assembles consciousness. Thus, Wundt gave subjects controlled sensory inputs and asked them for introspective reports about their conscious experiences. The careful application of stimuli required long hours of laboratory investigations that monitor the manner how subjects respond to the inputs. On the other hand, Americans, such as James, were not totally committed to laboratory research. James even implied in the *Principles of Psychology* (vol. 1, p. 192) that the German scientific method in psychology was boring. James wanted psychology to reach out and explore all facets of the human mind. Moreover, given his interest in Darwinism, radical empiricism, and pragmatism, James envisioned psychology as an applied science. Indeed, this is the direction that American psychology pursued.

The First American Psychologists

In the 1890s, an incredible amount of honor was accorded to Americans that studied in Germany with Wundt. In total, sixteen Americans received doctorate degrees with Wundt and "eleven of the group completed laboratory dissertations on topics such as touch, audition, vision, depth perception, emotion, aesthetics, memory, and the speed of mental processes" (Benjamin, Durkin, Link, Vestal, & Accord, 1992, p. 126). Thus, the first American psychologists were trained to be pure laboratory researchers in Wundt's laboratory. In addition, many of the Americans trained by Wundt came home to establish laboratories of psychology at various universities. Among those who started laboratories were: James McKeen Cattell at the University of Pennsylvania and Columbia University; Frank Angell at Cornell and Stanford Universities; George Stratton at the University of California, Berkeley; Charles Judd at Wesleyan and New York Universities; Edward Scripture at Yale University; Walter Dill Scott at Northwestern University, and Harry K. Wolfe at the University of Nebraska. After leaving Harvard with a doctorate in 1878, G. Stanley Hall spent the following year studying with Wundt, although the two had relatively little contact (Benjamin et al., 1992). Hall came to Johns Hopkins University to establish a laboratory in 1883. (Hall claimed that his laboratory was the first true research facility in the United States, a point which William James found contentious). In addition, five of Hall's students started laboratories at Indiana University, University of Wisconsin, Clark University, University of Iowa, and Bryn Mawr College (Hilgard, 1987).

Although Wundt's American students retained a strong emphasis for research, they moved the subject matter of psychology to more applied interests. Thus, Cattell (1860–1944) studied mental testing and started many business ventures to promote psychology for the general public; Judd (1873–1946) became a leading researcher in education; Scott (1869–1955) started the fields of organizational and industrial psychology. Another of Wundt's American students, Lightner Witmer (1867–1956), returned to the University of Pennsylvania and began the first psychological clinic to treat learning disorders in children and adolescents. Clearly, American psychology was becoming orientated toward practicality. In addition, by 1900, American psychology was so well established that it was no longer necessary to go to Germany for training. After 1900, Wundt had only two more American students.

American Assessment of Wundt

The year following Wundt's death in 1920, Bird T. Baldwin assembled in the journal, *Psychological Review,* reminiscences provided by several of his American students. George Stratton's (Baldwin, 1921, p. 170) words might best serve to indicate Wundt's legacy as viewed by the first-generation American psychologists:

> Wundt's greatest contribution to Psychology will, in my judgment, be not some particular doctrine or experimental discovery, but the impetus which he gave to the entire experimental activity in our field. It is largely due to him that Psychology is taking its place among the important sciences.

Charles Judd (Baldwin, 1921, pp. 173–177) provided the following physical and psychological profile of Wundt:

> Wundt was a tall, sparely built man with a slight stoop, a large head and a pleasant face. His features were strong and clear-cut. He wore thick, dark glasses which were the outward evidences of the conditions that made it possible for him to contribute to the literature of retinal pathology from his own introspective experience. He could use only part of one retina during the last half of his life. With this partial visual equipment, he did a prodigious amount of work, both of reading and composition . . .

> In personal ways Wundt was simple, even to the point of impressive modesty. He used sometimes to ask those of us who worked in the laboratory to Sunday dinner . . . At these dinners, he would reminisce about his American students

and plan trips to America which he felt he would never take because of the long ocean voyage . . .

I always found Wundt absolutely objective. I have read the controversial writings in which he took part and I know of his dislike for our great James's views . . . I have read his comments on the war and I have great difficulty in placing them in my thinking of him. I am disposed, for my part, to attribute all his scientific quarrels to his sensitiveness and modesty, and his devotion to truth as he saw it. I do not think that in scientific disputes he was partisan for personal reasons. He was absorbed in fact and wholly committed to what he believed to be the correct interpretation. The Wundt I knew never was anything but strictly empirical and objective.

The war referred to by Judd in the above quote was World War I. Wundt had expressed strong sentiments on behalf of the German cause and he blamed England for starting the war (Benjamin et al., 1992). Many historians have surmised that Wundt's strong support of German nationalism led to a denigration of his importance to the development of scientific psychology by British and American commentators. However, the sentiments expressed by Cattell (Baldwin, 1921, pp. 158-159) in the Wundtian eulogy are most fitting:

Wilhelm Wundt is dead. The London *Times* and other journals have impertinently remarked that he would have been more honored if he had died before signing the manifesto of the ninety-three German professors—that rather absurd, but truly pathetic and noble appeal to the good-will of the world. The civilization for which those men stood ranks in its fine distinction with the best periods of Greece, Italy, France, and England. It is now submerged in blood and ashes, sunk under the weight of its virtues and its sins, of specious idealism and crude materialism of its overlords, its allies, and its enemies. Let us hope that the brute arbitrament of force may once more yield to the generous rivalry of science and of diverse civilizations, and not hope only, but do our part to repay the debt that we owe to the dead.

Unfortunately, Cattell's plea for the restoration of civility and peace did not occur and an even more terrible World War II followed.

The First American Paradigm: Functional Psychology

The American approach to scientific psychology required a paradigm to express its commitment to practical issues. William James was persuasive in arguing that the applied nature of American psychology was consistent with the Darwinian emphasis upon adaptation to the social and cultural environment. Several of James's students, such as Edward Thorndike (1874–1949), Robert S. Woodworth (1869–1962), and James Angell (1869–1949) served to crystalize the focus of the American psychology upon the twin icons of natural selection and practical application. Finally, a loose confederation of ideas emerged as a paradigm and became known as "Functional Psychology." James Angell gave the most precise definition of Functional Psychology as part of his presidential address to the APA in 1906. Angell (1907, pp. 68–69) said that:

> The [Functional] psychologist is wont to take his cue from the basal conception of the evolutionary movement, i.e., that for the most part organic structures and functions possess their present characteristics by virtue of the efficiency with which they fit into the extant conditions of life broadly designated the environment. With this conception in mind, he proceeds to attempt some understanding of the manner in which the psychical contributes to the furtherance of the sum total of organic activities, not alone the psychical in its entirety, but especially the psychical in its particularities—mind as judging, mind as feeling, etc.

Angell (1907, p. 67) also concluded that Functional psychology searches for the "how and why" of mental processes whereas Structuralism searches for the "what."

However, one of Angell's students at the University of Chicago was troubled by the loose confederation of ideas that composed Functional Psychology. Its paradigm needed improvement to make experimental psychology consistent with the scientific model. The troubled student was John B. Watson (1878–1958), who was motivated to deal with Functionalism's inadequacies by creating Behaviorism.

The Behavioristic Paradigm

John Watson is a legend in the history of psychology, partly due to controversy that he enjoyed creating. He was a methodologist who campaigned for the Newtonian view of science. However, he spoke out on other issues. As Bergmann (1956) explains,

Watson was also a philosopher and a social commentator. These distinctive roles were often self defeating as Watson came to believe that he was a revolutionary figure. For his valuable contributions in methodology, Bergmann ranks Watson as the second greatest psychologist of all time, but far to the rear of the greatest. Watson was reduced to second place in psychology's hall of fame due to his theoretical mistakes made in the defense of Behaviorism. A short look at Watson's biography follows before his Behaviorism is discussed.

Watson's Life

In his autobiography, Watson (1936) described the rustic conditions of his early life growing up in the country surrounding Greenville, South Carolina. His rebel spirit was manifested early as he was prone to physical aggression and committed minor violations of the law. Somehow, he was able to enter Furman University at age sixteen and received a Master's degree in five years, bypassing the Bachelor's degree. He studied Latin, Greek, chemistry, mathematics, philosophy, and psychology and said he only enjoyed the latter two subjects. Wishing to pursue graduate study, Watson entered the University of Chicago whose psychology department was a major center of Functionalism due to the presence of James Angell, John Dewey, and H. H. Donaldson. Watson devoted himself to diligent laboratory work at Chicago investigating both learning and physiological processes in the rat. He also studied the major philosophers such as Locke, Hume, and Kant as well as Wundt's approach to experimental psychology. After three years, Watson graduated with a Ph.D., the youngest at that time to have earned a doctorate from the University of Chicago. Watson elected to stay on faculty following his graduation, but, in 1907, Johns Hopkins University offered him an appointment at the full professor level. A major opportunity was given to Watson in 1909 when the head of the psychology department, James Mark Baldwin, suddenly resigned. Watson filled the void created by Baldwin's departure and also inherited from Baldwin the editorship of the prestigious journal, the *Psychological Review*. At age thirty-one, Watson had the status to begin his campaign for objectivity in psychology. Watson's formal argument for an experimental psychology based upon observational facts that excluded the study of private mental states, such as consciousness, was presented in a 1913 paper entitled, *Psychology as a Behaviorist views it*. In 1915, Watson became president of the American Psychological Association, a tribute to his dedicated effort to improve American psychology.

In 1909, Freud made a triumphant journey to America to present his theory. Watson immediately became attracted to Freud's work, especially with regard to the importance of childhood experiences in the etiology of adult psychopathology. However, Watson disliked the theoretical language used by Freud and wanted to empirically establish the principles of child development. This interest in childhood psychopathology led Watson in 1916 to become associated with the Phipps Psychiatric Clinic supervised by Adolf Meyer at Johns Hopkins University. He also became interested in studying the reactions and learning abilities of newborn infants. World War I momentarily disrupted Watson's academic career. He, like so many other prominent American psychologists, was commissioned to serve in personnel selection. Watson was assigned the task of devising tests for picking air force pilots (Boakes, 1983). Soon, Watson came to hate the army and clashes with his superiors led to battlefield duty in Europe. However, the war came to an end before any combat, and Watson happily returned to Johns Hopkins in 1918 to continue his work with infants and development of Behaviorism.

In the autumn of 1919, Watson began his notorious "Little Albert" experiments which investigated whether children are capable of early emotional learning, a key premise in Psychoanalytic theory. Albert was nine months old when he was conditioned to fear a rat that before elicited curiosity and play (Harris, 1979). Not only were the Little Albert experiments important to the development of Watson's account of psychopathology, but they led to a major turning point in his life. Watson's research assistant was Rosalie Rayner, a member of a wealthy and prestigious family. At the time of the Little Albert studies, Watson, the handsome professor, and Rayner, the beautiful assistant, were in love. This affair eventually led to a stormy and public divorce from his wife, Mary. The University was greatly embarrassed by the situation and Watson was in jeopardy of loosing his professorship if he continued with Rosalie. Watson, the ardent Behaviorist who despised theorizing about internal feelings, chose on the side of love. He resigned from the University and in 1921 married Rosalie despite being in a penniless condition (Boakes, 1983).

Good luck now came Watson's way. He was able to secure a position in New York City doing advertising for the J. Walter Thompson Company. Within a few years, Watson became a major business success and earned as much money in 1928 as Babe Ruth. He continued to be an advocate for Behaviorism and wrote about child development. He and Rayner published in 1928, *The Psychological Care for Infant and Child,* that influenced the nurturing of children until the work of Benjamin Spock in the 1940s. However, in 1936, Rosalie Rayner Watson died from an intestinal illness. Watson was never the same and wrote no more about psychology (Cohen, 1979). In 1957, The American Psychological Association belatedly wanted to honor Watson for his achievements by presenting him a gold medal. Watson had planned to receive the award in person, but, in the end, sent his son to represent him. This gesture served to indicate Watson's indignation over the harsh criticisms he endured from psychologists over his defense of Behaviorism. At age 80, the Great Behaviorist died. His passing deeply influenced his sons, with one seeking understanding and insight in Psychoanalysis and the other committing suicide within a few years.

Watson's Behavioristic Contributions

Watson is not important for any of his theories about learning and child rearing. His value lies in the establishment of an objective method for conducting the science of psychology. In addition, Watson was a strong defender of materialism and empiricism regarding human nature. Watson's valuable impact, along with his dogmatic errors hindering psychology, have been clearly explained by Bergmann (1956). The following analysis of Watson's influence is taken from Bergmann's assessment.

Watson's true contribution to psychology is in the area of methodology. He transformed Functionalism into Behaviorism by insisting that experimental psychology have an objective subject matter, namely behavior. The essential message of methodological behaviorism is that: In principle, it should be possible to predict behavior from environmental, physiological, and experiential causes. With methodological behaviorism, Watson aligned psychology to follow the positivistic doctrines for science as formulated by Issac Newton. For a phenomenon to be studied scientifically, it must occupy physical space. Behavior can be studied scientifically because it has physical, measurable existence. Moreover, Bergmann praised Watson for removing the "teleological blur" from Functionalism. As seen in Angell's view, Functional Psychology "searches for the how and the why." Interest in the why question requires a purposive explanation, since intention must be specified. In contrast, the search for the how dwells upon knowing objective efficient causality of a phenomenon. Since mental states are not admissible to study, scientific psychology can only be concerned with knowing efficient causes for behavior, not final ones.

In Bergmann's assessment, Watson erred by articulating an unnecessary philosophical position to support methodological behaviorism. Watson's philosophical behaviorism denied the existence of internal mental states such as consciousness and thinking. No need to study mental processes, as Functionism and Gestalt Psychology were advocating, because the mind did not exist! If the mind did not exist, the study of the brain becomes a trivial matter. In his book, *Behaviorism,* Watson (1924) discusses the organs of the human body with a notable deletion. No mention of the brain was made. Watson became a unique materialist in that he did not argue for reduction of the mind to brain since the mind did not exist. Finally, Watson was a vigorous supporter of empiricism in that he contended human behavior is the sole product of experience. Connect the individual to his/her experiences and the efficient causes for that person's behavior are manifested. In a deliberate exaggeration, Watson (1926) defended empiricism with the hypothetical argument that he could take healthy babies and make them have any kind of adult personality solely based upon experiences. For all of his efforts, Bergmann concludes that Watson was the greatest of the Functional Psychologists and the first Behaviorist.

Reactions to Watson's Behaviorism

Watson's Behavioristic formula was studied by several eminent psychologists. For example, the Functional psychologist, Robert Woodworth (1918, pp. 29–43), noted that Watson's approach was too narrow to fulfil the purpose of psychology. Woodworth explained that Watson wanted to remove from psychology the study of consciousness. With the study of consciousness banned, there would be no further need for the unreliable method of introspection. Woodworth examined whether it would be useful for psychology to follow Watson's advice. Woodworth's conclusion was NO. First, Woodworth cleverly reminded his readers that psychology as a science had already adopted objective methods of research before Watson's introduction of Behaviorism. As Woodworth correctly acknowledged, psychologists such as Ebbinghaus (1885/1964) used objective methods to study human memory and Thorndike (1898) employed such methods to study animal learning. Reaction time experiments done by Wundt and others provided objective data regarding perceptual processes. Also, the study of abnormal psychology was well underway and used objective methods. Woodworth (1918, p. 34) also stated that the major aim of psychology is to understand the "workings of the mind." Introspection by itself will not be able to resolve the mysteries of the mind. However, the method is useful and should not be removed from the arsenal of research tools available to psychologists. Woodworth supported a middle ground between Watson's extreme Behavioristic position and those who were unwavering supporters of the introspective method. In this regard, Woodworth advocated a position he called *dynamic psychology*. In supporting dynamic psychology, Woodworth (1918, pp. 42–43) offered the following observation:

> Behavior we can observe, consciousness we can observe with some difficulty, but the inner dynamics of the mental processes must be inferred rather than observed. Even so, psychology is in no worse case than the other sciences. They all seek to understand what goes on below the surface of things, to form conceptions of the inner workings of things that shall square with the known facts and make possible prediction of what will occur under given conditions. A dynamic psychologist must utilize the observations of consciousness and behavior as indications of the "workings of the mind"; and that, in spite, of formal definitions to the contrary, is what psychologists have been attempting to accomplish since the beginning.

Woodworth's dynamic psychology focussed upon the drives or motives that energize the mental apparatus to produce behavior. The connections between drive and mental mechanism serve to show the "workings of the mind." In conclusion, Woodworth did not object to Watson's call for psychology to use objective research techniques. Instead, Woodworth charged that Watson went too far by robbing psychology of its subject matter (the study of the mind).

Mary Calkins (1863–1930), a former student of James and the only person elected to be president of both the American Psychological Association (1905) and the American Philosophical Association (1918), also disapproved of Behaviorism. Calkins (1921) did acknowledge that it is important to know how individuals react to their environments, a theme found in Behaviorism. However, Calkins rejected Watson's position as too extreme since it does not allow for the study of the mental apparatus. Instead, Calkins advocated "self psychology" which is defined as a complete study of mental processes as they help an individual cope with the environment. Calkins (1921, p. 13) claimed that, *"Self-psychology . . . is behavioristic when it stresses the relation of self to environment."*

Support for Behaviorism

Despite the protests of Woodworth, Calkins, and many others to Watson's views, Behaviorism's influence upon the conduct of scientific research grew stronger. In particular, two important developments from physics and philosophy were incorporated into psychology and aided the Behavioristic cause. These movements were operationism (from physics) and logical positivism (from philosophy).

Operationism

As psychologists in America were debating the direction their science should take, physicists were also concerned about the revolution taking place in their field. With the advent of Einstein's work and speculations about the quantum, physics began to adopt a new paradigm. A Harvard physicist, Percy W. Bridgman, was concerned that experimentation with exotic concepts might prove nettling. Therefore, in his book, *The Logic of Modern Physics,* Bridgman (1928) proposed that researchers should include in their methodologies specifications of the measurement procedures used to quantify concepts. In other words, a concept is to be defined by the methods of measurement. The operational definition insures the continuation of objectivity in physics research. Prominent experimental psychologists soon realized the value of operationism. For example, S. S. Stevens (1939) argued that operational definitions of concepts allow for the accumulation of research that is reproducible. Therefore, the development of psychology would be greatly aided by using concepts that are translated into experimental operations controlling behavior.

Logical Positivism

In 1924, a group of philosophers in Vienna joined forces to promote a new philosophy of science called logical positivism. The leader of the group, Moritz Schlick (1882–1936), came to America in 1931 as a visiting professor at the University of California, Berkeley, and spoke elaborately about the movement. Logical positivism had much in common with operationism. Whereas operationism stressed that concepts had to be defined by methods of measurement, logical positivism argued that theories had to be stated so precisely as to allow for their experimental testing. If a theory is held together by loosely defined concepts, then such a theory has no scientific merit since it could not be scientifically evaluated.

Ironically, the logical positivistic movement originated in Freud's city. Of course, the logical positivists would have frowned on Psychoanalytic theory as a prime example of useless language since its major principles have no measurable referent.

Logical positivism was prominent in the United States from 1930 to 1960 as several proponents of the movement escaped Nazi tyranny and joined American universities. Logical positivism supported the Behavioristic cause by emphasizing the need to be clear and precise in scientific theories. In particular, the development of Clark Hull's (1943) learning theory within Behaviorism was inspired by logical positivism.

Logical positivism also advocated an ambition first enunciated by Leibnitz in 1666, namely to unite all the sciences into one grand field. Leibnitz considered that one day all scientific disputes would be settled by mathematical calculation. Thus Leibnitz saw the unity of all sciences as resulting from the formulation of mathematical principles governing the phenomena of the Universe. Watson, not as ambitious as Leibnitz, nevertheless pointed out that psychology and biology had much in common. In fact, Watson's critics, such as Calkins (1921), accused him of reducing psychology to zoology. In modern times, the hope of uniting all the sciences has been essentially abandoned. Instead, scientists continue to search for unity within their specific fields.

Behaviorism's Impact upon Experimental Psychology

Behaviorism gave to psychology a paradigm that was consistent with the Newtonian view of science. Moreover, experience is the only major determinant of behavior. Given this unbridled commitment to empiricism, it became necessary for the Behaviorists to study learning. Gradually, the Behaviorists came to rely upon experiments with animals, especially rats, to indicate the major principles of learning. Since Darwinism accepts a continuity among living forms, animal experiments should reveal the fundamental principles of learning. Moreover, experimental control over confounding variables is afforded with animals.

The Great Learning Theorists

Behaviorism committed psychology to an objective subject matter, a materialistic view of human nature, and to the study of learning. However, Behaviorism was not monolithic in the area of theory construction. This is demonstrated in the divergent explanations of learning developed by Edward Tolman (1886–1959), Clark Hull (1884–1952), and B. F. Skinner (1904–1990).

Tolman recognized the limitations of Watson's approach for the development of theory. It was necessary for experimental psychology to address the internal states of the organism in order to explain behavior. Factors, such as drives, wants, and even learning, refer to events taking place within the organism. Tolman (1936/1951) represented internal processes by "intervening" variables which were defined as connective links between the environment and the organism's behavior. As a Behaviorist, Tolman maintained that the antecedent conditions must be specified that allow a particular intervening variable to operate. Therefore, intervening variables must be defined in terms of the operations that determine their involvement upon behavior. For example, the operational definition of learning requires a specification of the presumed conditions allowing learning to occur (i.e., number of training trials, delivery of reinforcements following a response, etc.) and the effects of learning upon behavior (increases in the frequency of the response).

Tolman (1932) had sympathies for Gestalt psychology and accepted that the organizing feature of behavior is that it is purposive. However, more traditional Behaviorists, while thanking him for introducing intervening variables, accused him of slipping back into mentalism (Spence, 1944). Concepts, such as purpose, are descriptions of behavior but are useless in explaining it.

Clark Hull (1943) refrained from using mentalistic concepts in developing behavioral theory. Instead, Hull maintained that theories in psychology should be completely objective. He believed that the behavior of a living organism can be fully explained by looking for efficient causes. Hull used several intervening variables in the development of his learning theory, and each one had to be operationally defined in terms of antecedent conditions and consequences upon behavior. Moreover, the intervening variables controlling behavior are solely determined by the antecedent conditions. No internal mental states, operating independently of the environment, were proposed by Hull. The organism is viewed as a passive participant in its behavior since the activity of internal states are solely determined by environmental inputs. Hull's style of theorizing for psychology was meant to emulate as closely as possible the Newtonian approach for physics.

B. F. Skinner (1938, 1950), was the most conservative Behaviorist. Modelling his approach to psychology after the philosophical beliefs of Francis Bacon, Skinner consistently maintained that behavior can be completely predicted on the basis of empirical rules discovered in experimental research. More specifically, the one environmental variable that has the greatest control over behavior is reinforcement, and the Skinnerian dictum, drawn from pragmatic philosophy, is that behavior is governed by its consequences (reinforcement). Skinner demonstrated the value of his approach by discovering the schedules of reinforcement that show how the strength of behavior varies with the empirical rule that governs the delivery of reinforcement (Ferster & Skinner, 1957). Since psychology is new as a science, Skinner concentrated on the discovery of empirical laws of behavior and was disinterested in developing theory.

Friendly Departure from Behaviorism

The hold of Behaviorism upon experimental psychology was to slip noticeably beginning around 1960. Researchers began to recognize that a tactical error had been made in not including the brain in the study of psychology. Therefore, a movement became identified, called psychobiology, which was determined to bring the nervous system back to psychology. However, psychobiology had no essential quarrel with Behaviorism regarding the commitment to the Newtonian view of science. In fact, the creation of psychobiology was welcomed since it allowed the full implementation of methodological Behaviorism by including the nervous system as the principle physiological cause for behavior.

Psychobiology

Watsonian Behaviorism expressed a disinterest in pursing the neural basis of psychology due to a bias that such activity would lead to the speculation about internal mental states (Bergmann, 1956; Spence, 1944). For years, the only major Behaviorist interested in the brain was Karl Lashley (1890–1958). Behaviorism's cavalier attitude regarding the importance of the brain was not shared by others. Ivan Pavlov (1927) developed the technique of classical conditioning to infer how the brain regulates learning. The biological basis of animal behavior was the research interest of American comparative psychologists, such as Robert Yerkes and Frank Beach, and of the European ethologists, such as Nicolaus Tinbergen and Konrad Lorenz. The importance of behavioral genetics was indicated in the early work of Robert Tyron (1929) who selectively bred rats for their ability to learn mazes.

By the 1950s, fascinating research was being reported showing that the understanding of the brain was indispensable for the explanation of behavior. For example, Delgado, Roberts, and Miller (1954) discovered that electrical stimulation of deep brain structures appeared to induce pain reactions that controlled the behavior of rats. Then, Olds and Milner (1954), also using electrical stimulation, found the pleasure system of the brain next to the pain system. The role of the brain in memory function was documented by the sad case of patient H. M., who suffered temporal lobe-hippocampal damage, resulting in a permanent form of anterograde amnesia (Scoville & Milner, 1957). Finally, the neurophysiological correlates of mental disorders were being investigated with the development of psychotropic medications (Craig & Stitzil, 1982).

The formal implementation of psychobiology occurred in 1964 when James McGaugh established the first graduate training program for the discipline at the University of California, Irvine. Subsequently, many other programs have been developed guaranteeing the success of the movement. Psychobiology, in defining its domain of research, has concentrated upon the neural basis of learning, memory, motivation, perception, and cortical pathologies such as Alzheimer's disease (Gormezano, Prokasy, & Thompson, 1987; Lynch, McGaugh, & Weinberger, 1984).

The success of psychobiology has allowed it to develop as an interdisciplinary field incorporating neurobiology, biochemistry, Behaviorism, cognitive psychology, and artificial intelligence. Thus, psychobiology has now become neuroscience and continues to enjoy great success in explaining behavior.

Unfriendly Departure from Behaviorism

Another defection from Behaviorism began in the 1950s. However, unlike the case of psychobiology, the development of cognitive psychology involved a hostile dialogue with Behaviorism. The tension between Behaviorism and cognitive psychology results from a basic philosophical difference regarding mental states. As previously discussed, Behaviorism was committed to the "blank slate" view of the mind embraced within the philosophy of empiricism. In contrast, cognitive psychology is premised upon rationalistic philosophy that requires the mind to be active. The mission of cognitive psychology is to identify the internal principles governing linguistic skill, perception, thinking, and memory. The tension between cognitive psychology and Behaviorism is not really surprising given that the philosophical difference between rationalism and empiricism has provoked enmity since the days of Plato and Aristotle.

Cognitive psychology proclaimed itself to be a revolution for psychology; however, history reveals that research interest in cognitive processes was present before the arrival of Behaviorism and were continued during its era. For example, the early opposition to Wundt's psychology by the Wurzburg and Gestalt psychologists was strongly motivated by the need to study internal mental processes. William James (1890a, b) wanted American Functionalism to focus upon mental states as they contribute to survival. Alfred Binet, at the beginning of the 20th century, became interested in measuring individual differences in mental aptitude that eventually produced intelligence tests and the search for the mental factors responsible for academic success (Anastasi, 1982). Frederick Bartlett (1932) began a program of research showing that the storage of information in human memory involves transformations of meaning from the original text material. Edward Tolman's (1932) Behavioristic approach to learning was filled with cognitive intervening variables. Finally, the penultimate cognitive psychologist was Sigmund Freud in that he explained the normal and abnormal adjustment of the human mind in terms of mental processes operating at both the conscious and unconscious levels.

The modern recurrence of cognitive psychology has produced a change in the formula of methodological behaviorism. The importance of internal mental states must be acknowledged by defining methodological behaviorism to now read: In principle, it should be possible to predict behavior from environmental, physiological, experiential, and *mental* causes. One of the major tasks of cognitive psychology is to devise the means of investigating internal mental processes so that their rules of operation may be known.

Modern Cognitive Psychology

Contemporary cognitive psychology began to be defined in 1955 when a conference was held at St. John's College at Cambridge University. This conference brought together an impressive array of psychologists, neurobiologists, and researchers in the new field of artificial intelligence and computers. The need to implement a theoretical approach to replace Behaviorism was clearly evident at this meeting. Present at this conference was Norbert Weiner whose book *Cybernetics* (1949) explained that machines could act purposefully and intelligently if they were equipped with feedback mechanisms. Also present was Noam Chomsky who later attacked Skinner's Behavioristic analysis of language skills. Chomsky (1959) reasoned that the human brain is predisposed to learn language and uses it to understand symbolically. Moreover, language use in the human is a creative and interpretative effort since there are many ways to express an idea through language. Its use requires internally active cognitive mechanisms whose processes cannot be exclusively programmed by environmental experiences as claimed by Skinner. Finally, George Miller and Jerome Bruner were at Cambridge that fateful year, and they later became the driving forces leading to the establishment of the Center for Cognitive Studies at Harvard University in 1960 (Bruner, 1988).

The theoretical approach for cognitive psychology was dictated in two important publications in the 1960s. George Miller, Eugene Galanter, and Karl Pribram (1960) issued their influential book, *Plans and the Structure of Behavior*. The importance of this work was to illustrate a method by which internal mental states can be studied. The internal workings of the human mind are analogous to the hardware and software of computers. With the advancement of computer technology occurring after World War II, cognitive psychology was afforded a way to simulate mental processes. The second publication was Ulric Neisser's (1967) book, *Cognitive Psychology*. Neisser reviewed the major cognitive research on thinking, memory, perception, and language. This book demonstrated that cognitive psychology is capable of producing rigorous scientific research.

Just as in the case of psychobiology, cognitive psychology became very successful and has evolved into an interdisciplinary approach incorporating mathematicians, computer scientists, neurobiologists, and psycholinguists. Now, the term *Cognitive Science* is often used to represent this diverse collection of interests. The cognitive approach has even been used in the field of learning theory, the traditional home of the Behaviorists. For example, Prokasy (1972) as well as Rescorla and Wagner (1972) began to develop theories of classical conditioning that require the computation on the part of the subject of the probability that the conditioned stimulus signals the occurrence of the unconditioned stimulus.

Unfortunately, modern cognitive psychology and traditional Behaviorism have not engaged in a useful amalgamation of ideas. Cognitive psychology belittles Behaviorism as "conceptually impoverished" (Mandler, 1985, p. 2) while Behaviorism chastises cognitive psychology for being "inimical to science" (Skinner, 1985, p. 300). The history of physics reveals that Einstein's relativity theories incorporated the earlier work of Newton. Thus, Einstein's theories did not deny Newton's but provided a larger context for understanding. Unfortunately, Behaviorism and cognitive psychology have not been able to emulate the history of physics and combine to produce a powerful paradigm for psychology. However, it may not be too late. Neisser (1984) has been advocating that experiential and cognitive factors must be included in any grand schema for explaining behavior.

Psychoanalysis

Perhaps the closest attempt to provide psychology with a grand unified theory has come from the development of Psychoanalysis. Accordingly, Bergmann (1956) gives to Freud the honor of being the greatest psychologist of all time. Freud's brilliance, in part, was due to his ability to synthesize a view of human nature that combined rationalism with empiricism, included the Darwinian emphasis upon adaptation, accepted determinism for human behavior, and leaned toward materialism in solving the mind-body problem. Also, Freud changed the views regarding the etiology of mental disorders. A common belief in the second half of the 19th century was that mental illness only befell those of inferior genetic stock. Freud allowed for the influence of inheritance, but also emphasized that anyone is susceptible to mental illness if subjected to excessive life stress. Mental illness results from the psychic attempt to adapt to mental pain by cognitively and emotionally restructuring reality. Before the historical development of Psychoanalysis is addressed, a brief glimpse of Freud's life is given based upon two excellent biographies (Gay, 1988; Sulloway, 1983).

Freud's Life

Sigmund Freud was born of Jewish parents on May 6, 1856 in Freiberg, Moravia. At the early age of six, he was taken to Vienna which would become his home until the Nazi invasion of Austria. In 1881, Freud received a medical degree from the University of Vienna and wanted to continue doing research with his mentor Ernst Brucke, Austria's leading physiologist. However, in June 1882, Brucke advised

Freud to seek a career in private practice since research assistants were paid low wages with little opportunity for advancement. For the next three years, Freud acquired clinical experience through his association with the Vienna General Hospital and he was given the opportunity to meet the leading scientific minds of Vienna.

When Freud was a boy, his mother kept telling him that he was destined to become great. Consequently, he began to seek his fame as foretold by his mother's intuition. In the Spring of 1884, Freud began to experiment with cocaine as an agent that might improve depression and relieve the symptoms of heroin withdrawal. However, the medical establishment began to criticize the use of cocaine in clinical practice calling it a very dangerous drug. Research on cocaine did not appear to be the route to fame. Also, in 1884, Freud began to collaborate with Josef Breuer who was working with a patient, Anna O. The strange case of Anna O. stimulated Freud's interest in mental disorders that led to a career move.

To gain valuable clinical experience, Freud, in 1885, received a traveling fellowship to study in France with Jean-Martin Charcot, the internationally famous psychiatrist. Only Louis Pasteur enjoyed a higher reputation than Charcot in France. The mental illness that Anna O. suffered was hysteria (now known as conversion disorder) and was of epidemic proportions at this time. Hysteria involved patients showing paralysis and general decompensation following a severe emotional trauma. Charcot demonstrated that the symptoms of hysteria could be removed by hypnosis. While in France, Freud made an important discovery that hysterical paralysis could not be due to neurological damage. Consequently, hysterical paralysis comes from a patient's psychic reactions to the traumatic events of life.

Upon concluding a successful stay in Paris, Freud returned to Vienna and, at the end of 1886, started his private practice. Also, in that year, he married Martha Bernays and their union endured for fifty-three years until Freud's death and produced six children.

In the treatment of hysteria, Freud learned that hypnosis was often ineffective. In 1889, Freud again went to France for advice, this time to Hippolyte Bernheim who verified that hypnosis was an unreliable clinical treatment. Bernheim did convey to Freud information that people hypnotized to a state of amnesia, nevertheless could be prodded to remember while conscious what had transpired under hypnosis. Freud now knew the importance of the unconscious mind and was determined to develop techniques to explore it.

Still searching for a way to attain fame, Freud, in 1895, began his truly ambitious *Project for a Scientific Psychology*. The purpose of the *Project* was to give an explanation of mental processes in terms of brain substrates. In a sense, the *Project* was to upgrade the approach initially started by Gall in phrenology. However, not enough was known about neuroanatomy to make the *Project* feasible. Disgusted, Freud abandoned the *Project* in 1896 after compiling three notebooks. Freud's friend,

Wilhelm Fleiss, had two of the notebooks when Freud decided to give up. Freud destroyed the third notebook and asked Fleiss to get rid of the other two. Fleiss, perhaps sensing Freud's future greatness, kept them. Currently, there is interest in returning to the rationale of the *Project* as a way to show how to merge cognitive science with neuroscience (Pribram & Gill, 1976). Also, Freud's penchant for obliterating his work was a remarkable character feature. In 1885 and 1907, Freud completely did away with his notes and manuscripts so that future biographers, other than Ernest Jones who was picked by Freud, would have difficulty chronicling his life.

With the *Project* gone, Freud devoted his efforts to the full development of Psychoanalytic theory and eventually found the key to success. He eliminated the use of hypnosis in his work and began to develop other techniques such as dream analysis, free-association, and behavioral analysis to explore the unconscious part of the mind. The development of Psychoanalysis as a theory of human personality and a method of psychotherapy occurred in three stages. From 1895 to 1905, Freud explored ideas regarding the role of anxiety and the defense mechanisms in the etiology of mental disorders. From 1905 to 1925, Freud concentrated upon the explanation of personality as involving the forces of the id, ego, and superego with the whole psychic structure motivated by biological energy. From 1925 to 1939, Freud answered his critics and worked also to perfect his theories.

In 1909, Freud, after once declining, accepted an invitation from G. Stanley Hall to come to the United States and be part of the celebration of Clark University's twentieth anniversary. In September, 1909, Freud, accompanied by his most famous supporter, Carl Gustav Jung (1875–1961), came to Clark University. He was given his only honorary degree and then delivered in the presence of a distinguished American audience, that included William James and Edward Bradford Titchener, five lectures that were subsequently published as the *Origin and Development of Psychoanalysis* (1910). Freud's own estimation was that his American visit was the turning point for the acceptance of Psychoanalysis.

In 1923, Freud, an avid cigar smoker, was diagnosed as having cancer of the mouth. In the next sixteen years, he received thirty-one operations to contain the cancer. As his face continued to show the ravages of the disease, he became reclusive. Yet, he continued to work diligently, saw five patients daily for psychotherapy, and continued to smoke cigars.

The final chapter of Freud's life opened on March 12, 1938, the day of the Nazi invasion of Austria. The Jews in Austria, already under attack before the arrival of the Nazis, were at great risk. Anna Freud began to wonder whether it would be better for the whole family to commit suicide before the Nazis killed them. However, Freud's international reputation helped to dissuade the Nazis from personally harming him. Freud's many admirers outside Austria began a campaign to get him out of danger.

Even the President of the United States, Franklin Roosevelt, was kept informed of Freud's situation. Eventually, international pressure and the payment of a ransom persuaded the Nazis to let Freud and his family go. On June 4, 1938, Freud left Vienna for political asylum in England. As in the case of Einstein a few years earlier, the Nazis were determined to rid the German culture of "Jewish science." During the last year of his life, Freud was accorded great respect. On June 28, 1938, Freud was made a member of the Royal Society of Science. Since Freud was too weak to travel, the Royal Society abridged its rules and brought to him the registration book to sign. He added his signature to the grand list that included Newton's and Darwin's. However, the ravages of old age and the persistent cancer continued. In great pain and dying, Freud reminded his physician of their pact regarding euthanasia. On September 21, 1939, Freud was given large doses of morphine. He slumped into sleep and then a coma. On September 23, 1939, Freud emulating the last days of Socrates with Stoic majesty died.

Psychoanalytic Theory

It is impossible to detail the scope of Psychoanalytic theory in this work. What can be done is to connect some of Freud's ideas to the great themes developed within the history of psychology. The following review should indicate that Psychoanalysis is really a synthesis of several major themes. In a true sense, Psychoanalysis as a paradigm of psychology has come the closest in fulfilling the expanded definition of methodological behaviorism.

The commitment to the materialistic position is seen in Freud's acceptance of Darwinian theory. Freud believed that humans are a product of biological evolution. Although he developed many constructs to indicate the operations of internal mental processes, Freud was clearly a materialist viewing the mind to be ultimately reducible to brain activity as presented in his *Project.* Freud allowed for the incorporation of rationalism by claiming that the id is a mental structure that is inherited. Humans come into the world with a set of emotions and needs already determined by evolution. The mental structure of the id represents the nativistic aspects of human nature and is programmed to seek pleasure and avoid pain. The great needs of the id are self-preservation and aggression and all human motivation is ultimately tied to the operation of these needs.

The individual cannot remain id and hope to survive. Experience allows part of the id to become the ego with the responsibility of satisfying the demands of the id. The ego obeys the reality principle in that it must seek objects to satisfy the id without jeopardizing the self. The major experiences determining ego formation and function are derived from child-parent interactions. Finally, the superego develops and represents an internalization of parental ethical values (Freud, 1964a). As Freud noted, the ego has to serve three cruel masters, the environment, the id, and the superego. Ego strength determines the success of the individual in coping with stress and maintaining mental stability. Inspired by Darwinism, Freud characterized the human as under constant pressure to adapt to changing conditions of life that cause stress. The developmental history of the individual often predicts the degree of success in adapting. However, if the ego is exhausted and cannot find an adaptive solution to stress, pathological ones will be tried. Neuroses, or anxiety disorders, result when the ego cannot find objects to satisfy the demands of the id. Psychosis occurs when the ego creates a false reality (splitting from reality) in order to contain the intolerable demands from the id.

The inner workings of the mind in the struggle for psychological adaptation are revealed by the dream process. In his famous work, *The Interpretation of Dreams,* Freud (1900/1938) developed the famous theory that dreams are depictions in disguised form of the individual's subjective status. Dreams reveal the concerns of the individual and often portray both rational and irrational solutions to dilemmas. Dreams act to fulfill wishes and dream content reflects the capacity of the mind to operate at the unconscious level.

In tracing down the origin of a particular mental disorder, Freud, following a pattern reminiscent of Aristotle's theory of causality, said that four factors must be specified (Sulloway, 1983). First, there are *preconditions* which refer to any inherited tendencies or constitutional weaknesses. Secondly, a mental disorder has a *specific* cause that serves to initiate the psychopathological process (i.e., childhood sexual abuse). Third, *concurrent* causes that refer to factors in the individual's immediate life which weaken ego function must be known (i.e., worry about finances, fatigue, sickness). Lastly, a mental disorder has a *releasing* cause that initiates the immediate appearance of the psychopathology. For example, in the case of Anna O., the precipitating cause for her hysteria was the death of her father.

Freud (1964b) was well aware of the criticism of his theory as lacking scientific rigor. However, he claimed to be a very careful investigator who used the case studies of his patients and other information from psychotherapy to derive, test, and modify his theories. He considered himself to be much in the same position as astronomers who cannot directly manipulate what they study. Instead, careful observation and application of valid scientific principles should allow for the success of astronomy and, in Freud's assessment, Psychoanalysis also.

Neo-Freudian Developments

Freud's theory has continued to develop through the efforts of European and American contributors. In England, a movement was initiated called Object Relations Theory that specifies the type of interactions between infants and their caregivers producing healthy and pathological personalities. Two branches of the Object Relations School emerged in England, one headed by Melanie Klein and the other by Anna Freud. Since Anna Freud was designated by her father as the guardian of Psychoanalysis, it was not surprising that the dialogue between the Kleinians and the Freudians was not always conciliatory.

More recently, another neo-Freudian movement has emerged which is called Self Psychology by its founder Heinz Kohut (1913–1981). Kohut has integrated Object Relations Theory with the humanistic views of Carl Rogers (1902–1987). Self psychology advocates that children try to adapt to the environments created for them by their parents. A child develops a kind view of the world if the parents are empathic about meeting its needs. However, a child has a hostile view of the world if the parents repeatedly disregard its needs. Without proper parental care, a child suffers an arrest of personality development that eventually is manifested in adulthood as a psychopathology. The child stores in memory the experiences with the parents and uses such memories as the means for coping with stress in later life. The developmental arrest of the personality results in the adult acting like a child in trying to cope with life stress (Baker & Baker, 1987).

Status of Psychology at the end of the Twentieth Century

Our work in this chapter has shown that psychology has been successful in establishing its scientific credentials. However, when compared to physics, psychology reveals a fundamental problem. Unlike physics, psychology has no dominant paradigm. Without the paradigm, the various specialties within psychology are not joined together by an articulate theory. Will psychology ever have a paradigm? Exploration of this issue is the focus of the next chapter.

The Search for Psychology's Scientific Paradigm

7

When the historical developments of physics and psychology are compared, a very noticeable difference emerges. Physics has been immensely successful in developing paradigms. In contrast, psychology has had great difficult generating a single paradigm acceptable to all members of its scientific community. Several (Kuhn, 1973; Popper & Eccles, 1977) have speculated why the two fields enjoy differential theoretical success. One reason for the lack of progress in psychology may stem from the incorrect view of reality. All past paradigms of psychology, such as Behaviorism, have been predicated on a world view supplied by classical physics. As we have explored, this perspective worked well for physics until research began exploring quantum effects within the atom. Physics adjusted its paradigm to include quantum phenomena. Accordingly, principles contained in quantum physics may be useful in outlining a paradigm for psychology.

Messages from Quantum Physics

The portrait of reality depicted by quantum physics is incredible in that it defies the classic view of the World machine advocated by Newton and Comte. Basically, Newton and Comte treated the Universe as being composed of isolated objects that only interacted when there were energy exchanges. Thus, Newton and Comte were committed to a strong determinism based upon the use of efficient causes to explain physical events. The quantum perspective of the World is much different. As we revealed in Chapter 4, quantum physics regards existence as energy. Breaking down the atom into more elementary states, such as quarks and leptons, leaves only energy and not mass. Secondly, determinism appears to break down in explaining the workings of the atom. In place of determinism, quantum physics has embraced an acausal approach that still allows for lawfulness in nature. The need for acausal explanations is reinforced by the experimental tests of Bell's theorem indicating that particles that once interacted inside the atom continue to have mutual influences upon one another after the particles have left the atom (i.e., action at a distance). Lastly, nature is not defined until it is measured. This startling realization is dramatized by the experiments on the nature of light. Light has wave and particle properties. No experiment has been able to capture simultaneously the dual nature of light. Instead, light behaves as a particle or a wave in accordance with the measuring procedures of the experimenter.

All of the claims of quantum physics are difficult to understand. However, one psychologist realized the significance of quantum physics and tried to give real-life examples of quantum principles. Specifically, Carl Jung illuminated the meaning of acausal connections operating in human existence by developing the ancient Chinese principle of synchronicity.

Jung and Synchronicity

As all psychology students know, Jung, early in his career, was Freud's close colleague. However, the two parted company after a bitter exchange of letters. Ostensibly, the split between Freud and Jung was over theoretical issues in Psycho- analysis. However, at a metatheoretical level, Freud and Jung had very different views of reality. Freud, captured by materialism and determinism, tried to explain the human personality in terms of experiential and biological causes. On the other hand, Jung, familiar with the new quantum physics, saw the human personality as constantly evolving to a state of stable unity called individuation. Most strikingly, the course of individuation is influenced by events that operate acausally.

Synchronicity

Jung (1973, p. 10) defined synchronicity as the meaningful coincidence of events. By the term *meaningful,* Jung held that synchronicity contributes to the individuation process. In other words, synchronicity is relevant to the evolution of the self, the most important aspect of personality. By the term coincidence, Jung meant that synchronicity is acausal because the events in question have no physical connec- tion. Usually what is connected in synchronicity is an inner state of mind to an outer state or event. Synchronicity's inner states can involve dreams, consciousness, intui- tions, and archetypes drawn from the unconscious. Synchronicity's outer states refer to occurrences in the physical world.

The following true story illustrates the principle of synchronicity. A few years ago, a friend began dating a lovely woman. Both had been married before, so they were very cautious in approaching romance. After dating for three weeks, both came to the conclusion that a decision whether to continue or terminate the relationship had to be made. At that point in time, the man involved, named John, had to take a business trip to Japan. To pass the hours on the long plane ride to the orient, John began to do a crossword puzzle. As John proceeded through the puzzle, he came to a three letter word defined as a "climbing plant." John thought for a while and came up with the answer IVY. A few items later, John came to another three letter word that answered the query, "name of the actor Jack on the TV show *Barney Miller.*" John checked his memory and came up with the name SOO. At that moment, John was incredulous because the name of his new love interest was IVY SOO! John took this as a favorable sign and upon returning from Japan began a serious relationship with Ivy that culminated in marriage.

The above story is a classic illustration of synchronicity. There is no causal connection between John's thought processes completing the crossword puzzle (inner state) and his acquaintance with Ivy (outer state). Yet, somehow the two events were brought together at a critical moment. Jung would probably add that the archetype active in John's unconscious mind is that of lover. This synchronicity led to a fulfillment of John's life or as Jung would say, the development of the self through individuation. Of course, the ego, which represents the rational conscious mind, cannot understand any of this. That is why Jung concluded that "the experience of the self is always a defeat for the ego" (Jung, 1974, p. 546).

Synchronicities are quite commonplace and occur to everyone. From Jung's perspective, it is unfortunate that many people do not realize the significance of the meaningful coincidence since synchronicities carry information about the unfolding of one's life.

Unity of Mind and Matter

The reality of synchronicity has substantial meaning for any development of a successful paradigm for psychology. Physicist Victor Mansfield (1997), after reviewing instances of the transforming power of synchronicity, concluded that the inner state of mind and the outer state of the World are connected. This realization is inconsistent with Newton's view that the external world runs independently of the human mind. Also, the question of interconnectedness of the inner and outer worlds revives the dilemma of Cartesian dualism. Somehow the realms of mind and matter communicate. As we have reviewed in Chapter 5, Spinoza resolved Descartes's dilemma by postulating the one substance theory in which mind and matter are aspects of a single underlying reality. Leibnitz's solution to Descartes's problem was to propose the existence of the monad whose mental structure contained a mirror image of the physical world. The harmony of the inner and outer worlds was realized in the perceptions taking place in the monad. Spinoza's and Leibnitz's views are helpful in suggesting that the paradigm for scientific psychology must indicate how the inner and outer worlds of experience are joined.

Interconnectedness

Quantum physics stands on the premise that all entities in the Universe are connected. This assumption allows for action at a distance phenomena. Briefly stated, action at a distance indicates that objects continue to exercise mutual influence independent of their location in space or time. In physics, actual tests of the Einstein-Podolsky-Rosen (EPR) hypothetical experiment, reviewed in Chapter 4, show that subatomic entities continue to influence each other despite being separated in time and space.

Regarding psychological experience, action at a distance phenomena are also known to occur. One of the best examples of this phenomena in psychology is the experience in which a person has an intuition that something terrible has happened to a loved one. Somehow, the two people are in contact despite their separation in space and time.

Action at a distance phenomena are not well regarded by mainstream psychologists committed to the Newtonian view of reality. Only in the suspicious area of parapsychology, also known as psi, is there serious study of the subject matter. However, with the improvement in experimental techniques, parapsychologists have been able to make a forceful case for the existence of informational transfer between a human observer and outerworld events.

The Ganzfield Procedure

Daryl Bem and Charles Honorton (1994) have co-authored the first review of parapsychology to appear in a major journal of scientific psychology. Their article in the *Psychological Bulletin* reported evidence for psi based upon data using the ganzfield procedure.

The word *ganzfield* means "total field" and the *ganzfield* procedure was initially developed to test principles of Gestalt psychology. However, the procedure was adapted in the 1960s to the study of psi phenomena. Basically, in the psi *ganzfield* experiment, two subjects are used; one is called the "sender" and the other is the "receiver." The sender first undergoes relaxation before studying material. The intention of the sender is to communicate the information in the material to the receiver. In turn, the receiver is located in another room with no obvious connection to the sender. At the conclusion of the communication period, lasting as long as 30 minutes, the receiver is given four stimuli and asked to select the one studied by the sender. In more recent experiments, items for viewing by the sender, such as video tapes, are randomly selected by a computer. Another computer will then present the four alternatives to the receiver. As reviewed by Bem and Honorton (1994), the results from several ganzfield experiments indicate that untrained subjects in psi have a hit rate of 35% in selecting the correct target with chance performance being at 25%. With well-practiced subjects, the hit rate can climb to 50%. The interpretation given to the *ganzfield* effects is that psi involves a weak informational exchange between two human beings. Since the signal is not prominent, most people in daily life would overlook such informational inputs since consciousness is constantly bombarded with sensory information. Nevertheless, if psi is accepted as a real phenomenon, the quantum principle of interconnectedness of entities separated in space and time is realized in the macro World.

General System Theory

The relevance of acausal explanations and the interconnectedness of all existent things has been recognized in the field of biology through the pioneering work of Ludwig von Bertalanffy (1968). His approach, called general system theory, has many interesting features, consistent with quantum physics, that may guide the development of a promising paradigm for the science of psychology. Since biology is conceptually closer to psychology than is quantum physics, the relevance of general system theory becomes more apparent. Von Bertalanffy's intention was to create a theoretical approach that is applicable to the understanding of the relationship among all forms of existence by defining principles common to all systems.

System Principles

Von Bertalanffy's major contribution was to provide a framework for integrating seemingly unrelated phenomena into a cohesive pattern. He was convinced that a system could not be understood by looking at its parts in isolation. The component parts are less important than the transactional process taking place between the parts. Thus, **interactions** or interconnectedness between the parts determine the activity of the whole system. A system is defined as a collection of objects and the interactions among them. Systems are organized to act in lawful ways. Moreover, the interactions within the system are governed by acausal principles. For example, in reductionistic thinking, **A** may be claimed as the cause of **B**. However, in general system theory, **A** may have an influence upon **B** which then returns influence back to **A**. Thus, causality in general system theory is not linear but circular. Nevertheless, the acausal patterns produce orderly outcomes.

Another important concept in general system theory is *hierarchy*. The movement of evolution is certainly in the direction of complexity. For example, the systems that compose the planet Earth may be arranged in the following sequence:

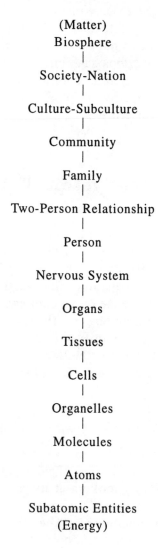

(Matter)
Biosphere
|
Society-Nation
|
Culture-Subculture
|
Community
|
Family
|
Two-Person Relationship
|
Person
|
Nervous System
|
Organs
|
Tissues
|
Cells
|
Organelles
|
Molecules
|
Atoms
|
Subatomic Entities
(Energy)

At each level, there is a system; but, in addition, the vertical connections between the systems represent the interconnectedness of everything (Goldenberg & Goldenberg, 1991).

Application to Psychology

General system theory has found a refuge in psychology in an area called family therapy (Glick, Clarkin, & Kessler, 1987). The aim of this approach is to understand the individual as a product of a system known as the family. In other words, to comprehend the meaning of an individual's behavior, an observer must know the interactions that operate to organize the family.

Family as a System

A family is a self-regulating system since it is able to maintain order while changes occur. Families try to remain constant even though individuals within it are continually changing. If family stability is threatened, family members will attempt to restore equilibrium so as to insure stability (Jackson, 1969).

The functioning of the individual cannot be understood until the dynamics of the family of origin are understood. In addition, individuals bring into marriage a background of family relationships that influence the interactions between the spouses. Murray Bowen (Papero, 1990), a major family therapist, maintained that spouses develop a comfortable level of emotional distance. In addition, each marriage has a certain level of conflict. According to Bowen, greater levels of conflict denote higher levels of tension within the family. Bowen also noted that children within the family must be influenced by the level of family tension. For example, a mother's emotional response to a child is dictated by the quality of the relationship with her husband. Finally, Bowen concluded that all aspects of family life are influenced by the degree of spousal dysfunction. Bowen's principles serve to indicate that interconnected factors operate to shape the personality of the individual.

Psychology as a Science of Wholeness

Newton's and Comte's World view requires a commitment to objectivitism, positivism, and reductionism (Harman, 1994a). An objective world is one that is separated from the individual observer and is studied through detached and careful observation. Positivism allows the physical world to be measured. Reductionism means that any system is understood by studying the causal connections among parts that compose the system. Thus, reductionism is based upon determinism. Certainly, objectivism, positivism, and reductionism have worked well in science to produce an understanding of the macro-world of matter. However, in psychology, these assumptions have failed to produce a viable paradigm.

Physicists such Bohr, Bohm, and Mansfield have abandoned the World view of Newton and Comte. In place of objectivism, physics realizes that the observer and the observed are somehow tied together. This is illustrated by the nature of light. Simply put, light behaves as a wave or a particle dependent upon how the observer wishes to measure it. In place of positivism, physics acknowledges Einstein's theory of relativity that makes space and time obey the parameters of the observer. In place of reductionism, physics proposes the interconnectedness of events on the sub-atomic level, as illustrated by Bell's theorem.

It is to their credit that the German Gestalt psychologists (Kohler, Koffka, and Wertheimer) emphasized the study of whole processes. However, the Gestalt message was not heeded and psychology toiled throughout the twentieth century without a functional paradigm. Now, a greater number of voices can be heard advocating a reformulation of the paradigm, not only for psychology, but for all of science. As it applies to psychology, the new paradigm is based upon a holistic approach incorporating interconnectedness and acausality.

Characteristics of the New Paradigm

Harman (1994b) has provided insights as to the nature of an inclusive paradigm suitable for psychology based upon a holistic approach. This approach begins with the premise that all phenomena are connected together and dismisses reductionism. According to Harman (1994b, p. 377):

> Thus, a "wholeness science" would seek understanding, rather than singular, exclusive "causes." Its aim would be illumination more than the ability to

predict and control. It would contain most of present science, but in an expanded context. It would not foster the temptation to assume that consciousness is nothing but brain function, or to insist that the course of evolution can be explained by mutations and natural selection, or to extrapolate physics from the laboratory back to a completely mechanistic "Big Bang" origin of the physical universe.

In addition, the new paradigm stresses that there are two ways to "know." The first way of knowing is based upon empiricism. The readings taken by the senses have provided the data for traditional science. However, the second way of knowing is through intuition or "inner knowing" (Harman, 1994b, p. 377). Sometimes, inner knowing comes through synchronicities; other times through imagination and creativity. Thus, one can be both tough- and tender-minded as William James noted. Finally, a new paradigm of psychology must allow for acausality. Action at a distance phenomena occur in physics and they occur in psychology. In summary, a new paradigm for psychology acknowledges the interconnectedness of everything, empirical and rational ways of knowing, and acausality.

The new paradigm does not invalidate past scientific progress. Harman's conclusions are most appropriate (1994b, p. 390):

> To re-emphasize the point, none of present science is invalidated in the limited domains where it was generated. However, some of the common extrapolations of scientific findings into the area of human affairs become questionable. For example, the fact that genetic characteristics are involved in behavior should not be extrapolated to conclude that the complete explanation for behavior is ultimately to be found at the molecular level. The fact that random mutation and natural selection are clearly factors in evolution should not be extrapolated to conclude that they are sufficient to account for the forms and diversity of organisms actually found. It is even in doubt whether we are justified in extrapolating the scientific laws we observe today back to the time of a hypothetical "Big Bang."

Implications of the New Paradigm

The new paradigm acknowledges William James's doctrine of radical empiricism (reviewed in Chapter 6). According to this doctrine, scientific psychology should be allowed to study whatever occurs within the context of human experience. The task of scientific psychology is then to determine the nature of the experience. In the new paradigm, psychology is permitted to study such behaviors as sychronicities, paranormal events, and religious events such as "miracles." Thus, the entire spectrum of the human experience, including consciousness, is now open to investigation (Harman, 1994b).

The new paradigm carries a special meaning for humanity. If interconnectedness is accepted as a cardinal principle, then the condition of each human being affects the status of everyone. All the joys and sorrows are shared experiences. Sometimes, business is viewed as an enterprise that is exploiting. However, there are examples of enlightened captains of industry who realized the interconnectedness of humanity. For example, Konosuke Matsushita founded his Japanese manufacturing company in 1917 with an investment of 100 yen. The company eventually grew into a multinational economic giant with a highly recognized brand name—*Panasonic*. Some of Matsushita's guiding principles were: treat people you do business with as if they were family members; sell customers products that will benefit them; and the goal of the manufacturer is to conquer poverty and rid society of misery by producing shared capital (Kotter, 1997).

The Problem of Consciousness

Consciousness has been a troublesome issue for the traditional paradigms of psychology. William James was an advocate for its study; however, with the advent of Behaviorism and its successor paradigms, the study of consciousness was banned from scientific psychology. Psychology's reluctance to study this quintessential process has not deterred others from the pursuit. Since 1990, neuroscientists, physicists, artificial intelligence experts, and philosophers have all concentrated on the task of defining consciousness. Horgan (1996, pp. 159–190) has provided a detailed summary of this work given below.

Approaches from Materialism

As to be expected, the reductionistic heritage embedded in science has led to attempts to explain consciousness as the product of neural activity. A leader in this direction is Francis Crick, who, along with James Watson, gained international fame in 1953 by working out the molecular structure of DNA. Since 1990, Crick and his colleagues have taken a biological approach to the study of consciousness. Crick's basic premise is that consciousness is the result of two interacting neural systems, attention and short-term memory. Once the neural activity responsible for these processes are understood, then consciousness will be explained.

Computer Simulation

The androids depicted in science fiction films suggest that, one day, machines will be built that can simulate all human mental processes including consciousness. The field of Artificial Intelligence (AI) concentrates upon building machines that can duplicate the functions of the human mind. A prominent developer of AI is Marvin Minsky who believes that the human mind is really an organic device that can be mimicked by a silicon computer. Just as a computer is an assemblage of different components performing unique functions, so too is the human mind. The interaction of mental processes is the cardinal principle organizing the mind. From Minsky's perspective, the complex computer, loaded with interacting devices that simulate the human mind, is the best chance we have to demonstrate the nature of consciousness without ever really explaining it.

Anti-Reductionistic Approaches

The dualistic philosophy of Descartes has been revived in an attempt to explain consciousness. Karl Popper, the philosopher, and John Eccles, the neuroscientist, eschew the possibility that consciousness will ever be reduced to neural activity. Instead, consciousness is an event that has a correlational, but not causal, connection to brain activity. Popper and Eccles (1977) are also advocates of free will. It is free will that ultimately drives the machinery of the human brain.

In place of an extreme commitment to dualism, the physicist Roger Penrose has offered a treatment of consciousness that relies on principles from quantum mechanics. In the quantum world, one subatomic entity can affect another entity instantaneously and without a physical connection. Penrose hypothesizes that consciousness is the product of quantum effects taking place within the neurons. He has even suggested the location of the critical quantum activity. Neurons contain microtubules which are thin shafts of protein that are embedded within the cell walls. Quantum activity along the microtubules may generate consciousness. Penrose draws support for this claim from the work of Stuart Hameroff, an anesthesiologist, who discovered that electrical activity within microtubules decreases as an individual loses consciousness.

Philosophy Strikes Back

Contemporary philosophers have commented on the scientific quest to understand consciousness. For example, Thomas Nagel offered that consciousness is a process that is found in humans and other higher animals. Therefore, an understanding of higher life forms requires a way to penetrate consciousness. Nagel expressed this sentiment in the following way. Science may be able to understand biological systems; however, science will never know what it is like to be a bat until one shares the consciousness of a bat. Another philosopher, Colin McGinn, echoes the views of Kant by holding that the human mind is limited in its ability to understand complex issues. The question of consciousness may be one of those problems that is beyond the human mind to provide a comprehensive answer. However, another philosopher, David Chalmers, holds out hope that science combined with philosophy will eventually solve the consciousness problem. Chalmers argues that science must adopt a new organizing principle, called information, in order to understand mental and physical reality. Information is as important an organizing principle as are the concepts of time and space. The importance of information as an interconnecting principle was stressed by David Bohm in his explanation of action at a distance effects in quantum physics (reviewed in chapter 4).

Hope for the Future

As the above treatment indicates, consciousness is a topic still shrouded in mystery. However, with the emergence of a new paradigm in psychology based upon wholeness, interconnectedness, and acausality, the study of consciousness is a highly feasible enterprise.

Conclusions

The understanding of what is real is still a work in progress. In fact, in the field of psychology, the search for a viable paradigm keeps the field vibrant. We will always continue to need inquisitive minds open to new possibilities. But what propels the mind to engage in the hard work of knowing? The following quote from Albert Einstein (taken from Demartini, 1997, p. 211) may provide the answer:

The most beautiful and most profound emotion we can experience is the sensation of the mystical. It is the dower of all true science. . . . to whom this emotion is a stranger, who can no longer wonder and stand rapt in awe, is as good as dead. To know that what is impenetrable to us really exists, manifesting itself as the highest wisdom and the most radiant beauty which our dull faculties can comprehend only in their most primitive forms—this knowledge, this feeling, is at the center of true religiousness.

Bibliography

Ackerknecht, E. W. (1956). *Franz Joseph Gall: Inventor of phrenology and his collection.* Madison, WI: University of Wisconsin Medical School.

Albert, D. V. (1994). Bohm's alternative to quantum mechanics. *Scientific American,* May, 58–67.

Anastasi, A. (1982). *Psychological testing* (Fifth Edition). New York: Macmillan Publishing Company.

Andrade, E. N. de A. (1954). *Sir Isaac Newton.* London: Collins.

Angell, J. R. (1907). The province of functional psychology. *Psychological Review,* 14, 61–91.

Armitage, A. (1957). *Copernicus: Founder of modern astronomy.* New York; A. S. Barnes and Company.

Baker, H. S. & Baker, M. N. (1987). Heinz Kohut's self psychology: An overview. *American Journal of Psychiatry,* 144, 1–9.

Baldwin, B. T. (1921). In memory of Wilhelm Wundt. *Psychological Review,* 28, 153–188.

Barthell, E. E. Jr. (1971). *Gods and goddesses of ancient Greece.* Coral Gables, FL: University of Miami Press.

Bartlett, F. C. (1932). *Remembering: A study in experimental and social psychology.* Cambridge University Press.

Bem, D. J., & Honorton (1994). Does psi exist? Replicable evidence for an anomalous process of information transfer. *Psychological Bulletin,* 115, 4–18.

Benjamin, Jr., L. T., Durkin, M., Lomk, M., Vestal, M., Accord, J. (1992). Wundt's American doctoral students. *American Psychologist,* 47, 123–131.

Bergmann, G. (1956). The contribution of John B. Watson. *Psychological Review,* 63, 265–276.

Bernal, J. D. (1972). *The extension of man.* Cambridge, MA: The M.I.T. Press.

Bethe, H. A., Gottfried, K, Sagdeev, R. Z. (1995). Did Bohr share nuclear secrets? *Scientific American,* May, 85–90.

Boakes, R. (1983). *From Darwinism to behaviorism.* Cambridge: Cambridge University Press.

Bohm, D. (1980). *Wholeness and the implicate order.* London: Routledge & Kegan.

Boring, E. G. (1950). A *history of experimental psychology.* New York: Appleton-Century-Crofts.

Boslough J. (1985). *Stephen Hawking's universe.* New York: Quill/William Morrow.

Bridgman, P. W. (1928). *The logic of modern physics.* New York: Macmillan.

Bronowski, J. (1973). *The ascent of man.* Boston: Little, Brown & Company.

Bruner, J. (1988). Founding of the center for cognitive studies. In W. Hurst (Ed.), *The making of cognitive science: Essays in honor of George A. Miller.* Cambridge: Cambridge University Press.

Burtt, E. A. (1952). *The metaphysical foundations of modern science.* New York: Humanities Press.

Bury, J. B. (1913). *A history of Greece.* London: Macmillan and Co., Limited.

Butterfield, H. (1957). *The origins of modern science.* New York: The Free Press.

Cadden, J. (1995). Science and rhetoric in the middle ages: The natural philosophy of William of Conches. *Journal of the History of Ideas, 56,* 1–24.

Calkins, M. W. (1921). The truly psychological behaviorism. *The Psychological Review, 28,* 1–18.

Cann, R. L. (1987). In search of Eve. *The Sciences,* September/October, 30–37.

Caudill, E. (1994). The Bishop-Eaters: The publicity campaign for Darwin. *Journal of the History of Ideas, 55,* 441–460.

Chomsky, N. (1959). Review of B. F. Skinner's verbal behavior. *Language, 35,* 26–58.

Clagett, M. (1955). *Greek science in antiquity.* Freeport, NY: Books for Library Press.

Cohen, D. (1979). *J. B. Watson: The founder of behaviorism.* London: Routledge & Kegan Paul Ltd.

Cohen, N. (1988). *Gravity's lens: Views of the new cosmology.* New York: John Wiley & Sons.

Copleston, S. J., F. (1985a). A *history of philosophy—Book One.* Garden City, NY: Image Books.

Copleston, S. J., F. (1985b). A *history of philosophy—Book Two.* Garden City, NY: Image Books.

Craig, C. R., & Stitzel, R. E. (1982). *Modern pharmacology.* Boston: Little, Brown and Company.

Crowther, J. G. (1960). *Founders of British science.* Westport CT: Greenwood Press, Publishers.

Darwin, C. (1859/1963). *The origin of species.* New York: Washington Square Press.

Darwin, C. (1872). *The expression of emotions in man and animals.* London: Murray.

Davies, J. D. (1955). *Phrenology: Fad and science.* New Haven: Yale University Press.

Davies, P. (1983). *God and the new physics.* New York: Simon & Schuster.

Davies, P. C. W., & Brown, J. R. (1986). *The ghost in the atom.* Cambridge: Cambridge University Press.

De Beer, G. (1971). Charles Robert Darwin. In C. C. Gillispie (Ed.), *Dictionary of scientific biography.* New York: Charles Scribner's Sons.

Delgado, J. M. R., Roberts, W. W., & Miller, N. E. (1954). Learning motivated by electrical stimulation of the brain. *American Journal of Physiology,* 179, 587–593.

Demartini, J. F. (1997). *Count your blessings.* Rockport, MA: Element Books.

Devlin, K. *(1994). Mathematics: The science of patterns.* New York: Scientific American Library.

De Santillana, G. (1955). *The crime of Galileo.* Chicago: University of Chicago Press.

Dressler, A. (1987). The large scale streaming of galaxies. *Scientific American,* 257, 46–54.

Durant, W. (1938). *The story of philosophy.* New York: Garden City Publishing Co.

Ebbinghaus, H. (1885/1964). *Memory: A contribution to experimental psychology* (H.A. Ruger and C. E. Bussenius, Trans). New York: Dover.

Erdman, I. (1956). *The works of Plato.* New York: The Modern Library.

Erwin, D. E. (1996). The mother of mass extinctions. *Scientific American,* July, 72–78.

Ferster, C. S. & Skinner, B. F. (1957). *Schedules of reinforcement.* New York: Appleton-Century-Crofts.

Feynman, R. P. (1985). *QED: The strange theory of light and matter.* Princeton, New Jersey: Princeton University Press.

Forward, R. L., & Davies, J. (1988). *Mirror matter: Pioneering antimatter physics. New* York: John Wiley & Sons.

Freedman, W. (1992). The expansion rate and size of the Universe. *Scientific American,* November, 54–60.

Freud, S. (1900/1938). The interpretation of dreams. In A. A. Brill (Ed.), *The basic writings of Sigmund Freud.* New York: The Modern Library.

Freud, S. (1910). The origin and development of psychoanalysis. *American Journal of Psychology,* 21.

Freud, S. (1964a). *The standard edition of the complete psychological works of Sigmund Freud. Vol. XIX. The ego and the id and other works.* London: Hogarth Press.

Freud, S. (1964b). *The standard edition of the complete psychological works of Sigmund Freud. Vol. XXII. New introductory lectures on psychoanalysis.* London: Hogarth Press.

Freud, S. (1966). *The standard edition of the complete psychological works of Sigmund Freud. Vol. I. Prepsychoanalytic publications and unpublished drafts.* London: Hogarth Press.

Frost, Jr., S. E. (1942). *Basic teachings of the great philosophers.* New York: Barnes & Noble.

Gammow, G. (1961). *Biography of physics.* New York: Harper & Row.

Gay, P. (1988). *Freud, A life for our times.* New York: W. W. Norton & Company.

Geanakoplos, D. J. (1979). *Medieval western civilization and the Byzantine and Islamic worlds.* Lexington, MA: D. C. Heath and Company.

Glick, I., Clarkin, J., & Kessler, D. (1987). *Marital and family therapy* (third edition). Orlando: Grune & Stratton.

Goldenberg, I. & Goldenberg, H. (1991). *Family therapy: An overview.* Pacific Groves, CA: Brook/Cole.

Gormezano, I., Prokasy, W. F., & Thompson, R. F. (Eds.) (1987). *Classical conditioning* (3rd edition). Hillsdale, NJ: Lawrence Eribaum Associates.

Grant, E. (1971). *Physical science in the middle ages.* New York: John Wiley and Sons.

Gribben, J. (1984). *In search of Schrodinger's cat: Quantum physics and cosmology.* New York: Bantam Books.

Gribben, J. (1986). *In search of the Big Bang: Quantum physics and cosmology.* New York: Bantam Books.

Gribbin, J. (1995). *Schrodinger's kittens and the search for reality: Solving the quantum mysteries.* Boston: Little, Brown and Company.

Griffiths, B. (1994). *Universal wisdom: A journey through the sacred wisdom of the world.* San Francisco: HarperCollins.

Gruber, H. E., & Barrett, P. H. (1974). *Darwin on man.* New York: E. P. Dutton & Co.

Hackforth, R. (1952). *Plato's Phaedrus.* Indianapolis: The Bobbs-Merrill Company.

Hamilton, Edith (1940). *Mythology.* Little, Brown & Company.

Hansen, B. (1978). Science and magic. In D. C. Lindberg (Ed.), *Science in the middle ages.* Chicago: University of Chicago Press.

Harman, W. (1994a). A re-examination of the metaphysical foundations of modern science: Why is it necessary? In W. Harman (Ed.), *New metaphysical foundations of modern science.* Sausalito, CA: Institute of Noetic Sciences.

Harman, W. (1994b). Toward a "science of wholeness." In W. Harman (Ed.), *New metaphysical foundations of modern science.* Sausalito, CA: Institute of Noetic sciences.

Harris, B. (1979), Whatever happened to little Albert? *American Psychologist, 34,* 151–160.

Harrison, E. (1985). *Masks of the universe.* New York: Macmillan Publishing Company.

Harrison, P. (1995). Newtonian science, miracles, and the laws of nature. *Journal of the History of Ideas, 56,* 531–553.

Haskins, C. H. (1960). *Studies in the history of medieval science.* New York: Frederick Ungar Publishing.

Hawking, S. W. (1988). *A brief history of time.* New York: Bantam Books.

Heidbreder, E. (1933). *Seven psychologies.* New York: Appleton-Century-Crofts.

Herbert, N. (1985). *Quantum reality: Beyond the new physics.* Garden City, New York: Anchor Press.

Hibler, R. W. (1984). *Happiness through tranquility: The school of Epicurus.* Lanham, NM: University Press of America.

Hilgard, E. R. (1987). *Psychology in America: A historical survey.* San Diego: Harcourt Brace Jovanovich, Publishers.

Hirst, W. (1988). *The making of cognitive sciences: Essays in honor of George A. Miller.* Cambridge: Cambridge University Press.

Horgan, J. (1996). *The end of science.* Reading, Massachusetts: Addison-Wesley Publishing Company.

Hull, C. L. (1943). *Principles of behavior.* New York: Appleton-Century-Crofts.

James, W. (1890a). *The principles of psychology. Volume 1.* New York: Henry Holt.

James, W. (1890b). *The principles of psychology. Volume 2.* New York: Henry Holt.

James, W. (1902/1958). *The varieties of religious experience.* New York: New American Library.

James, W. (1907/1991). *Pragmatism.* Buffalo, New York: Prometheus Books.

James, W. (1912/1976). *Essays in radical empiricism.* Cambridge, MA: Harvard University Press.

Johnson, G. (1995). *Fire in the mind.* New York: Alfred A. Knopf, Inc.

Jung, C. G. (1973). *Synchronicity: An acausal connecting principle* (R. F. C. Hull, Trans.). Princeton, NJ: Princeton University Press.

Jung, C. G. (1974). Mysterium Coniunctionis. In *Collected works. Vol. 14.* Princeton, NJ: Princeton University Press.

Kernberg, O. (1975). *Borderline conditions and pathological narcissism.* New York: Jason Aronson.

Kessel, F. S., & Bevan, W. (1985). Notes toward a history of cognitive psychology. In C. E. Buxton (Ed.), *Points of view in the modern history of psychology.* Orlando: Academic Press. 198.

Kibre, P. & Sirasi, N. G. (1978). The institutional setting: The universities. In D. C. Lindberg (Ed.), *Science in the middle ages.* Chicago: University of Chicago Press.

Klein, D. B. (1970). *A history of scientific psychology.* New York: Basic Books.

Klein, M. (1986). A contribution to the psychogenesis of manic-depressive states. In R. P. Buckley (Ed.), *Essential papers on object relations.* New York: New York University Press.

Kohler, W. (1925/1976). *The mentality of apes.* New York: Liveright.

Kotter, J. P. (1997). Matsushita: The world's greatest entrepreneur. *Fortune,* March 31, 135, 6, 105–111.

Kuhn, T. S. (1957). *The Copernican revolution.* Cambridge, MA: Harvard University

Kuhn, T. S. (1973). *The structure of scientific revolutions.* Chicago: University of Chicago Press.

Latzer, M. (1994). Leibniz's concept of evil. *Journal of the History of Ideas,* 55, 1–15.

Leary, D. E. (1992). William James and the art of understanding. *American Psychologist,* 47, 152–160.

Lerner, L. S. & Gosselin, E. A. (1986). Galileo and the specter of Bruno. *Scientific American,* 256, 120–133.

Levinton, J. S. (1992). The big bang of animal evolution. *Scientific American,* November, 84–91.

Lindberg, D. C. (1978). Transmission of Greek and Arabic learning to the west. In D. C. Lindberg (Ed.) *Science in the middle ages.* Chicago: University of Chicago Press.

Litke, A. M., & Schwarz, A. S. (1995). The silicon microstrip detector. *Scientific American,* May, 76–81.

Lynch, G., McGaugh, J. L., & Weinberger, N. M. (1984). *Neurobiology of learning and memory.* New York: Guilford Press.

Maor, E. (1994). The story of e. *The Sciences,* July/August, 24–29.

Mandler, G. (1985). *Cognitive psychology: An essay in cognitive science.* Hillsdale NJ: Lawrence Erlbaum Associates.

Mansfield, V. *The challenge of synchronicity.* http://www. lightlink/com/vic (21 March 1997).

Martin, S. G., Clark, G. H., Clarke, F. P., & Ruddick, C. T. (1941). *A history of philosophy.* New York: Appleton-Century-Crofts.

Maslow, A. H. (1970). *Motivation and personality,* 2nd edition. New York: Harper & Row.

Miller, G. A., Galanter, E., & Pribram, K. H. (1960). *Plans and the structure of behavior.* New York: Holt, Rinehard, and Winston.

Milner, R. (1996). Keeping up Down House. *Natural History,* 105, 8, 54–57.

Morford, M. P. O. & Lenardon, R. J. (1985). *Classical mythology.* New York: Longman.

Mulligan, L. (1994). Robert Boyle, "right reason," and the meaning of metaphor. *Journal of the History of Ideas,* 55, 235–257.

Mukerjee, M. (1996). Explaining everything. *Scientific American,* January, 88–94.

Multhauf, R. P. (1978). The science of matter. In D.C. Lindberg (Ed.), *Science in the middle ages.* New Chicago: University of Chicago Press.

Myers, G. E. (1986). *William James: His life and thought.* New Haven: Yale University Press.

Nash, L. K. (1957). The atomic-molecular theory. In J. B. Conant (Ed.), *Harvard case histories in experimental science.* Cambridge: Harvard University Press.

Neill, T. P., & Schmand, R. H. (1957). *History of the Catholic church*. Milwaukee: Bruce Publishing.

Newman, J. H. (1927/1958). The real function of the university. In M. B. McNamee (Ed.), *Reading for understanding*. New York: Rinehart.

Neisser, U. (1967). *Cognitive psychology*. New York: Apple-Century-Crofts.

Olds, J., & Milner, P. (1954). Positive reinforcement produced by electrical stimulation of septal area and other regions of the rat brain. *Journal of Comparative and Physiological Psychology, 48*, 14–16.

Pagels, H. R. (1983). *The cosmic code: Quantum physics as the language of nature*. New York: Bantam Books.

Pais, A. (1988). Knowledge and belief: The impact of Einstein's relativity theory. *American Scientist, 76*, 154–158.

Parsons, E. A. (1967). *The Alexandrian library: Glory of the Hellenic World*. New York: American Elsevier Publishing Company.

Pavlov, I. P. (1927). *Conditioned reflexes*. London: Clarendon Press.

Peters, R. S. (1962). *Brett's history of psychology*. Cambridge, MA: M.I.T. Press.

Pinsent, J. (1985). *Greek Mythology*. New York: Peter Bedrick Books.

Pitts, E. (1986). Spinoza on freedom of expression. *Journal of the History of Ideas, 47*, 21–35.

Popper, K. R., & Eccles, J. C. (1977). *The self and its brain*. Berlin: Springer-Verlag.

Pribram, K. H., & Gill, M. M. (1976). *Freud's "Project" reassessed*. New York: Basic Books.

Prokasy, W. F. (1972). Developments with the two-phase model of classical conditioning. In A. H. Black & W. F. Prokasy (Eds.), *Classical conditioning II*. New York: Appleton-Century-Crofts.

Read, J. (1957). *Through alchemy to chemistry*. London: G. Bell and Sons.

Redgrave, H. S. (1969). *Alchemy: ancient and modern*. New Hyde Park, NY: University Books Inc.

Rescorla, R. A. & Wagner, A. R. (1972). A theory of Pavolovian conditioning: Variations in the effectiveness of reinforcement and nonreinforcement. In A. H. Black & W. F. Prokasy (Eds.), *Classical conditioning II*. New York: Appleton-Century-Crofts.

Riordan, M. (1992). The discovery of quarks. *Science, 56*, 1287–1292.

Roberts, L. (1988). New targets for human gene therapy. *Science, 241*, 906.

Robin, L. (1928). *Greek thought and the origins of the scientific spirit*. New York: Alfred A. Knopf.

Robinson, D. N. (1981). *An intellectual history of psychology*. New York: Macmillan Publishing Company.

Rogers, A. R. (1932). *A student's history of philosophy*. New York: Macmillan Publishing Company.

Russell, B. (1959). *The A.B.C. of relativity.* New York: The New American Library of World Literature, Inc.

Russell, B. (1972). *A history of western philosophy.* New York: Simon & Schuster.

Ruthen, R. (1993). Adapting to complexity. *Scientific American,* January, 130–140.

Sambursky, S. (1963). *The physical world of the Greeks.* London: Routledge and Kegan Paul.

Schneer, C. J. (1960). *The search for order.* New York: Harper & Row.

Schneer, C. J. (1984). *The evolution of physical science.* Lanham, MD: University Press of America.

Schramm, D. N., & Steigman, F. (1988). Particle accelerators test cosmological theory. *Scientific American,* 258, 66–72.

Schwarz, J. H. (1985). Completing Einstein. *Science 85,* 6, 60–63.

Scoville, W. B., & Milner, B. (1957). Loss of recent memory after bilateral hippocampal lesions. *Journal of Neurology, Neurosurgery, and Psychiatry,* 20, 11–21.

Segre, E. (1980a). *From falling bodies to radio waves: Classical physicists and their discoveries.* New York: W. H. Freeman.

Segre, E. (1980b). *From X-rays to quarks: Modern physicists and their discoveries.* New York: W. H. Freeman.

Shumaker, W. (1972). *The occult sciences in the Renaissance.* Berkeley, CA: University of California Press.

Siegel, R. E. (1968). *Galen's system of physiology and medicine.* Basel, Switzerland: S. Karger AG.

Singer, D. W. (1950). *Giordano Bruno: His life and thought.* New York: Schuman.

Skinner, B. F. (1938). *The behavior of organisms.* New York: Appleton-Century-Crofts.

Skinner, B. F. (1950). Are theories of learning necessary? *Psychological Review,* 57, 193–216.

Skinner, B. F. (1985). Cognitive science and behaviorism. *British Journal of Psychology,* 76, 291–301.

Smith, T. V. (1956). *Philosophers speak for themselves: from Thales to Plato.* Chicago: University of Chicago Press.

Smith, W. D. (1979). *The Hippocratic tradition.* Ithaca, NY: Cornell University Press.

Snyder, E. E. (1969). *History of the physical sciences.* Columbus, OH: Charles Merrill Publishing Company.

Spence, K. W. (1944). The nature of theory construction in contemporary psychology. *Psychological Review,* 51, 47–68.

Spurzheim, J. S. (1908). *Phrenology.* Philadelphia: J. B. Lippincott.

Strayer, J. R., & Munro, D. C. (1970). *The middle ages 395–1500.* New York: Appleton-Century-Crofts.

Stevens, S. S. (1939). Psychology and the science of science. *Psychological Bulletin*, 36, 221-263.

Sulloway, F. J. (1983). *Freud: Biologist of the mind.* New York: Basic Books.

Talbot, C. H. (1978). Medicine. In D. C. Lindberg (Ed.), *Science in the middle ages.* Chicago: University of Chicago Press.

Taylor, A. M. & Taylor, A. M. (1993). *Science and causality: A historical perspective.* Sausalito, CA: The Institute of Noetic Sciences.

Taylor, E. (1994). An epistemological critique of experimentalism in psychology or, why G. Stanley Hall waited until William James was out of town to found the American Psychological Association. In H. M. Adler & R. W. Rieber, *Aspects of the History of Psychology in America: 1892–1992.* New York: New York Academy of Sciences.

Thorndike, E. L. (1898). Animal intelligence: An experimental study of associative processes in animals. *Psychological Review,* Monograph Supplement, 2(8).

Tolman, E. C. (1932). *Purposive behavior in animals and men.* New York: Appleton-Century-Crofts.

Tolman, E. C. (1936/1951). The intervening variable. In M. H. Marx (Ed.), *Psychological theory: Contemporary readings.* New York: Macmillan Publishing Company.

Tomlin, E. W. F. (1963). *The western philosophers.* New York: Harper & Row.

Trefil, J. S. *(1985). Space, time, and infinity.* Washington, Smithsonian Books.

Tryon, R. C. (1929). The genetics of learning ability in rats. *University of California Publications,* 4, 71–8.

Ueberweg, F. (1888a). *History of Philosophy. Vol I.* New York: Charles Scribner's Sons.

Ueberweg, F. (1888b). *History of Philosophy. Vol II.* New York: Charles Scribner's Sons.

Vilenkin, A. (1987). Cosmic strings. *Scientific American,* 257, 94–102.

von Bertalanffy, L. (1968). *General system theory: Foundation, development, applications.* New York: George Braziller.

Wallbank, T. W., & Taylor, A. M. (1960). *Civilization: Past and present (Vol 1).* Chicago: Scott, Foresman and Company.

Watson, J. B. (1913). Psychology as a behaviorist views it. *Psychological review,* 20, 158–177.

Watson, J. B. (1924). *Behaviorism.* Chicago: University of Chicago Press.

Watson, J. B. (1926). What the nursery has to say about instincts. In C. Murchison (Ed.), *Psychologies of 1925.* Worchester, MA: Clark University Press.

Watson, J. B. (1936). John B. Watson. In C. Murchison (Ed.), *A history of psychology in autobiography.* Worchester, MA: Clark University Press.

Watson, R. 1. (1971). *The great psychologists* (Third Edition). Philadelphia: J. B. Lippincott Company.

Wheelwright, P. (1959). *Heraclitus.* Princeton, NJ: Princeton University Press.

Weinberg, S. (1992). *Dreams of a final theory.* New York: Pantheon.

Wiener, N. (1948). *Cybernetics.* New York: John Wiley & Sons.

Williams, T. H., Current, R. N., & Freidel, F. (1961). *A history of the United States (Since 1865).* New York: Alfred A. Knopf.

Wilson, M. D. (1980). Body and mind from the Cartesian point of view. In R. W. Reiber (Ed.), *Body and Mind.* New York: Academic Press.

Woodworth, R. S. (1918). *Dynamic psychology.* New York: Columbia University Press.

Wundt, W. (1911/1973). *An introduction to psychology.* New York: Arno Press.

Young, R. M. (1971). Franz Joseph Gall. In C. C. Gillispie (Ed.), *Dictionary of scientific biography.* New York: Charles Scribner's Sons.

Zeilik, M., & Smith, E. V. P. (1987). *Introductory astronomy and astrophysics* (Second Edition). New York: CBS College Publishing.